Praise for *Relational Judaism*

"Consecrate the new: rejuvenate the old. With these two imperatives, Ron Wolfson demonstrates that without belonging, believing and behaving are orphaned.... His writing confirms the insight of the philosopher of relationship, Martin Buber: 'all real living is meeting.'"
—**Rabbi Harold Schulweis**, Valley Beth Shalom, Encino, California

"A highly readable description and analysis of the most exciting and innovative programs and personalities in North American Judaism today.... This book should be read and studied by all concerned with the modern American Jewish condition."
—**Rabbi David Ellenson**, president,
Hebrew Union College–Jewish Institute of Religion

"Any book that quotes Steve Jobs and Rabbi Joseph Soloveitchik in the span of a few pages knows how to apply some of the best thinking from the business and non-profit sectors, along with the wisdom of Jewish text and tradition, to address the question of how we can live lives of meaning and purpose. A must read."
—**Rachel Levin**, executive director, Righteous Persons Foundation

"Open[s] doors of engagement and learning that make life more profound and wondrous. Takes a theology of relationship and translates it into lives well lived, and communities more vibrant!"
—**Rabbi Bradley Shavit Artson**, dean, the Ziegler School of Rabbinic Studies, American Jewish University; author, *Passing Life's Tests: Spiritual Reflections on the Trial of Abraham, the Binding of Isaac*

"A needed dose of truth from someone who has done his homework. An honest tour through today's Jewish landscape, skipping the all too familiar nostalgia in favor of concrete ideas, commitment and hope."
—**Rabbi Noa Kushner**, The Kitchen, San Francisco

"Challenges the Jewish community to embrace a wholly new and boldly different paradigm.... Brings much-needed fresh thinking to a Jewish community striving to reinvent itself, and seeking to engage new generations with renewed depth, vibrancy and relevance."
—**Larry Moses**, senior philanthropic advisor and president emeritus, The Wexner Foundation

"The definitive account of how Jewish institutions are moving from programs, turf and walls to relationships, openness and engagement. A must read for anyone serious about transforming today into a successful and significant tomorrow."

—**Rabbi Lawrence A. Hoffman, PhD**, author,
Rethinking Synagogues: A New Vocabulary for Congregational Life

"An invaluable resource full of common sense wisdom.... What emerges is a vision for a Jewish future full of meaning and purpose and most of all engagement. A must read for every Jewish leader."

—**Rabbi Naomi Levy**, author, *Hope Will Find You*; spiritual leader,
Nashuva: The Jewish Spiritual Outreach Center

"Combines a clear understanding of purpose and meaning with a detailed and useful description of how relationships empower all of our institutions."

—**Barry Shrage**, president, Combined Jewish Philanthropies, Boston

"Essential reading.... It calls to all of us in leadership: Reclaim that which is sacred in Jewish life by encountering the other!"

—**Rabbi Jonah Dov Pesner**, senior vice president,
Union for Reform Judaism

"Hits on the key challenge for us as Jewish leaders—engagement of Jews with each other.... Reading this book will serve to focus all of us on our common work in today's new reality."

—**Allan Finkelstein**, president and CEO,
Jewish Community Centers Association

"A superb organizational roadmap for any synagogue willing to put substance behind their aspiration to be warm and welcoming."

—**Rabbi Peter J. Rubinstein**, Central Synagogue, New York City

"If you worry about the Jewish future, read this book and then send a copy to every Jewish leader you know."

—**Rabbi Ed Feinstein**, Valley Beth Shalom; author,
Tough Questions Jews Ask: A Young Adult's Guide to Building a Jewish Life

"With compassion, stark honesty and enduring hope, tells the story of the next chapter of institutional Jewish life.... Any person, team or community struggling with creating and practicing a relevant Judaism in this very consumerist day will benefit tremendously from the transformative dialogue ... stories and well-articulated challenges woven throughout the pages of this book."

—**Rabbi Stephanie Kolin**, co-director,
Union for Reform Judaism's Just Congregations

"Groundbreaking ... call[s] us to return to the central mission of Judaism and offer[s] practical guidance on how to get there. A must read."
—**Rabbi Baruch HaLevi**, co-author, *Revolution of Jewish Spirit*; spiritual leader, Congregation Shirat Hayam, Greater Boston

"Exemplifies how Judaism and its institutions will only grow stronger if the focus is on the personal relationships they create. I hope Jewish leaders across the board read this book and allow for the transformation to happen within their organizations."
—**David Cygielman**, CEO, Moishe House

"A must read if you want to learn how to make the *tikkun* that the Jewish community is desperate for: places that will nurture real relationships, human connectedness, personal engagement, holy community."
—**Rabbi J. Rolando Matalon**, Congregation B'nai Jeshurun (BJ), New York City

"Challenge[s] every congregational leader, seminary educator and community professional to rethink how they will reshape their institutions and embrace twenty-first-century Jews."
—**Steven Windmueller**, Rabbi Alfred Gottschalk Emeritus Professor of Jewish Communal Service, Hebrew Union College–Jewish Institute of Religion

"With his usual charm, humor and intellect, Wolfson provides us with the next steps following welcoming."
—**Rabbi Steven C. Wernick**, CEO, United Synagogue of Conservative Judaism

"A must read for anyone who cares about the future of Jewish life in America, or anywhere for that matter."
—**Rabbi Daniel G. Zemel**, Temple Micah, Washington, DC

"Eloquent and persuasive ... provocative and practical, [this book] can be the spark for a revolution in Jewish organizational life that is both sorely needed and enormously exciting.... I guarantee that you'll be glad you found this book."
—**Dr. Jonathan S. Woocher**, chief ideas officer and director, Lippman Kanfer Institute, JESNA

"A must read for all professionals and lay leaders who want their Jewish organizations to succeed in the age of networks ... [and] a roadmap for the new Jewish leader, one who listens and gathers Jewish people and their families to create meaning, purpose, belonging and blessing."
—**Lisa Farber Miller**, senior program officer, Rose Community Foundation, Denver, Colorado

"A vital resource for rabbis, cantors, educators and lay leaders striving to transform their communities into places where people care about one another, and where powerful internal relationships can be catalyzed into a force for creating a more just world."

> —**Rabbi Jill Jacobs**, executive director, Truah: The Rabbinic Call for Human Rights; author, *Where Justice Dwells: A Hands-On Guide to Doing Social Justice in Your Jewish Community*

"Important ... captures the spirit and drive behind the most profound transformation of American Judaism in a century.... A must read for rabbis, professionals and lay leaders who steward the Jewish community."

> —**Rabbi Noah Farkas**, Valley Beth Shalom, Encino, California

"Readable and usable ... it is about how to ensure Judaism's and the Jewish people's contribution to the world as we near completion of the fourth millennium of Jewish history. As he asks on the last page, 'What are we waiting for?' I, for one, will not."

> —**Dr. Bruce Powell**, head of school, New Community Jewish High School, West Hills, California

"Brilliantly takes the emphasis [on our communal nature] and shows how it can become a reservoir of meaning in our lives, a strong tie to God and to the Jewish community, and a way for Jewish institutions to regain the allegiance of Jews of all ages."

> —**Rabbi Elliot Dorff**, rector and distinguished professor of philosophy, American Jewish University

"An extraordinary resource.... No one will ever think about the significance of building enduring relationships in quite the same way."

> —**Rabbi Peter S. Berg**, The Temple, Atlanta, Georgia

"Codifies what would seem to be uncodifiable, the secret of how to rejuvenate Jewish life.... Gives practical and inspiring advice on how to build relationships in every sphere of life—and at the end we will not only have happier people, happier friends and happier synagogues, but we will also have a vibrant Jewish community. We will no longer be asking 'Will Judaism in America survive?' as we will be too busy thriving."

> —**Rabbi Joseph Telushkin**, author, *Jewish Literacy* and *A Code of Jewish Ethics*

For more praise for *Relational Judaism*, please visit www.jewishlights.com.

Relational
Judaism

Other Books by Dr. Ron Wolfson

God's To-Do List
103 Ways to Be an Angel and Do God's Work on Earth

Be Like God
God's To-Do List for Kids

The Seven Questions You're Asked in Heaven
Reviewing and Renewing Your Life on Earth

The Spirituality of Welcoming
How to Transform Your Congregation into a Sacred Community

What You Will See Inside a Synagogue
(co-authored with Rabbi Lawrence A. Hoffman, PhD)

The Art of Jewish Living Series

Hanukkah, 2nd Ed.
The Family Guide to Spiritual Celebration

Passover, 2nd Ed.
The Family Guide to Spiritual Celebration
(with Joel Lurie Grishaver)

Shabbat, 2nd Ed.
The Family Guide to Preparing for and Celebrating the Sabbath

A Time to Mourn, a Time to Comfort
A Guide to Jewish Bereavement

Relational Judaism

Using the Power of Relationships to Transform the Jewish Community

Dr. Ron Wolfson

For People of All Faiths, All Backgrounds
JEWISH LIGHTS Publishing
Woodstock, Vermont

Relational Judaism:
Using the Power of Relationships to Transform the Jewish Community
2013 Hardcover Edition, First Printing
© 2013 by Ron Wolfson

Library of Congress Cataloging-in-Publication Data

Wolfson, Ron.
Relational Judaism : using the power of relationships to transform the Jewish community / Dr. Ron Wolfson.
pages cm
Includes bibliographical references and index.
ISBN 978-1-58023-666-9
  1. Fellowship—Religious aspects—Judaism. 2. Communities—Religious aspects—Judaism. 3. Hospitality—Religious aspects—Judaism. 4. Synagogues—United States—History—21st century. 5. Judaism—United States—History—21st century. 6. Jewish leadership—United States—History—21st century. I. Title.
BM720.F4W65 2013
296.6'7—dc23

                                    2012049487

10   9   8   7   6   5   4   3   2   1

Manufactured in the United States of America

Jacket and Interior Design: Heather Pelham

Published by Jewish Lights Publishing
A Division of LongHill Partners, Inc.
Sunset Farm Offices, Route 4, P.O. Box 237
Woodstock, VT 05091
Tel: (802) 457-4000   Fax: (802) 457-4004
www.jewishlights.com

For Rabbi Myer S. Kripke
Scholar, teacher, philanthropist.
My first rabbi.

יֵלְכוּ מֵחַיִל אֶל־חָיִל
(Psalm 84:8)
May you go from strength to strength.

In memory of Dorothy K. Kripke
My first author.
May her memory forever be a blessing.

Contents

A Note to the Reader

DEAR READER,

As I set about the research for this book, I sought out the leading professionals, lay leaders, and institutions of our time who are pioneering a relationship-based approach to Jewish communal vitality in the twenty-first century. A benefit of my position as an academic action-based investigator (and instigator!) and my longevity in the field is the opportunity to befriend many of these colleagues and to visit their institutions. I conducted more than 150 interviews, attended an array of conferences and convenings, and visited numerous cutting-edge organizations. You will find extensive "Voices from the Community" quotations from this research within the narrative, as well as in "Spotlight on Best Practices," all of which are designed to support my vision of a new Relational Judaism and offer concrete suggestions and best principles for those wishing to adapt these strategies in their own professional and volunteer work.

In a way, the book itself is a relational conversation among you, me, and these extraordinary voices. In the introduction and chapters 1 and 2, I present the case for Relational Judaism. I then offer in chapter 3 the framework of Nine Levels of Relationship—the substantive goal for engaging our people in a Relational Judaism. Chapter 4 presents six case studies of institutions, initiatives, strategies, and individuals who employ a relational approach to engagement of the affiliated, the unaffiliated, and the under-affiliated. In chapter 5, I present Twelve Principles of Relational Engagement, a toolbox, if you will, for those interested in applying the strategies of Relational Judaism in their own work. Finally, in chapter 6, I chart some of the challenges facing our community today and put forth a bold new approach for engaging new people in our communities and deepening the relationships with those already in our midst. If you are studying the book with your organization's leadership team, I recommend reading one chapter at a time. In the Hebrew transliteration, the letters "ch" (representing the Hebrew letter *chet*) and "kh" (representing the Hebrew letter *kaf*) are sounded as in the word "Bach." The same is true for certain words beginning with "h" as in *havurah* and Hanukkah.

So, as I always do in person at scholar-in-residence appearances, classes, and lectures, I stand at the open door of our meeting, shake your hand, introduce myself ("Hi, I'm Ron"), and welcome you into the conversation about how we can create a Relational Judaism that informs—and transforms—our institutions, denominations, and continental organizations, a Relational Judaism that I believe presents the best hope for engaging our people in a community that offers them a path to meaning and purpose, belonging and blessing. Thanks for joining me!

—Ron Wolfson

In the beginning is the
relationship.

MARTIN BUBER

Introduction

A Cautionary Tale

Recently, I was invited to be scholar-in-residence at what was once
one of the largest synagogues in the United States. The congregation
was celebrating its one-hundredth anniversary. The campus was dominated by a huge building, built in the 1960s. The sanctuary was enormous, and a labyrinth of hallways led to dozens of classrooms, offices,
and meeting halls. In the year 2000, the community had no mortgage,
no debt, and a balanced budget. Most synagogues would love to be in
such great shape.

Yet, there were signs that the coming decade would be challenging.
The building was aging and in need of renovation. The senior rabbi
who had served the congregation for decades was retiring. Most omi-
nously, the demography of the community had changed; young people
were moving north. The synagogue membership was slowly but surely
declining from a high of nearly 1,500 households. The leaders of the
synagogue knew that something had to be done.

Here's the something they did.

In the year 2000, they decided to borrow one million dollars to
invest in the future growth of the congregation. After the long-serving,
beloved rabbi retired, they hired a high-priced rabbi … who lasted
less than two years. That cost one-half million dollars. The other

half-million was spent on programming, all kinds of programming—big events, concerts, community lectures with high-priced nationally renowned speakers, highly touted initiatives to get more people into the synagogue on Shabbat—all sorts of things. Many of the programs had clever names, good marketing, and high appeal to specific segments of the community. Lots of people showed up for these programs and, by all accounts, enjoyed them. And then ... they left. Nothing was done to change the ambience of the congregation, which was widely considered cold and unwelcoming. Nothing was done to engage the people with others in attendance. Nothing was done to connect individuals with the congregation itself. Nothing was done to find out who they were. Nothing was done to follow up. Nothing was done to convince the members that the institution truly cared about them.

The result: after ten years of this initiative, the congregation was a million dollars in debt, and membership had shrunk to 300 households. By the time I got there, the leaders were kicking themselves, asking me what they could do to reinvigorate their community.

I told them what I will tell you.

It's all about relationships.

People will *come* to synagogues, Jewish Community Centers, Jewish Federations, and other Jewish organizations for programs, but they will *stay* for relationships. Programs are wonderful opportunities for community members to gather, to celebrate, to learn. There is nothing "wrong" with programs; every organization has them. But, if the program designers have given no thought to how the experience will offer participants a deeper connection to each other, with the community, and with Judaism itself, then it will likely be another lovely evening, afternoon, or morning ... with little or no lasting impact.

For those interested in living a Jewish life and for those professionals and lay leaders seeking to increase Jewish engagement, permit me to put my cards on the table, up front:

It's not about programs.

It's not about marketing.

It's not about branding, labels, logos, clever titles, websites, or smartphone apps.

It's not even about institutions.

It's about relationships.

The Beating Heart of My Jewish Soul

I love Judaism, and I love the institutions of Jewish life. I have spent my entire career working for them, with them, and through them to engage others in the Judaism I love.

And I love the people who work for Jewish institutions, both professionals and laypeople. They are talented, dedicated, overworked, and often underpaid and/or underappreciated, and they are passionate advocates for Jewish life. They are my esteemed colleagues and partners.

I learned to love being Jewish through relationships. My Jewish self was shaped by my relationships with family, with friends, with Jewish texts and ritual, with synagogue and community, with Jewish peoplehood, with Israel, with social justice work, and with God.

These relationships form the beating heart of my Jewish soul. It is because of them that I am a passionate and fully engaged Jew. I feel most Jewishly connected when I am with my family and friends, when I am engaged in the activities of a community, when I learn about and "do" Jewish, when I support the Jewish people, when I stand up for Israel, when I work to repair the world, when I wrestle with—and thank—God.

Judaism in its very essence is a relational religion, born of a covenant between God and the people Israel, sustained for millennia by a system of behaving, belonging, and believing that grows and evolves through time and space. But Judaism is even more than a religion. It is a people, a community of communities, a culture, a language, a history, a land, a civilization, a technology, a path to shape a life of meaning and purpose, belonging and blessing.

After more than forty years of living and teaching the Jewish way, I have come to an understanding about the essence of Judaism:

It's all about relationships.

Beyond Welcoming

In *The Spirituality of Welcoming*, I posited that the first step in transforming congregations into sacred communities must be establishing a "welcoming ambience" for newcomers and spiritual seekers. Since the publication of the book in 2006, I have continued my visits to synagogues of all types, sizes, and geographic locations throughout North America and across the globe. I have taught workshops on welcoming for synagogue leaders in communities ranging from New York City to San Diego, from London to Hong Kong. Invariably, a synagogue president will greet me during these visits, a well-marked copy of the book in hand, proclaiming, "I bought a copy for every member of our board!"

Of course, I am thrilled when this happens. The greatest compliment an author can receive is to see a copy of one's book with multiple pages dog-eared, highlighted, and Post-It noted ... or with the comment, "I have your book on my e-reader!" I become even more excited when I detect evidence that the synagogue leaders are serious about taking to heart the lessons we learned in Synagogue 2000/3000—that the synagogue as sacred community must offer engaging worship, life-long learning, social justice, and a healing community and begin the process of building relationships by implementing strategies that lead to extending a warmer welcome to members and strangers alike.

Surprisingly, I have also been invited to teach this approach to leaders of Jewish day schools, Federations, Hillels, summer camps, JCCs, Jewish women's and men's groups, youth educators, Jewish teachers, cantors, rabbis, and executives of major Jewish organizations. It is as if the entire Jewish community understands the truth that, with few exceptions, newcomers to our *mishpachah* (family) often feel ignored, intimidated, and put off by the reception they receive when they walk into a Jewish setting.

But improved signage, greeters at the door, and name tags represent only the beginning of a transformative process that moves an institution from an ostensibly busy place with a calendar full of programs to an organization deeply committed to becoming a community of relationships. What really matters is that we care about the people we seek to engage. When we genuinely care about people, we will not only welcome them; we will listen to their stories, we will share ours, and we will join together to build a Jewish community that enriches our lives.

In this volume, I intend to push deeper into this vision. I will suggest a new term to conceptualize the Jewish experience: *Relational Judaism.*

The vision of Relational Judaism is to strengthen Jewish consciousness and commitment by encouraging individuals to build relationships with Nine Levels of Jewish experience: self, family, friends, Jewish living, community, peoplehood, Israel, world, and God.

The methodology of creating Relational Judaism rests on Twelve Principles of Relational Engagement, strategies that leaders of Jewish institutions can employ to attract new people and deepen relationships with those already in the ranks.

The mission of Relational Judaism is to transform Jewish institutions and organizations seeking to engage Jews and those living with Jews from program-centric to relational communities that offer meaning and purpose, belonging and blessing.

The questions I invite you to consider are these: How do we transform our communities from institutions of programs to communities of relationships? How do we shape a relational community? How do organizational leaders spend their time differently when the goal is to engage people in relationship, not simply invite them to programs? When are the key points of recruitment, engagement, and retention during the life cycle of affiliation in a relational community? How might we transcend denominational boundaries, ideological differences, and institutional walls to develop a Relational Judaism in the twenty-first century?

Let me blunt: the stakes are high. Until recently, we have done pretty well to engage Jews through some connection with the Jewish community. Estimates suggest 80 percent of Jews affiliate with some institution—a synagogue, a Jewish Community Center, a Federation, a school, a youth group—at some point in their lives. We get 'em, but then, we lose 'em, usually at key transition points. Why? Because we have failed to develop deep relationships with many of the individuals who come into our midst, and we are, frankly, terrible at transitioning our people from one organization to another, from one city to another, from one life stage to another.

We can do better.

Telling Stories, Asking Questions

Our starting point is an amalgam of two of the fundamental and most beloved activities that define the Jewish experience: telling stories and asking questions. The Torah itself is accurately called "the greatest story ever told." One of the most popular of all Jewish holidays is the Passover Seder, the goal of which is to tell the story of the Exodus—a master narrative, stimulated by questions. Jews have been telling stories for millennia. Building relationships begins by engaging in conversation and sharing our stories.

After all, is there anything more common to Jewish conversation than the asking of questions? The Torah records the first question God asks a human being: "*Ayeka?*"—"Where are you?" (Genesis 3:9). At the other end of the Bible, the book of Lamentations, attributed to the biblical prophet Isaiah, contains the same four Hebrew letters, arranged in the word *Eikhah*, "How?"—the question that Jews ask God when confronted by unfathomable destruction and devastation.

The Talmud is built on the art of asking questions. The Four Questions of the Passover Seder stimulate the telling of the Exodus narrative. This propensity for questions extends to the oft-observed query about the Jews of Eastern European heritage, "Why do Jews seem to always answer a question with a question?" as in the old joke:

> Morris and Izzy were sitting over a bowl of tuna salad discussing the meaning of the cosmos.
>
> "Life," said Morris, "is like a bowl of tuna fish."
>
> Izzy pondered the statement and then asked Morris, "So, why is life like a bowl of tuna fish?"
>
> "How should I know?" Morris replied. "What am I, a philosopher?"

Two Questions

As we will explore shortly, a widely used strategy to build relationships in community organizing is based on both storytelling and question asking. In a "one-on-one" meeting, two people share a cup of coffee and begin the conversation by telling each other their personal stories. When the time seems right, the organizer will ask a provocative question, such as "What keeps you up at night?" The purpose of the question is to tease out concerns the person has, concerns that could reveal the person's self-interest. By hearing similar answers to this question during a "listening campaign" with dozens or even hundreds of members of an organization, the community could embrace a justice "action" to effect change, to ameliorate a wrong, to bridge a gap in social services.

While "What keeps you up at night?" is clearly a provocative question, Rabbi Sharon Brous of IKAR, an independent spiritual community in Los Angeles, has chosen a different tack with her congregation. When small groupings of members and curious guests gather in "house parties," Brous says she would rather "ask a question that comes from a place of hope and dreams. I want my people to find a sense of purpose in their lives. So, I ask them, 'What gets you up in the morning?'"

The two questions are important … and I am compelled to answer them both as I tell you my story.

Why I Get Up in the Morning

"What gets you up in the morning, Ron?"

Relationships.

I first learned about relationships from observing how the people closest to me interacted with other human beings. My parents, Alan and Bernice (may they rest in peace), enjoyed a wonderful relationship for sixty-one years. Even as a child, I marveled at how they seemed to always be in sync with each other. Though they were both busy in their professional careers, they nevertheless made time for each other, for their three sons, and for our extended family. Mom was extraordinarily devoted to her parents—my Bubbie Ida and Zaydie Louie—visiting them nearly every day. She called her three sisters every morning, just to check in or to share a story about what one of the nine grandchildren in the family had said or done. Once Bubbie's health began deteriorating, Mom understood the importance of keeping the family relationships close—organizing and hosting the large family holiday meals on Rosh Hashanah and Passover. When she founded the Nebraska Foundation for Visually Impaired Children to improve the lives of blind children, she found her volunteer calling, establishing relationships with other advocates for the blind that lasted fifty years.

My father taught me how to begin a relationship with a stranger. He was the kind of guy who got onto an elevator on the first floor, engaged you in conversation, and by the time you reached the sixth floor of the building, he knew your story and you certainly knew his. This gregariousness came from a deep place in Dad's heart: he treated every human being he met as someone created "in the image of God." And, frankly, he just loved to schmooze. Somehow, when you met him, you felt like you were reuniting with a long-lost friend.

My grandfather, Zaydie Louie, was a larger-than-life figure in Omaha. Beginning as a peddler of fruits and vegetables, he built the first modern supermarket in the state of Nebraska in the 1950s by offering his customers low prices, truckload quantities, and friendly customer service. At the entrance of Louis Market was a "courtesy counter," where you could find Louie greeting his customers by name, extending a handshake, offering credit for those low on funds, and building relationships with everyone involved in the enterprise: the public, vendors, employees, and his four sons-in-law, who were given equal partnerships in the business upon marrying one of his daughters. Dad claimed that in all the years he worked side by side with his father-in-law, he never once heard a critical comment or a raised voice. Louie regularly donated food, flowers, and Christmas trees to Boys Town and the public schools in Omaha. He sponsored the Triple-A baseball team and hobnobbed with politicians. All this by force of his loving personality; the man had never gone to school in Russia and signed his name with an "X." It mattered not. When Louie took the family out to dinner at local restaurants, inevitably a stream of people would come by the table to say hello. I thought he was the mayor.

I learned the importance of friendships from a group of eight boys who first met in preschool and navigated childhood and adolescence together until we graduated high school. We were brought together by our mothers, who understood the importance of relationships. They enrolled us in the same schools and invited each other's children to birthday parties. They sent us to the same afternoon Hebrew school, summer camp, and youth group. They brought us with them to synagogue, and several of the moms sang every Friday night in the volunteer choir at Beth El Synagogue. We boys learned to *layn* (chant) Torah for our Bar Mitzvah celebrations and continued to do so nearly every week through high school. We all loved to sing, forming a "Boys' Barbershop Octet" in junior high school that came to be known as "The Bunch." We were leaders of our high school A Cappella Choir, scoring the leads in our annual Broadway musical performances and the solos at school concerts. We were pals, hanging out together on weekends, studying together for exams, pulling pranks on talk radio shows, running a fictitious teenager for president of Central High School Student Council. When we see each other now, nearly fifty years later, we pick up our friendship as if it were yesterday.

The most important relationship in my life began on a Sunday night in 1965 when I walked down the stairs into the basement of Marsha Elkon's house for a "Bible Quiz Bowl," a joint program of the Conservative and Orthodox synagogue youth groups in Omaha. There, across a crowded room, I saw the cutest girl I had ever seen. She was wearing a madras-print blouse with the initials "S.K." stitched on the pocket. I made a beeline to her and introduced myself. Her name was Susie Kukawka, and I engaged her in conversation the entire evening. Four years later, we were engaged, and we've been married now for forty-two years.

Susie is the reason I get up in the morning. Our son, Michael, our daughter, Havi, and our son-in-law, Dave … and our grandchildren, Ellie Brooklyn and Gabriel Elijah … they are why I get up in the morning. My brothers, Bob and Doug, and their families … they are why I get up in the morning. My many friends and colleagues from around the country and throughout the world … they are why I get up in the morning.

And I get up in the morning to continue to pursue my passion: engaging Jews with a joyful Judaism that gives them meaning and purpose, belonging and blessing.

What Keeps Me Up at Night

"What keeps you up at night, Ron?"

The future of Jewish institutions.

I have been a leader in Jewish organizational life since I was fourteen years old. In 1963, I became a member of my local synagogue youth group when I joined the BILU chapter of United Synagogue

Youth at Beth El Synagogue in Omaha, Nebraska. My first job was regalia chairman—I was in charge of the pins and T-shirts. Two years later, I was elected the president of the chapter and a vice president of the regional board. In my senior year of high school, I was elected the regional president of EMTZA, representing a thousand Jewish teenagers from the Midwest states. During that year, I spent seventeen weekends in synagogues spanning our region, from Winnipeg in the north to St. Louis in the south, from Denver in the west to Iowa City in the east. At Washington University in St. Louis, I was the president of Hillel and began my teaching career at Congregation B'nai Amoona. I have been a Jewish educator since 1967, working in religious schools, summer camps, and youth groups. During my thirty-seven-year career in academic life at the American Jewish University (formerly the University of Judaism), I have been a professor, dean, vice president of a university, director of a center for the Jewish future, creator of an institute for Jewish family education, scholar-in-residence at hundreds of synagogues, cofounder of Synagogue 2000/3000, and participant in innumerable conferences on all levels of Jewish communal life. Through it all, I have been an optimistic observer of the North American Jewish community, a cheerleader for making Judaism accessible to all. Not once have I worried about the Jewish future. I have slept well at night.

Until now.

Now, I have trouble falling asleep. Now, I worry.

I'm not worried about the Jewish future. I am worried about the future of Jewish institutions.

I am worried that the "tried and true" strategies for engaging Jews with Judaism are not working. I am worried that the communal organizations of Jewish life have been slow to respond to the changing demography and the changing reality of how Jews—and the substantial numbers of non-Jews living in Jewish households—encounter Judaism. I am worried that a large percentage of our young people are not at all interested in "belonging" to existing institutions, even as they show interest in things Jewish. I am worried that Jews have become so successful at integrating themselves into the mainly Christian society at large and that the (mainly Christian) society at large has become so extraordinarily accepting of Jews in their lives that the distinctiveness of our people—our ethics, our culture, our religion—is losing its edge.

This worry is not new. More than one hand-wringing pundit has called Jews "the ever-dying people." Nonsense. My colleague Rabbi Lawrence A. Hoffman likes to remind audiences that *Look* magazine in the 1970s ran a cover story titled "The Vanishing American Jew," predicting the disappearance of North American Jews by the year 2000. "Look what vanished," Larry quips. "*Look* magazine!" I have no concerns about Jews and Judaism surviving on this continent. But, I have never been satisfied that a small number of committed Jews will sustain Judaism. As I wrote in *The Spirituality of Welcoming*:

> In an age-old debate, some leaders have argued that the Jewish community has always survived because of a "saving remnant," a small group of dedicated Jews who keep the religion and culture alive. Others have dismissed this view as pessimistic and fatalistic, preferring to believe that Judaism as a religion, culture, and people is so deep, so inspiring, so meaningful that the only reason we have not grown is a centuries-long resistance to proselytizing. In other words, we have a great product; our marketing stinks.[1]

Some may argue that our institutions are on a plateau or in decline due to the economic crisis that hit the community hard these past numbers of years. "When the economy improves, campaigns will be more successful, and membership levels will come back." Perhaps. But there are new factors at play: lower birthrates, longer young adulthood, delayed marriage, intermarriage, and an exodus of aging baby boomers from synagogues and other groups.

Others will say, "So what?" Institutions come and go. Those that meet the needs of people will do fine; those that do not will disappear or become much smaller. Besides, look at all the exciting start-up organizations, many of which are the creation of young Jewish entrepreneurial leaders. Isn't that a sign that the incredible drive of Jews to organize is alive and well? Absolutely. I come not to bury Jewish institutions, but to praise them when they take up the rallying cry of engagement and work to transform themselves into vehicles for a Relational Judaism.

A Different Worry

What a radical shift in the "worriness quotient" from a time not so long ago when the hand-wringing was about how modern Jews pined to escape the shackles of a Judaism that felt like an obstacle to success! Here is how one astute observer of Jewish life characterized "the present crisis in Judaism" not so long ago:

> Before the beginning of the nineteenth century all Jews regarded Judaism as a privilege; since then, most Jews have come to regard it as a burden.... The number of Jews who regret they are not Gentiles is legion. "If I had my choice," a prominent American-Jewish woman is quoted as saying, "I would have asked God to make me a Gentile, but since I had no choice I pray to Him to help me be a good Jewess." ... "The great majority of Jewish youths at the colleges," writes a Harvard graduate, "consider their Jewish birth the real tragedy of their lives. They constantly seek to be taken for Gentiles and endeavor to assimilate as fast as their physiognomy will allow."[2]

These words mark the opening chapter of the groundbreaking book *Judaism as a Civilization* by Mordecai M. Kaplan, published in 1934. Kaplan argued that the problem with viewing Judaism simply as a "religion" and not as a broad and deep "civilization" shackled Jews with an outdated, depressive, and ultimately unappealing yoke, dragging down a proud people and hastening a wholesale exodus to other religions or, more likely, to the ranks of American secularists. His proposal: envision Judaism as far more than a "religion," but rather as an "evolving civilization," in which

> [a Jew's] life should consist of certain social relationships to maintain, cultural interests to foster, activities to engage in, organizations to belong to, amenities to conform to, moral and social standards to live to as a Jew. Judaism ... is thus something far more comprehensive than Jewish religion. It includes that nexus of history, literature, language, social organization, folk sanctions, standards of conduct, social and spiritual ideals, aesthetic values, which in their totality form a civilization.[3]

After mercilessly critiquing the dominant forms of Jewish religious life at the time, including Reform, Conservative, and modern Orthodox, Kaplan set forth his new vision for "reconstructing" Judaism by emphasizing the totality of the Jewish experience, beginning with a land (Israel), language (Hebrew), mores, laws and folkways, folk arts, and social structure. Kaplan's ideas were revolutionary, controversial, and hugely influential to an entire generation of rabbinical students in the 1940s and 1950s. The Orthodox excommunicated him, and his colleagues at The Jewish Theological Seminary barely tolerated him, but Kaplan never backed down. Although the majority of his students did not embrace the organizational structures of Reconstructionism—the denomination emanating from Kaplan's teachings—preferring to take Conservative and Reform pulpits during the explosive postwar years of synagogue expansion, they effectively adopted the Kaplanian plea for broadening the conception of Judaism beyond religion. The modern synagogue-center with its vast array of programming was the direct result of Kaplan's vision.

Kaplan's influence can be seen in the institutions of Jewish life that exploded with growth during the post–World War II years. Fueled by the legion of newly married young couples and their baby-boomer children, hundreds of new synagogues sprouted up in suburban communities across North America. At its peak, the number of Jewish children enrolled in religious schools exceeded half a million. Jewish Community Centers also thrived, building magnificent campuses with swimming pools, health clubs, auditoriums, preschools, and libraries. The economy was robust, Jewish businesses were making money, philanthropy was on the rise, and Jews were nudging their way onto previously inhospitable college campuses and into previously unattainable professions.

Beginning with the student-led protests at the General Assembly of the Federations in 1969, the call for a deepening of content and commitment in Jewish institutions and a period of exciting experimentation grabbed the imagination of the community. *Havurot*—small friendship circles—gained favor, liberal Jewish day schools were founded, and a kind of "do-it-yourself" Judaism was promulgated by the publication of the enormously popular *Jewish Catalog* books. Jewish studies programs on campuses sprouted up across the continent, and with it came a new crop of professors and academic researchers interested in Jewish history, Bible, Hebrew language, sociology, and all manner of Jewish cultural expression.

Yet, there were ominous signs that the newfound acceptance Jews enjoyed at all levels of society came at a cost. Intermarriage, considered by most a palpable sign of assimilation, was on a precipitous rise, culminating in the oft-cited but overestimated figure of 52 percent in the community-shaking 1990 National Jewish Population Survey.[4] The "official" Jewish communal establishment searched for a rallying cry; they found it in the call for "Jewish continuity." Sociologists, convinced that earlier claims of the "vanishing American Jew" were unfounded, nevertheless warned that the Jewish community of the late twentieth and twenty-first centuries would likely be smaller, its numbers shrinking due to later marriage, lower birthrates, and a steadily aging population.

Two influential voices, sociologists Arnold M. Eisen and Steven M. Cohen, identified another challenge for communal leaders. The rebellious young people who grew up in the 1960s had turned into the "sovereign selves" of the 1990s. Imbued with a fierce independence born of American individualism and a rejection of authoritarianism, no one—not the clergy, not communal norms, not even family— would tell these Jews how to live their lives. Their choices about how "Jewish" they would be, sometimes on a daily basis, presented a new formidable challenge to participation and affiliation.

This assertion of individualism has impacted all religious communities. The fastest growing segment in North American religion is the "Nones." The "Nones" report they have no religious preference, they belong to no spiritual community, and they feel no particular loyalty to a political party or ideology. In a world of unlimited choice, they are choosing the sidelines. Despite all the attempts at engagement, despite all the aggressive work of evangelicals and recruiters of all stripes, more and more people, both young and old, are opting out.

We can no longer count on a steady influx of young Jews with young children in tow entering synagogues and JCCs. If they come at all, they arrive in their late thirties and early forties, necessarily busy with two careers to make ends meet, with little or no time to volunteer in a volunteer-driven system. Even when the young become empty nesters, the institutions barely know what to do with them. With the extraordinary advances in medical care, it may be true that sixty is the new forty, but only recently has the Jewish community begun to think about how to engage the huge numbers of aging baby boomers, even as the question of how to reach young Jewish adults between the ages of twenty-one and fortysomething rages.

Compounding the challenge exponentially is the current economic climate, which, at this writing, may be inching into a slow recovery, but the flat fundraising campaigns of Federations, the sinking or flat membership rolls and revenues at synagogues and JCCs, and the difficulty in securing funds plaguing virtually every nonprofit institution in the Jewish community have cast a cloud over the sunniest of dispositions ... even mine.

Now, What?

So, what to do?

In the first decade of the new millennium, policy makers looked for the "next big idea" for engaging Jews with Judaism and the community: "get more kids into Jewish day schools," "expand the available beds in summer camps," "send young Jews who had never been to Israel on an all-expenses-paid ten-day trip," "entice adults into serious Jewish learning"—to be sure, all wonderful and important goals. In synagogue life, the call for "transformation" was loud and clear: "warm up the welcome for newcomers," "create spiritual seeker–sensitive worship experiences," "become a congregation of learners," "offer a 'synaplex' of parallel programming to attract higher turnout to events," and "move from 'functional' to 'visionary' communities." Jewish Community Centers added Jewish educators to their staff rosters. Hillel Foundations trained "engagement workers," bringing programs out of the building and into the dorms. New initiatives such as Synagogue 3000's Next *Dor* (generation), Birthright NEXT, and Moishe House mounted events to attract young Jewish adults. National religious movements launched campaigns for teenage engagement and new leadership training efforts.

And yet, after countless hours spent in all this effort, there is a palpable feeling of impending dread descending on the Jewish community. Synagogue membership is declining, sometimes precipitously. Federation campaigns are down. JCC membership is flat. The relationship between Israel and Diaspora Jewry is complex and complicated. The cost of Jewish education, particularly day school tuition, is pricing families out of the market.

To be sure, there are promising developments as well. Jewish cultural arts—books, music, art, film, architecture, dance, journalism—are flourishing. Young Jewish entrepreneurs are exploring social media and technology strategies for engaging Jews with all things Jewish. The growing Orthodox population, supplemented in certain large Jewish communities by recent immigrants from Iran, Russia, and Israel, has fueled an explosion of kosher products, restaurants, tours, and holiday retreats. The number of seminaries has tripled in the past twenty years, graduating many more rabbis, cantors, educators, and communal professionals than ever. European Jewry is reborn. Israel, for all its challenges, enjoys a thriving economy and is a beacon of democracy in only, lest we forget, six decades of existence.

I'm still worried.

I worry that we are failing to provide our people with that most basic experience of community life: *relationships*.

In our rush to turn out numbers, in our frantic search for ways to get people through our doors, our institutions spend most of their time, energy, and money devising programs for one target audience or another. "Let's have a lecture series for the seniors!" "How about an afternoon at the zoo for families?" "Why not a once-a-month worship experience with a band?" "A cooking class for the foodies?" Moreover, we are good at this ... clever even. A Jews and Brews for young Jewish adults to celebrate Purim. Lamaze-l Tov for expectant parents. The People versus Abraham, a faux trial of the biblical Abraham, accused of child endangerment, featuring a well-known television courtroom judge and two outstanding lawyers, one for the prosecution, one for the defense.

These are wonderful programs. They are often done with panache and style. They regularly attract a crowd.

But, what happens after the crowds go home? Has anything happened during the time they were at the program to deepen their relationship to the community, to the sponsoring institution, and most importantly, to each other? Or, will they check it off their to-do list, another consumable activity, demanding little or no commitment other than a couple of hours of their time? And, will they continue their relationship with the institution? A rabbi confides in me, "A woman who was a member of my synagogue for twenty years resigned. I was shocked because she showed up to all of our programs. So, I called her to ask why she was leaving. You know what she said? 'I came to everything, and I never met anybody.'"

Something is missing. Something critically important. Something so crucial, it could determine the health of the North American Jewish community in the twenty-first century.

It's time to shift our paradigm. It is time to shift the shape of Jewish engagement.

1

Shifting the Shape of Jewish Engagement

ON A WARM AND BEAUTIFUL Sunday morning in June, a local Federation invited me to be the keynote speaker at a symposium on synagogue life, the culmination of a yearlong conversation among leading rabbis and lay leaders concerned with the precipitous decline in congregational membership. The numbers had shocked the community into action. The synagogues were discussing collaborative religious schools, mergers, and selling buildings. The Federation, understanding full well that the majority of givers to community fundraising campaigns are also synagogue members, was hopeful that their planning capacity and financial acumen could somehow help the synagogues regain or maintain their economic footing. Everyone was concerned about an affiliation rate that had dipped below 15 percent.

And so I was not surprised that 150 representatives of synagogues showed up for a full day of conversations about the future of congregational life in particular and Jewish communal life altogether. I listened carefully to a prominent rabbi accurately detail the challenges facing mainstream synagogues, a synagogue executive director bemoan the duplication of services each congregation represents, and a chief executive officer of the Federation offer creative approaches to managing the situation. Each presentation was thoughtful and delivered with passion. During breakout groups on "Alternative Synagogue Models" and "Approaches to Membership," the conversations were urgent and respectful. And, yet, I was chagrined to hear that almost every suggested solution centered on ways to downsize the community. Sell buildings. Merge congregations. Eliminate Jewish schools. Abandon initiatives. Lay off staff.

This scenario is not unusual; it is becoming more and more common every week. Hardly a day goes by without some plea from some corner of the community that we need to get smaller; that we cannot sustain membership-based organizations; that we will find it increasingly difficult to recruit and engage the next generation.

The latest demographic survey of a major Jewish population center—*the* major American Jewish population center, New York City—confirms the anecdotal evidence. In June 2012, the UJA-Federation of New York published the *Jewish Community Study of New York: 2011*.[1] The findings shocked but hardly surprised institutional leaders. While the Conservative and Reform movements each lost about forty thousand member households in the past ten years, the self-defined category "Just Jewish" nearly doubled from 19 percent in 2002 to 37 percent of the 1.54 million Jews in the eight-county area. Sociologist Jacob B. Ukeles, one of the authors of the study, noted that the Conservative movement has lost almost half its membership in New York City during the past thirty years, with only 46 percent of those raised in Conservative households choosing to remain "Conservative," the lowest retention rate among denominational groups. The Reform movement loses a high percentage of their children once the Bar/Bat Mitzvah party is over. The two growing population centers are the Orthodox, especially the very religious, and the "Just Jewish," who eschew denominational labels.

These "Just Jewish" Jews are a complicated group. Clearly, some are Jewish in name only, rarely involved in Jewish activities that classically define Jewish identity. Yet others show up at Passover Seders, light Hanukkah candles, and fast on Yom Kippur. This is particularly common among young Jews who have been raised with many of the predictors of strong adult Jewish engagement: day school education, an Israel experience, and attendance at a Jewish summer camp. They just don't like to be ideologically pigeonholed. It is well-known, for example, that many of the entrepreneurial leaders of independent minyanim are products of the Conservative movement, deeply committed Jews who consider the label "Conservative" as either a barrier to entry or irrelevant. Whatever the reasons, "Just Jewish" is today the second largest population in New York City. We write them off at our peril, especially because a large number of them are in the demographic of young Jewish adults.

Another troubling indicator that the non-Orthodox community is in decline is the response to the question "Do you feel that being Jewish is very important?" In the 2002 survey of New York Jewry, 65 percent of respondents answered affirmatively[2]; ten years later, the number had fallen to 57 percent. Even one of the most observed of all Jewish holidays took a hit: the percentage of people who said they never participate in a Passover Seder grew from 8 percent in 2002 to 14 percent in 2011.

It may be that we cannot do much about the effects of demography, geography, and societal change. But I, for one, do not want to stand idly by while our community shrinks. I didn't sign up for closing synagogues, schools, and centers; selling Torah scrolls; and going out of business. As a baby boomer, I lived through the tumult of the 1960s, which was every bit as challenging to Jewish institutional life. I recall vividly the shock reverberating through the community when students "took over" the General Assembly in Boston in 1969, when Havurat Shalom (the forerunner of what we now call independent minyanim) was condemned by mainstream synagogue leaders, and when a respected demographer predicted that intermarriage would cause the disappearance of the American Jewish community by the year 2010.

I believe we are much too resilient and resourceful to give up and settle for less. Will Jewish institutions need to change to adapt to the new realities? Absolutely. Will we need our smartest, savviest leaders to step up and think creatively about developing new sources of revenue? You bet. Will our institutions need to "up their game" to recruit, engage, and retain people and their support? Undoubtedly.

The question is, how? How will we do this transformational work? Changing the conversation, engaging in courageous dialogue, developing strategic plans, conducting studies, writing analytic white papers and blogs—all of these are interesting, perhaps even useful. Yet, every day we talk, we fail to act. Every day we debate, we avoid the work that needs to be done. Every day we spend wringing our hands is a day wasted.

Rather, let us shift the shape of our work. Let us figure out what to do that can fundamentally restore the faith, trust, and engagement of our people with the Jewish experience … and then do it. Let us figure out how to build relational experiences that enrich our people's lives. Let us not procrastinate. The future of the Jewish community in North America is at stake.

A New Goal

The shape shifting begins with this question: What's the goal?

The goal of Jewish institutions is not self-preservation; it is to engage Jews with Judaism. It's not gaining more members; it's gaining more Jews. It's about people, not programs. It's about deep relationships, not fee-for-service transactions.

It is time we turn the paradigm of programming-to-engage-Jews on its head, envisioning a new approach that *begins* with engaging Jews in a personal relationship with other Jews and Judaism and then program events for them. Ironically, this was Kaplan's goal all along. As leading Modern Orthodox theologian Rabbi David Hartman so insightfully teaches:

> Soloveitchik, Heschel, and Berkowitz thought they could adapt a traditional Judaism to the modern world. Kaplan did not. Kaplan thought there needed to be a total rethinking, a reconstruction, of Judaism for the modern world.… He had a passion for the *mishpachah* [family] called the Jewish people. For him, religion is meant to serve the Jewish people, and not that the Jewish people should serve the religion.[3]

Our new goal is served by putting people before programs. Let's learn who they are before we try to figure out what they want. Let's inspire them to see Judaism as a worldview that can inform the many different levels of relationship in their lives. Let's work toward a rededication of our *mishpachah*, our people, to a renewed Relational Judaism.

Today, the big concern of foundations and funders is "engagement" and "follow-through." What level of engagement does the institution create with its people? Is it simply transactional—"I pay you dues, you give me a rabbi on call, a Bar Mitzvah for my kid, High Holy Day seats," or "I pay your JCC membership fee, you give me access to the gym, an early childhood program for my toddler, a few cultural programs," or "I pay your day school tuition, you give my kids a quality education (in secular studies, first and foremost)"? Or, is the level of engagement relational, beyond servicing my immediate needs? And what of "follow-through," especially after impactful Jewish experiences like summer camp, youth group, Birthright Israel trip, and day school? If the "experience" is simply a one-off, then what's the point? What if each of the institutions sponsoring these programs does virtually nothing to guide the participants to the next experience, the next step on their Jewish journey? When we don't consider these questions—or worse, when we consider them and then do nothing about it—we will pour more millions of dollars into stand-alone programs with little attention to "follow-through," "linking the silos," or "integration." I wish Jewish life were like Apple, a totally integrated, closed system. But, it is not. Maybe it was in ghetto days, but not in North America, not now.

Success is not butts in seats, not more programs, not more one-offs. The question Jewish institutional leaders should ask is not, did people enjoy the event or the experience? The key question is: *Did we engage each person in significant relationship with Jews and Judaism through their participation in the organization? Did we deepen their commitment to the values of our institutions? Did we create new leaders willing to engage peers and others in community? Did we guide them to grow in their relationship with Judaism in one or more of these ways: connection to self, to family, to friends, to Jewish expression, to community, to Jewish peoplehood, to Israel, to the world, to God? Did we demonstrate how Judaism is a path toward meaning and purpose, belonging and blessing?*

Relationships as Drivers for Engagement

How shall we do this? What drives engagement?

Sacha Litman created a consulting firm in 2003 called Measuring Success (http://measuring-success.com) to help its nonprofit clients succeed in achieving their mission by providing measurement tools and teaching clients how to make data-driven decisions. In their work with the Jewish community, Measuring Success gathers hard data in its surveys on the "drivers" of two key indicators of Jewish engagement: (1) does participation in the organization impact Jewish growth, and (2) does a member of a synagogue or JCC, a school parent, or a donor to Federation recommend the organization to others? The first driver, "Jewish Growth," is measured by a series of questions about spiritual and intellectual growth as a Jew, a sense of belonging to something larger than self, feeling like a better human being, and connection to God. The second outcome variable is known as a "Net Promoter Score," a predictive indicator of how likely a member/client/customer is to recommend the organization to a friend. There is a direct correlation between "likely to recommend" and the ability of the organization to retain the person as a member/client/customer/donor (continuity of engagement), even if the organization raises the cost of engagement, even in a down economy. On the other hand, if the organization provides a poor experience, then not even lower cost will prevent customers from abandoning it. For comparison purposes, the famously engaging Apple Stores earn a Net Promoter Score of 80 percent or better; US Airways scores negative 12 percent. The aggregate average Net Promoter Score of all Jewish institutions surveyed by Litman's group: 35 percent.

I asked Litman to weigh in on whether "relationships" impacted either of these drivers, how the professionals in the institutions spend their time, or based on the findings, how Jewish organizations might rethink their approach to engagement. The quotations are in Litman's own words.

- *Federations.* In 2004–07, Measuring Success studied self-reported data from the top one thousand donors in the largest thirty-five Federations in North America. When Federation professional staff met with the top one thousand donors monthly rather than quarterly, the increase in the annual gift went up by an average of $30,000. In a study of the top four hundred donors to UJA-Federation of New York conducted in 2010, one of the strongest drivers of a jump from mid-level gift ($1,000–10,000) to major donor ($50,000 and up) was the "strength of the relationship between the professional solicitor and the donor *before* the increase." The data "turned the time spent on cultivation tasks by development professionals on its head."

- *Jewish Community Centers.* A key factor for improving both outcome scores is "a personal relationship with a staff member at the JCC, in addition to the quality of an individual program. Yet, in our 2006–2007 study, the majority of members report not interacting with any staff while in the building." The Measuring Success study also revealed a weakness common in most organizations, according to Litman. "Cross-selling, the concept of encouraging someone to explore other Jewish opportunities for what they could do beyond the gym or the early childhood center, was not happening. Why? Because it requires a staff person to interact with the member ... and that was not happening." The JCC Association now encourages and trains staff to interact with members while walking the halls, in the various facilities, and at programs and works more diligently at building relationships rather than "sitting in their offices, organizing and running the programs." As we will learn below, this emphasis on relational work has significantly improved reported interactions between staff and members and cross-selling.

- *Synagogues.* Measuring Success surveyed members in more than twenty congregations in New York City, Montreal, and Chicago from 2009 to 2012. The top drivers of "likelihood to recommend" and "growth as a Jew" are whether the member "resonated with the vision and values of the congregation." "Social connectedness" was the number three driver. Most strikingly, a meeting with the rabbi for even one hour was associated in a jump of nearly 25 percentage points in scores. "Yet, rabbis only met one on one with about 10 to 15 percent of congregants during the course of the year. There is more. Even though social connectedness is a top driver of engagement, the largest expenditures in synagogue budgets were early childhood programs and religious schools. Very few synagogues spend significant human or budgetary resources on building relationships among the adult members of the congregation." When presented with the data, synagogue leaders began to reassess time on tasks and budgets.

- *Jewish Day Schools.* Measuring Success has studied hundreds of Jewish day schools, with a focus on drivers of enrollment, a key concern because of flat growth in many day schools throughout North America. "How much you charge in tuition or the purchase/lease of a new facility makes no difference in enrollment—these are red herrings. The only driver for enrollment is perceived quality of the education." Day schools are doubling down on improving the quality of the product and hiring the best teachers and administrators they can find.

Litman summarizes a few "common themes" that emerge in all the organizations:

1. We are better at "consumerist, transactional Judaism" than Jewish growth. You wanted a Bar Mitzvah, we gave you a good one, but you still dropped out.

2. "Likelihood to recommend the institution to a friend" is a strong predictor of an individual's likelihood to renew or drop membership. But it only measures responsiveness to a consumer's expressed need. To switch from transactional to relational, we need to tackle the loftier goal of "growth as a Jew," a "latent need" that can only be achieved through relationships.

3. For institutions like JCCs and synagogues that attempt to maintain members from womb to tomb and have an array of programs to serve them, the key is to cross-sell. But that requires staff to be retrained to interact with members on a regular basis, and to keep track of individual needs and interests.

4. Almost all institutions surveyed do a miserable job at tracking their people. Even for those with customer relationship management (CRM) programs, the value of the data depends completely on whether staff enter the data in a timely fashion. The top driver of long-term engagement is whether the individual's values align with the institution's stated values. These values are transmitted most effectively through relationships, not brochures and mission statements. When you look at independent minyanim, megachurches, and Chabad, they each have found a way to connect with each person to discuss his or her religious journey. To do this in our mainstream institutions will require a major culture shift from transactional to relational.

A Relational Jew

A beginning point for institutional transformation from programmatic to relational communities is to think differently about how we empower individuals to build relationships with the totality of the Jewish experience. The goal is not to shape a "_____ (fill in the blank with a denomination—Reform, Conservative, Orthodox, Reconstructionist, Renewal) Jew," not a "secular Jew," not a "JCC Jew," not a "Federation Jew," not a "social justice Jew." The goal is to become a *Relational Jew*, a Jew who views Judaism as impacting virtually all of one's relationships. Jewish identity is not measured by how many services I attend a month, or how much money I give, or whether I light Shabbat candles. These are all indicators of Jewish *identification*. Internal Jewish *identity* is shaped by the relationships in my life.

> Do I see myself as Jewish? Does my Jewishness influence the way I live my life: my work, my purpose, my hobbies, my indulgences, the food I eat, the music I listen to?

> Do I see myself as part of a Jewish family? How do I relate to being a Jewish father, daughter, grandfather, sister, partner, spouse?

Do I locate myself among a network of good friends, friends who will be there for me in good times and bad?

Do I engage in lifelong learning about Judaism? Do I try on Jewish practice? Do I commit to living a Jewish life? Does Jewish observance shape the way I live: the rhythm of my week, the calendar of my year?

Do I belong to and support the community—a synagogue, JCC, Federation, Jewish defense organization?

Do I connect to the Jewish people, the "tribe"?

Do I care about the State of Israel?

Do I work to repair the world?

Do I wrestle with God?

The critic may say, "But, Ron, do people really want more than a transactional relationship with Jewish institutions? Maybe they're happy with fee-for-service. Just ask them what they want and provide it." Perhaps. Yet, I am reminded of the famous insight of Steve Jobs:

> Some people say, "Give the customer what they want." But that's not my approach. Our job is to figure out what they're going to want before they do. I think Henry Ford once said, "If I'd asked customers what they wanted, they would have told me, 'A faster horse!'" People don't know what they want until you show it to them.[4]

Some people, many people, don't know what they want in a Jewish institution until you show it to them. Listen to congregant Jill Seigerman reflect on her experience at Central Synagogue, a Reform congregation in New York City:

> *Never in a million years would I have believed I would become so involved in my congregation and in Jewish life. At age seven, my father asked if I wanted a Bat Mitzvah or to ski on weekends in Vermont; of course I chose skiing. I didn't grow up with any significant Jewish education, any affiliation with a synagogue. My husband was raised in a Conservative household;*

when our kids were little, we looked for a synagogue that we thought would be right for us as a couple.

From the moment we entered our first Friday night service at Central Synagogue, we wondered: How could so many people be so happy and connected to the service? Is this what it is like every Friday night? We immediately felt embraced by the clergy: Angela (Cantor Buchdahl), Peter (Rabbi Rubenstein), Rabbi Mo Salth, and Rabbi Michael Friedman. At our very first High Holy Day services at Central, they said, "If you are a new family in our synagogue, please come up and introduce yourself after services." Evan and I went up to meet them ... and they were so warm and welcoming. They chatted with us. It felt like they cared about getting to know us from that very moment. The outreach to new families really made an impact on us. The service itself was also embracing—with singing, swaying with our arms around our neighbors, introducing ourselves to congregants we didn't know—all of that made us feel part of the community the minute we were there.

We saw many of these same congregants at our evening cocktail parties and house meetings. These are small gatherings with the clergy at a congregant's home. They are community-building events that help to bring the congregation together. Our rabbi speaks about where we are as a synagogue, what we are doing, and what it means for the larger Jewish community. These events typically start with a d'var Torah, a member of the clergy speaks for twenty minutes or so, and then a conversation follows. The clergy are open to questions and the discussion can be enlightening, inspiring, and informative. This builds a relationship with the clergy and it builds a relationship with the community.

We have a very tight-knit nuclear family, but my husband and I believe that you can't really know who you are and where you're going unless you know where you came from. I think that our experience at Central Synagogue has helped us to know who we are, and has made us better parents, better friends, and better people ... really. And my kids feel connected there, too. They really enjoy it. We have Shabbat dinners with other families. We light candles together. We talk about things as a family that I don't think we would ever have talked about if not for Central. This is the value-added of a great synagogue.

Who Needs Institutions?

With all the talk of "post-denominational" Judaism—the blurring of the previously impermeable borders between Orthodox, Conservative, Reform, Reconstructionist, and Renewal Judaism—the real revolution is the specter of "post-institutional" Judaism. What if Jews really don't want (or need) institutions to be Jewish? What if I can get Jewish content, Jewish experiences, Jewish counseling, Jewish learning without the cost, both financial and otherwise, of affiliation?

As usual, North American Jews are once again influenced by the current zeitgeist. And today's zeitgeist is known as DIY—do-it-yourself. With the explosion of cable television channels, there is a never-ending stream of DIY shows, promising to show you how to renovate your home, host a dinner party, cook a meal, or restore an antique. Television hosts want to empower you to make over a part of your life, filling the airwaves with information on how to do it … yourself.

Moreover, we are served by companies that have made individuated experiences the hallmark of their strategy. Burger King tapped into this mind-set early on with their advertising slogan "Have it your way." Home Depot championed the idea with their line "You can do it. We can help."

The democratization of knowledge is perhaps the single greatest achievement of the Internet. The days when professionals, academics, and (I hasten to add) rabbis held exclusive access to information are over. I can search the Internet for just about any information I need. Need a diagnosis of an illness? WebMD. Stock market advice? E*trade. Write a will? LegalZoom. If we want personal recommendations from peers for a good restaurant, a reliable plumber, and a fabulous resort, Zagat.com, Angie's List, and Trip Advisor are instantly accessible on a smartphone.

Who needs face-to-face community when we have a Facebook community with which to commune? Why join a congregation to give kids a Jewish education (still the single most powerful motivator for synagogue affiliation) when we can have Jewish books mailed directly to our homes for free, watch streaming worship services, hire an online tutor to prepare children for a Bar/Bat Mitzvah, host the celebration in the backyard officiated by a rent-a-rabbi—all for far less than annual membership dues? Need to remember a loved one? Why buy memorial plaques in a synagogue when you can list names of the dearly departed on the National Jewish Memorial Wall website for eighteen dollars a year? In Los Angeles recently, this DIY Judaism has perhaps found its ultimate expression in Shiva Sisters, two women who saw the opportunity to step into the gap left by synagogues that can no longer afford or have the volunteers to help provide a meal of condolence after a funeral. Shiva Sisters will take care of everything: hire a rabbi for the ceremony, cater the meal, organize the minyan, and provide valet parking.

This new accessibility to Jewish knowledge and Jewish professionals represents a relatively new phenomenon, and we are just now feeling its impact. Exacerbating the situation is the current economic downturn, which has put financial pressures on discretionary income that would otherwise fund memberships and donations to Jewish organizations. The decline of synagogue membership has forced smaller institutions to merge or even disappear. Although Jewish Community Centers thrive in many communities, where there were once five JCCs in Los Angeles, there are now two. Central agencies for Jewish education in many communities are shut down. Publicly financed Hebrew charter schools are a growing option to day schools.

Jewish Federations have always thought of themselves as the "central address" of the community. For years, their sophisticated fundraising machines collected contributions to the "community" and doled out the money to local affiliated agencies (JCCs, Jewish Family Services, Bureaus of Jewish Education, and others), while the majority of the dollars were sent to Israel. In some communities, the Federations remain a strong force. But when major funders began to make "donor-directed" contributions directly to Israel and set up their own foundations to fund favored causes, when local agencies were forced to do their own fundraising, the rationale for a central address came under question. Again, the DIY culture has had an enormous impact on institutional life, and savvy Federation leaders have necessarily adjusted their appeal for funds and their role in the community, emphasizing to their lay leadership and professionals the crucial importance of building relationships with individual donors and convening arms of the community that otherwise would remain siloed.

Jewish communal professionals and clergy nearing retirement who have jobs cannot afford to stop working, closing off opportunities for the next generation of leaders. Meanwhile, the professional preparation institutions continue to graduate teachers, educators, communal service workers, cantors, and rabbis, who enter a shrinking job market, often laden with significant student loan debt. What shall these people do? Some will have no choice but to hang their own shingle and offer their services to an increasingly savvy population of Jews who, whether forced by the economic circumstances or because they do not see the value of spending hundreds or thousands of dollars over a number of years, decide to forgo "membership" in Jewish institutions and hire single practitioners, eager for their "business."

Let me be blunt: The days when Jewish institutions could count on people showing up are over. The days when newcomers to a community could be counted on to look for a school for their kids, a local market for food, and a synagogue to join are over. The days when a Federation could count on the vast majority of Jews to give a gift are over. The days when a Jewish Community Center was actually the center of the community are over. In this new reality, another program will not meet the need of the moment. If Jewish organizations are to survive and thrive, what they offer will need to change dramatically ... and soon.

Jewish institutions must rethink their value proposition. If the "value" offer is a calendar of programs, access to Jewish information, gyms, pools, health clubs, cultural events, even activities to "repair the world," our people can get all that for much less money than the high cost of Jewish institutional affiliation. But, if our value proposition is the opportunity to be in face-to-face meaningful relationship with Jews and Judaism in a relational community that offers a path to meaning and purpose, belonging and blessing, we have a shot at engaging our people in a twenty-first-century Relational Judaism.

2

Toward a
Relational Judaism

RELATIONSHIP. DEFINITION: CONNECTION; FRIENDSHIP.
Synonyms: affiliation, affinity, alliance, association, bond, exchange, interconnection, link, marriage, nearness, network, rapport, relation, relevance, similarity, tie.

Terms of Engagement

The Jewish idea of relationship is expressed best in the Hebrew word *brit,* "covenant." A covenant is a pact between two or more people, a social contract, in which one party promises something in return for something from the other. The model for *brit* comes from the earliest accounts in the Torah. God makes a pact with Adam and Eve—"Eat of all the trees in the Garden of Eden except one" (Genesis 2)—and then, of course, they do not hold up their end of the deal. God tells Noah to prepare for the devastating flood; he does, and humanity is saved. Then, Abraham becomes the ancestor of the Jewish people by accepting the covenant with God, who promises to make him and his descendants a great nation if he follows God's instruction to "go out" from everything he knows to "a place that I will show you" (Genesis 12). This relationship of reciprocity between the individual Jew and God is sealed through a ritual called *brit milah* (male circumcision) and *brit ha-bat* (female baby welcoming) in every generation.

Even the model for the covenant entered into between the Israelites and God at Sinai is based on reciprocity. This was most likely borrowed from the Hittite suzerainty treaties common in the ancient Middle East, where the "suzerain" was a "lord" in a power relationship with "vassals." Essentially, the form of the treaty includes a history of the relationship and a stipulation of what each will do for the other.

Jewish theologian and ethicist Rabbi Elliot Dorff teaches the difference between a contract and a covenant. A contract is an agreement to do a task. When the task is complete, the relationship is over. A covenant, however, is intended to create a relationship; it is intended for the long term. Like the covenant of marriage, you hope the partnership is lifelong.

Enlightenment philosophers John Locke and Thomas Hobbes both discuss "social contracts," what it means to leave the state of nature and enter into a social relationship. For Hobbes, every human being is out for herself/himself; since everyone is vulnerable, the social contract is intended to protect the self. For Locke, every human being is rational; the social contract is thus intended to maximize what people can do together. Contrast this with the Jewish tradition, which views every human being as created *b'tzelem Elohim*, "in the image of God." God creates community in order for people to do *mitzvot*—obligations; that is the purpose and mission of community. When you live a life according to the *mitzvot*, you work on perfecting yourself and perfecting the world.

Rabbi Dorff draws a vivid example to explicate the differences between American pragmatism, shaped by the social contract theorists, and Judaism, shaped by a covenantal relationship. Why should I care about my body? The American pragmatist answer is, "I will feel better, I will get better insurance, and I will live longer." The Jewish covenantal answer is, "I take care of my body in order to serve God by fulfilling the obligations that come by being in relationship with the Divine."

We may, however, be experiencing a shift in American individualism. Barack Obama tapped into it in his book *The Audacity of Hope*:

> If we Americans are individualistic at heart, if we instinctively chafe against a past of tribal allegiances, traditions,

customs, and castes, it would be a mistake to assume that is all we are. Our individualism has always been bound by a set of communal values, the glue upon which every healthy society depends. We value the imperatives of family and the cross-generational obligations that family implies. We value community, the neighborliness that expresses itself through raising the barn or coaching the soccer team. We value patriotism and the obligations of citizenship, a sense of duty and sacrifice on behalf of our nation. We value a faith in something bigger than ourselves, whether that something expresses itself in formal religion or ethical precepts. And we value the constellation of behaviors that express our mutual regard for one another: honesty, fairness, humility, kindness, courtesy, and compassion.[1]

Rabbi Dorff notes a similar shift in American religious life by recalling a comment made to him by Joseph Blau, his professor of religion at Columbia University in 1964:

> Blau told our class that the pendulum has swung to where religion means social action. But, he predicted, it will swing back to a point where religion is a search for individual spirituality. It was a prescient comment; that is exactly what has happened over the past fifty years.... I see all sorts of evidence that the pendulum may be swinging back again toward social justice, toward a realization that our task is to fix the earth. That is the purpose of the Jewish covenantal relationship. Maybe Barbra Streisand was right after all: "People who need people are the luckiest people in the world."

The words used in the Torah to describe the establishment of a covenant are *likhrot brit*—literally, "to cut a covenant." "Cut" is an interesting term. We "cut a check," a promise to pay. We "cut a deal," an agreed-upon transaction. But, we also "cut someone out of a will" and "cut off" a bad relationship. Cutting can mean both separating and binding, depending on the context. In either meaning, the individuality of the two parties in relationship is recognized.

The mutual covenant agreed to at Sinai was initiated in quite a dramatic form. As the Torah relates, Moses climbs to the top of the mountain, where God prepares the people to receive the Torah:

> Adonai called to him from the mountain, saying, "Thus shall you say to the house of Jacob and declare to the children of Israel: 'You have seen what I did to the Egyptians, how I bore you on eagles' wings and brought you to Me. Now then, if you will obey Me faithfully and keep My covenant, you shall be My treasured possession among all the peoples. Indeed, all the earth is Mine, but you shall be to Me a kingdom of priests and a holy nation.' These are the words you shall speak to the children of Israel."
>
> Moses came and summoned the elders of the people and put before them all that Adonai had commanded him. All the people answered as one, saying, "All that Adonai has spoken we will do!" And Moses brought back the people's words to Adonai.
>
> EXODUS 19:3–8

In Judaism, the individual is a member of a community with obligations. We left Egypt as a community; we experienced Sinai as a community. We are obligated to one another by a system of *mitzvot*, which means not rights, but responsibilities.

Relationships are a two-way street. They make claims on me. In Los Angeles, the mother of a neighbor dies, and I cancel my appointments to attend the funeral in order to be with my friend, although I barely knew his mother. Another friend is honored by a prominent Jewish communal organization; I send a check and attend the dinner. I react with concern and empathy to the news of anti-Semitic attacks in a European country. The community gathers together for a walk to raise consciousness and money for the victims of genocide in Darfur, and our *havurah* participates. A child tragically dies, and I rail at God.

Emanuel Levinas, a twentieth-century French Jewish philosopher, taught that from the moment of birth, we are obligated by the mere "gaze" of another.[2] The very essence of relationship is the responsibility to engage the Other, to respond. Philosopher Martin Buber called this the "I–Thou" relationship.[3] The Other is not an inanimate "It"; the Other is a personal "Thou" that demands a response. Social constructivists like Peter Berger and Kenneth J. Gergen argue that virtually everything we experience is a function of relationships, not some inherent quality of the thing itself. In a sense, we are all, always, in relation to someone or something else.

This obligation to each other is rooted in the biblical notion that every human being is made in the image of God. The *image* of God is within, but the *presence* of God is found "in the between," in our relationships. When I care for another person, I am taking on the responsibility of doing God's work on earth.

On a personal level, other important relationships in life follow this covenantal model. Marriage signifies a change in relationship between two individuals. A set of reciprocal agreements is made through vows and, in the Jewish instance, a formalized contract—the *ketubah*. The promise of this covenant is celebrated by the officiant—lifelong devotion, a sensitive companion on life's journey, children. Names often change—completely or hyphenated. The new relationship is celebrated in ritual, song, dance, and feasting. Bar/Bat Mitzvah marks another transitional moment, when children accept the responsibilities and privileges incumbent upon an adult Jew.

I am reminded that other covenants most people enter into during their lives are, in fact, a privilege, not a right. Obtaining a driver's license is one example. Driving is a privilege that comes with attendant obligations and responsibilities. Likewise, serving on a jury requires a covenant, a "swearing in" during which the juror accepts the burden of listening to evidence, negotiating with fellow jurors, and rendering judgment. As citizens of America and Canada, we have both the right and the responsibility to vote, the vehicle by which democracy ensures the inalienable relationship between individuals and government.

The idea of covenant is, as Rabbi David Wolpe, author and rabbi of Sinai Temple in Los Angeles, has noted, "the spine of Judaism."[4] We are constantly reminded of our covenantal relationship with God and each other. Shabbat is a sign of the covenant. The Passover Seder reminds us that God keeps promises: *V'hi she'amdah l'avoteinu v'lanu,* "God who safeguards God's promises to our ancestors and to us." The pageantry of the Torah reading service reenacts the revelation of the covenant at Sinai. The goal of the covenant is celebrated at the climax of the ceremony—the returning of the Torah to the holy ark: *Etz hayim hi l'machazikim bah*, "It is a tree of life for those who take hold of it," *v'tomkheha m'ushar*—"and those who support it are enriched." In other words, those who embrace the covenantal relationship discover how to live a life of meaning and purpose, belonging and blessing. Moreover, covenants form the foundation of "community"—a group of people bound together in relationship based upon reciprocal responsibilities.

We North American Jews are not only citizens of two great countries; we are also citizens of a people called *b'nei Yisrael*, "the children of Israel"—the descendants of Jacob, the descendants of Moses, the descendants of those who stood at Sinai and accepted a covenantal relationship with the God of Abraham and Sarah. The terms of agreement are specified, the consequences of success or failure if they are fulfilled or ignored are clear, and the covenant is initiated in a dramatic form. How we navigate between the rights of the sovereign self and the obligations of community is the challenge facing Jewish communal leaders in the twenty-first century.

The Challenge of Individualism

There is a flip side to the coin of individualism—loneliness. Ironically, in a world of hyper-connectivity, we are shockingly alone, glued to our computer and smartphone screens, texting each other from across the room, sending e-mails of condolence or posting on Facebook walls instead of picking up the phone or showing up in person, face-to-face. At Temple Emanu-El in San Francisco, one of the largest urban Reform synagogues in the country, the results of a yearlong "listening campaign" featuring hundreds of one-on-one conversations and dozens of house meetings designed to reveal the concerns people have that might lead them to engage in actions to improve society are instructive. The organizers were not surprised when the sorry state of public education rose to the top of the justice agenda. They were surprised, however, by the second issue that emerged from these revelatory dialogues: the isolation and loneliness felt by members of the congregation. "We come to services, to programs, and we don't know anyone." "Our kids go to preschool together, but we don't know the other parents." "We are lonely."

In his famous philosophical treatise *The Lonely Man of Faith*, Rabbi Joseph B. Soloveitchik unpacks the two images of Adam in the Torah.[5] In the first chapter of Genesis, Adam is created "in the image of God" and given dominion over his environment. Soloveitchik calls this first Adam a "majestic man" who, like an individualist, sees the world and relationships as functional, transactional, pragmatic. This Adam uses his creative abilities to impose his will on the world. The second Adam is different. In chapter 2 of Genesis, God proclaims, *Lo tov he'yot ha'adam l'vado*, "It is not good for man to be alone," and with God's intervention and Adam's contribution (a rib), Eve arrives to relieve the existential loneliness of the individual. More importantly, Soloveitchik teaches, this second image of Adam presents him as a "covenantal man" who is in relationship with God. By accepting the notion that he cannot thrive alone, Adam the "lonely man" in chapter 1 becomes Adam the "lonely man of faith" in chapter 2, understanding that living in a relational community, building a relationship with God and with other human beings, is the path to bringing a redemptive interpretation to the meaning of existence.

We are both Adams. We revel in our individualism, our incredible, ever-increasing dominion over all we see. Yet, we crave companionship, community, relationship—because through it, we find meaning and purpose, belonging and blessing.

Three Levels of Community

In our conversation, Arnold M. Eisen, chancellor of The Jewish Theological Seminary of America, reflected on the importance of relationships as the foundation of community:

> I have been saying my entire adult life that the quality of the Jewish community is what it's all about ... and given that "community" is all about relationships, relationships are the key. So, Buber was right. It's no coincidence that this tradition of ours mandates relationships and has a God who

invites us into relationship. Relationships build communities.
There is no doubt that it is the heart of the matter.

In his book *Taking Hold of Torah: Jewish Commitment and Community in America*, Eisen writes movingly of the three levels of community he believes can engage unaffiliated Jews. The first is the local Jewish community: face-to-face community "built on the basis of clear and present needs ... and held together primarily by the cement of personal connection linking each person and his or her *re'a*, or neighbor."[6]

The second level of community is global—that of North American Jewry or the Jewish people as a whole. Here, Eisen is arguing that North American Jews need connection to the idea of Jewish peoplehood.

> Although many Jews are no doubt in flight from the weight of their people's history and the quandaries it poses, most Jews also feel considerable pride at their people's achievements over the centuries and today. Counting the Jews among Nobel Prize winners and other lists of celebrities is a well-known Jewish sport. The benefits, real and imagined, of attachment to one's people and all it stands for are substantial.[7]

The third level of community Eisen calls "middle-range" because of its size, scope, and function. These are groups that are somewhere between the face-to-face smaller local Jewish community and the grand notion of "North American Jewry" or "world Jewry." They include larger synagogues, regional Federations, cultural organizations, and political causes. Community is created by commitment to a shared cause and "nurtured by the discovery that, only five minutes into the first encounter, one can abandon small talk in favor of shorthand conversation about things that matter. Middle-range communities are less homogeneous than local communities and necessarily embrace a wider diversity of opinions and needs. Such communities can create 'networks of affection' as a result of close work together on causes, through study experiences, and affinities."[8]

Eisen concludes that while it may be daunting to create community on all three levels—local, global, and middle-range—reaching for the goal is crucial for the future of North American Jewry.

The strength of community, as of ritual, lies in its potential to bring people together despite differing backgrounds and beliefs: to take them out of themselves into a space "between" and then return them to themselves, to their private spaces, transformed. The experience of Jewish community, the sense of lived connection to the covenants of fate and destiny, is what brings Jews back for more of the same ... and bonds them more tightly to the Jewish people and Jewish traditions despite their unwillingness to sacrifice autonomy or foreclose options.[9]

Eisen then lays down a bold challenge to communal leaders:

The magic does not work for all Jews ... and never will. Given its success thus far, however, the aim of actively involving another 10 percent of the community over the course of the next decade or so—half a million Jews—does not seem to me at all unrealistic. The resultant transformation of the community would be beyond measure.[10]

Eisen wrote these words in 1997. It has been "a decade or so." Yet, membership in community is down, donations are flat, organizations continue to struggle for support and attention. Why? I believe it is because most Jewish communal organizations invested in programs, not people; built buildings, not micro/local communities; focused on institutions, not relationships. Shortly, we will look at case studies of those organizations that are embracing the vision that relationships are the building blocks of community; they are thriving. Is it too late for others? I don't believe it is ... if we do the labor-intensive work to build communities of enduring relationships that engage and motivate Jewish identity and commitment.

Listening, Sharing, Doing, Trusting

As we will explore below, a Relational Judaism begins with listening and telling. Sharing the stories of your life is the essential bridge between two people, the connecting roadway of relationship. In our conversations, we reveal ourselves to others. At first, we reveal small-talk details: sports teams we support, weather we enjoy, traffic we endure. But, as the conversation proceeds, we reveal more important aspects of our lives: where we grew up, where we studied, whom we know, what we do. Eventually, as the relationship deepens, we reveal our innermost hopes and fears, achievements and disappointments, opportunities and challenges.

As contemporary scholar Rabbi Gordon Freeman observes, revelation is the first act of building a relationship.

> Revelation is an act of opening up, of revealing an inner essence. Revelation is very risky (for God, for everyone), for people can reject it. Revelation is glorious because people can accept the giver in unbound intimacy. If revelation is rejected, one's very existence is at stake. Without revelation, there is no relationship. Without relationship, one stands alone.[11]

In Judaism, revelation is an ongoing phenomenon. The giving of Torah only began at Sinai; Torah is revealed to us continuously. The blessing recited before and after the reading of the Torah emphasizes the point: *Barukh atah Adonai, notayn ha-Torah*, "Blessed are You, God, who gives the Torah." The tense is present, not past. The Torah is revealed at the instant of hearing, just as the person is revealed during the conversations that fuel relationship.

This is the essence of a one-on-one, face-to-face encounter with those we seek to engage with Judaism. "What's your story?" "Tell me about yourself." We Jews are good at telling stories. The Torah we read out loud four times a week is replete with compelling stories that illustrate the complexities of lives lived in relationship—with other human beings and with God. The Passover Seder is structured around a text called *Haggadah*—literally, "The Telling." In recent years, the extraordinary effort to record and catalog more than fifty thousand stories and testimonies of Holocaust survivors through Steven Spielberg's Shoah Foundation is a project of storytelling. Speaking of Hollywood, it is no surprise that the ranks of moviemakers, song lyricists, Broadway playwrights, novelists, and nonfiction authors are filled with Jewish names.

For Jewish institutional leaders, telling is the second most important step in building relationships. The most important first step is *listening.* In our rush to tell the Jewish story, we often forget to listen carefully to our target audience. Listening requires total attention. When people feel heard, the connection is deepened, the relationship progresses. When people feel ignored or dismissed, there is no chance for relationship.

This critical ability to listen is illustrated in this wonderful commentary on the people Israel's response to the dramatic giving of the Ten Commandments (Exodus 20:15). The commentator reflects on why the Hebrew terms *kolot,* "thunder," and *lapidim,* "lightning," are plural:

> "And all the people saw the thunderings and the lightnings."
> The thunderings upon thunderings, the lightnings upon lightnings. How many thunderings were there and how many lightnings were there? It is simply this: they were heard by each person according to his capacity.
>
> *M'KHILTA OF RABBI YISHMAEL, BACHODESH 9*

The midrash is saying something quite profound: each of us has an individualized capacity to hear revelation(s).

The relationship between listening and doing is a dynamic dialectic. In one famous quotation from the Torah, the people Israel at Sinai say, *Na'aseh v'nishma,* "We will do and we will hear" (Exodus 24:7). But, in two earlier texts, listening precedes deeds: "All that Adonai has spoken we will do!" (Exodus 19:8, 24:3). The watchword of the Jewish people—*Sh'ma, Yisrael!* "Hear, people of Israel"—is the imperative to listen. We too must listen carefully and hear our people if we hope to engage them in "doing Jewish."

"Doing" is the next step in building relationships. Think of your closest friends. How did you really get to know them? Not just from talking together, certainly. Sharing experiences is the glue that bonds people together. Having dinner together, watching a show or movie together, working on a project together, taking a trip together— these are opportunities to deepen relationships with others. In Jewish institutional life, most leaders will agree that being together on a "mission"—to Israel, to Africa, to rebuild homes in New Orleans, to support Jews in the former Soviet Union, to an AIPAC conference, a

General Assembly, or a biennial meeting of a denominational religious movement—does more to maintain relationships than any other single experience. Often these experiences of "doing" lead to the sharing of feelings, a further revelation of the innermost self. In a way, these are *lekh lekha* experiences, a "going out to one's self" that both heightens self-awareness and fosters engagement and connection.

Inevitably, relationships change as individuals grow and change through the years. Relationship maintenance requires an awareness of this expected development, further listening to concerns and issues as they arise, and an adjustment of the relationship moving forward. When this is done in good faith, the relationship grows even stronger, as does the trust between the parties.

Finally, it is this notion of trust that is the reward for the investment in building relationships with others. You trust that your dearest family and friends will be there with you in good times and be there for you in bad. You trust that the challenges you encounter in life will not be faced alone. You know that those who know you, who have shared life with you, who love you will be there to offer support, comfort, care, and help. For those who believe in a power beyond the self, the reward of being in relationship with God is similar. A reciprocal relationship with God, rooted in the notion of mutual covenant, can give a sense of assurance that even in the darkest hours of existence, "though I walk through the valley of the shadow of death, Your rod and staff will comfort me" (Psalm 23:4). The ultimate payoff for investing in relationships with others and with The Other is the knowledge that you are not alone.

3

The Nine Levels of Relationship

RELATIONSHIPS WITH WHOM? How? Where? When? For what?

What is the goal of shifting the paradigm of Jewish organizations from programmatic to relational?

The buzzword of the moment in Jewish communal conversation is "engagement." How will the community engage the unaffiliated, the under-affiliated, and even those who do affiliate with the Jewish experience? In thinking about this question, I look to a book of the Bible known as the Song of Songs.

Ostensibly, the Song of Songs is a love story told in lofty poetic language, illuminating the relationship between two people. The Rabbis, perhaps embarrassed over the erotic nature of the book, interpreted the story as a metaphor for the relationship between God and the people Israel.

As in any good love story, the relationship between two individual entities begins with telling stories, learning about each other, and building memories through shared experiences together. The process leads to a decision to become "engaged," a period of time in which to test the bonds, to ensure the long-term viability of the relationship. Ultimately, the two become one—"married"—a (hopefully) lifelong commitment to be in relationship, through thick and thin, good times and bad. It is this lifelong commitment that is the goal of Jewish engagement as well.

Look at the graphic image to the right. What do you see?

Do you see the outline of a chalice? Or, do you see the silhouetted profiles of two persons in face-to-face relationship? Focus your attention on the white, and you will see the cup; focus on the black, and you will see the people.

This is an apt symbolic representation of *relationship*. When two human beings engage each other in a face-to-face encounter, relationship exists *in the between*. It is in that space that relationship can turn into "engagement." The goal of Relational Judaism is to foster the relationships that will bring people into deep, lasting engagement with the Jewish experience.

The Sacred Fountain of Relationships

A number of years ago, I was celebrating Shabbat dinner with good friends who had just returned from Israel with the most wonderful souvenir. It was a "*Kiddush* fountain." The Hebrew word *kiddush*—from the root word *kadosh*—literally means "sacred."

The silver device stood about ten inches high and featured two tiers. The top tier was a single large *Kiddush* cup; on the bottom tier, eight small *Kiddush* cups sat in a circle, each one positioned below a spout. When it came time to recite the *Kiddush* prayer, the host filled the large *Kiddush* cup with wine and, with quite the flourish, poured it into a hole at the top of the fountain. Within seconds, the wine was distributed simultaneously to the eight small *Kiddush* cups on the bottom tier, much to the delight of everyone at the table. When the wine finished its journey through the fountain, the host handed each of the guests a cup, over which we, together, sang the prayer praising God and sanctifying the Sabbath day. It was both a communal and an individual experience, filled with surprise and joy, creating a memorable moment of Jewish celebration, not just of Shabbat, but of the relationships around the table.

When we are "in the between" with another, we share a bond, a sacred bond. Rabbi Edward Feinstein teaches:

A family, a circle of friends, gathers about the Shabbat or holiday table to share a celebration. A cup of wine is raised. The wine is not sacred. It's only Manischewitz. What is sacred, holy, are the bonds that gather us together to celebrate life. So together we recite a prayer called *Kiddush*.

Two individuals in love and devotion, determined to share a lifetime together. A ring—whole and unbroken—is slipped onto a finger, signifying a commitment whole and unbroken. And words are spoken. *Haray at m'kudeshet li*, you are *kadosh* to me. This rite that bonds two lives together is called *kiddushin*.

A loved one has died. And with tears we rise in the presence of a community at prayer to declare that even the catastrophe of death cannot sever the bond that holds us together. This prayer is called *Kaddish*.

Kiddush, kiddushin, Kaddish, kadosh, kedushah—all mean holiness, and all mean opening the self to embrace another, bonding with another, holding the other close, never letting go, making the other part of the self. We form around ourselves a circle, a circle of our intimate concern the people we care for, the ones we define as ours. For some, the circumference of that circle is so narrow it includes only the individual self; its diameter reaching only to the end of the nose. For others, the circle includes family, community, nation. We worship a God whose circle of concern is infinite. *Adonai Ehad*, God is the infinite circle of concern encompassing all of life.

Kedoshim tihiyu, "You shall be holy": this is the highest spiritual aspiration of Jewish life. Open up the self, draw your circle wider and wider, until it approaches the infinity of God's circle.

What is the opposite of holiness? In Hebrew, the opposite of *kadosh* is *hol*. Translated as "profane" or "ordinary," *hol* literally means "sand." Sand has no cohesion, no connection, no bonds. When you are in relationship, you share a bond with an Other. It's this world of *hol*, sand—of atomized individuals; of sovereign, lonely, unconnected selves—that you come to community to escape. When you tire of being a consumer, you seek intimacy, friendship, trust. When you weary of transactional relationships, you seek belonging. When Jewish institutions become places of sacred community, you discover *kadosh*.[1]

So, I went out and bought our family a "*Kiddush* fountain," a physical reminder that when we are "in the between"—in the sharing with others—we find relationship with others and with the Divine. Moreover, it is *ot hi l'olam*—"a sign of the everlasting relationship *between* God and the Jewish people."

The "*Bayns*" of Our Existence

If organizations are not focusing their energies and resources on mounting programs, how, then, will they strengthen the connectedness of Jews with the Jewish experience? Can we develop a vision for a fully realized, fully engaged Relational Jew?

Yes, we can. And it begins with the key word that characterizes "relationship." It is the Hebrew word *bayn*, "between."

What does "between" mean? The standard definition is "jointly engaging, in common to, serving to connect or unite in a relationship." Its origin is Old English: *be-* + *tweonum*, literally "be-two." It is the relationship of two. It is the dash between what Martin Buber called the "I" and the "Thou." The essence of "between" is connection, the bridging of the space between you and an Other. As we shall learn, building relationships requires filling the space with shared feelings and experiences that create trust, respect, even love.

These are the "*bayns*" of our existence:

1. *Bayn adam l'atzmo*—between you and yourself: a strong internal Jewish identity, a definition of self that includes "Jewish" as a key factor
2. *Bayn adam l'mishpachah*—between you and your family
3. *Bayn adam l'haveiro*—between you and your friend(s)
4. *Bayn adam l'Yahadut*—between you and Jewish living and learning
5. *Bayn adam l'kehillah*—between you and your community, both sacred and secular

6. *Bayn adam l'am*—between you and Jewish peoplehood, wherever Jews are

7. *Bayn adam l'Yisrael*—between you and the State of Israel

8. *Bayn adam l'olam*—between you and the whole world

9. *Bayn adam l'Makom*—between you and God: belief or disbelief; either way, a willingness to wrestle with the Divine

Jewish institutional life, in its totality, can empower individuals to create, sustain, and celebrate these Nine Levels of Relationship.

Before we go any further, let's talk about God. I fully realize there are many Jews who will say, "I don't believe in God." I meet them at lectures, especially when I speak about my books *God's To-Do List: 103 Ways to Be an Angel and Do God's Work on Earth* and *Be Like God: God's To-Do List for Kids* (both Jewish Lights Publishing). When I ask, "Tell me about the God you don't believe in," the response I inevitably get is a Sunday-school version of an old man with a long white beard, sitting on a throne in heaven. I don't believe in that God, either. Whether you are a believer, an agnostic, or an atheist, please do not let "God" be an obstacle to a relationship between you and something bigger, something beyond yourself. And, if that is too daunting, perhaps you can believe in the "godliness" within you. Whatever your belief—or nonbelief—you can still be counted in the Jewish experience. After all, Jews are called "*b'nei Yisrael*," the descendants of the one who wrestles with God (*El*), a reference to Jacob, who struggled with God before the encounter with his brother Esau, from whom he stole a birthright. Our birthright as Jews is to be God-wrestlers; that is who we are. As I often say to those who are nonbelievers, "Bring it on." When you wrestle with some idea, someone, or especially, some One, you are in relationship.

The First Level: *Bayn Adam l'Atzmo*—Self

An engaging Relational Judaism will speak directly to the following existential questions: Who am I? What is the meaning of my life? What is my purpose?

This is the first level of relationship—with my Self.

Likewise, Jewish tradition has always seen the individual as a relational being. The most well-known of Rabbi Hillel's teachings (*Pirke*

Avot 1:14) begins with this notion of self-identity: *Im ein ani li, mi li?* The usual translation of this aphorism is, "If I am not for myself, who will be for me?" But, the literal translation is, "If I am not for myself, who am I?" If I do not understand my self, how can I possibly be in relationship with an Other?

Lest one think this call for self-reflection is some sort of twenty-first-century version of the "me" culture, the intense navel-gazing period of self-actualization popularized in the 1970s, it is important to note that the root of the Hebrew term for prayer, *tefillah*, is *l'hitpalel*, a reflexive verb meaning "to examine oneself." The goal of Jewish prayer is not simply to praise God and ask for God's blessings. The goal of Jewish prayer is to be *moved*, to change one's self.

In his seminal work *Relational Being*, Kenneth J. Gergen presents an alternative construction of human existence that counters the view that the individual self is essentially independent and autonomous—a "bounded being." Instead, Gergen seeks to demonstrate that "virtually all intelligible action is born, sustained, and/or extinguished within the ongoing process of relationship." He calls the individual a "relational being," inhabiting a "world that is not within persons but within their relationships."[2]

Jewish tradition has always seen the individual not as a "bounded being," but as a *bonded* being. Judaism is rooted in community, responsibility, obligation, and commitment to things beyond the self. After all, is not one of the goals of a community and a religion the enculturation of a certain set of beliefs, behaviors, and belongings that have a profound influence on the self? This is not about the question "What's in it for me?" It is about the question "How will my life be different by engaging with Judaism?" And how are the lives of the people we engage—our congregants, students, supporters, members, leaders, and guests—*changed* as a result of their engagement with our institutions and community?

When do we move people? I mean, really *move* them. Does belonging or coming to a synagogue, a JCC, a defense organization, a Hillel, a youth group, help them become better human beings? Are we influencing, educating, socializing, empowering every individual to be the best person she or he can be?

This is the Zusya question. It is the question Martin Buber called the "Query of All Queries":

> Before his death, Rabbi Zusya said: "In the coming world, they will not ask me: 'Why were you not Moses?' They will ask me: 'Why were you not Zusya?'"[3]

In a Relational Judaism, perfecting the self—*tikkun atzmi*—is a worthy goal. When individuals understand that we have something to say about how to live a life of meaning and purpose, belonging and blessing, they will connect to this questing, curious people. Our task is to encourage people to lead a life that stands up to this ultimate question we are asked in heaven: *"Were you the best you that you could be?"*

For nearly twenty years now, I have been studying the evangelical megachurch, engaging their leaders in conversation, learning the principles of how they build relationships and sacred community. Every semester, I take my education students from American Jewish University and my rabbinical students from the Ziegler School of Rabbinic Studies to visit Saddleback Church, one of the leading megachurches in the world. I have become friends with Rick Warren, Saddleback's founding and visionary pastor, and many of his colleagues who lead the church.

The most striking reality of Saddleback Church is how "in your face" they are about how Christianity can change lives. In their study of religion in America at the turn of the century, *American Grace*, Robert Putnam and David Campbell present detailed sociological survey data and vignettes that illustrate how congregations are doing their work.[4] There is an excellent description of Saddleback and their overarching goal: they are in the business of *changing lives*. Pastor Warren likes to say, "When you come to Saddleback, you will hear something on Sunday that you can use in your life on Monday ... in your work, with your family ... for your community."

In a seemingly ironic twist, the first sentence in *The Purpose-Driven Life*, Rick Warren's best-selling book, is, "It's not about you."[5] He stares down American individualism, the "me-first" culture that drives his target audience, and unabashedly tells his readers and his congregants that there is a higher purpose for their lives beyond self-indulgent, narcissistic personal campaigns for ever-greater collections of material things. He and his colleagues have shaped a sacred community built on a "culture of transformation" that begins with how the self can transcend itself by creating relationships—with God, with other human beings, with the world, a path to a purposeful and meaningful life.

Our Selves

We live in an amazing time. As a result of medical advances that have lengthened life expectancy, we will be the first people in history to live in a community with four generations, each generation spanning twenty years, each with its own unique characteristics. Let's look at three distinct Jewish generations: baby boomers, generation X, and millennials.

1. THE JEWISH BABY-BOOMER SELF

The children born in the twenty years after World War II form the famous "baby boom" generation. Now nearing retirement, the boomers are often in positions of leadership in the Jewish community. The boomers are what sociologist Wade Clark Roof famously called "the generation of seekers." What are they seeking? Self-actualization, meaning, a belief that they have, in fact, changed the world. Most of the boomers married before age thirty, and many of them found their way into Jewish affiliation when their children were born.

2. THE JEWISH GENERATION-X SELF

Born between 1965 and 1982, Generation Xers are commonly thought to be "slackers" and unhappy. Not true, according to a longitudinal study of this generation by the University of Michigan. Jewish Xers are the first wired/wireless generation, with extensive social, work, and community networks beyond the immediate family. Despite the stereotype, most are industrious, settled into careers, establishing families, and beginning to engage in Jewish communal life, albeit slowly.

3. THE JEWISH MILLENNIAL SELF

The millennial generation consists of those born between 1982 and 2004. Studies of the millennials reveal this generation to be "confident, connected, and open to change." They resist "belonging," and they are nowhere near as loyal to jobs, career paths, and cities as previous cohorts were. Pursuing their passion is important to them, many abandoning their professions to "follow their dreams," "to live a meaningful life." They have been taught the value of social justice through a variety of service learning experiences. Like generation X, the millennials are in no hurry to partner off, but being a good parent and having a successful marriage are important to them.

Like other millennials, many of the Jewish young adults in this generation distrust institutions, prefer to shape their own experiences, and connect with others through their own microcommunities, hence the interesting development of independent minyanim. They are interested in Jewish expression, but not necessarily through synagogues, JCCs, or other organizations. Cultural arts, public-space Judaism, and do-it-yourself holiday celebrations are attractive.

Like the generations before them, Jewish millennials want to find meaning and purpose in Jewish life, but on their own terms. They ask: How does being Jewish inform my personal and professional choices? How do I take the next steps on my spiritual journey? Is there a small community of peers with whom I can build relationships? Who is there to mentor me when life takes unexpected turns, when parents divorce or die, when tragedy strikes, when it is time to settle into a career or start a family?

Engaging the Self

Recognizing these generational differences and proclivities can be instructive for institutions seeking to engage these Jews. Certainly, the leading lights in the Jewish community developed interesting strategies to do just that. For Rabbi Harold Schulweis in the 1970s, it was the establishment of small groups—*havurot*—in his congregation, a model adopted by scores of synagogues across North America. Writing at the turn of the millennium, sociologists Eisen and Cohen called on institutions to provide the vehicles (their metaphor is a fleet of busses, all perfectly timed to be at just the right place to pick up the suddenly interested sovereign self passenger) to transport individuals on their personal Jewish journeys. What will be the strategy for changing the lives of the generation Xers and millennials? I believe it must be based on hearing them, understanding them, and engaging them in meaningful relationships with the Nine Levels of Relationship with the Jewish experience.

Changing lives means moving people—not just intellectually, but also emotionally. David Brooks, in his book *The Social Animal: The Hidden Sources of Love, Character, and Achievement*, explores the "empire of emotion" that exists in the unconscious realm of the mind.

> If the study of the conscious mind highlights the importance of reason and analysis, study of the unconscious mind highlights the importance of passions and perception. If the outer mind highlights the power of the individual, the inner mind highlights the power of relationships and the invisible bonds between people. If the outer mind hungers for status, money, and applause, the inner mind hungers for harmony and connection—those moments when self-consciousness fades away and a person is lost in a challenge, a cause, the love of another or the love of God.[6]

To quote the great educator Shlomo Bardin, people need to be touched, not only taught. And yet, if you interview most Jews, you'll find they can count on one hand the number of times they have felt inspired, elevated, and elated with a Jewish experience.

Federations, Jewish social justice organizations, and defense organizations are good at this. They produce emotion-filled videos of immigrants kissing the ground upon arriving at Ben Gurion Airport in Israel, nurses caring for the elderly, and college students building houses in post-Katrina New Orleans. The goal is to move the heart and motivate the hand to write a check.

Synagogues, on the other hand, are coming late to this understanding. For most of the past decade the Synagogue 3000 Synagogue Studies Institute has served as the Jewish component for an annual nationwide study of congregational life called the FACT survey, "Faith Communities Today," sponsored by the Hartford Theological Seminary. In 2011, in answer to the question "Are your worship services joyful?" 74 percent of Reform leaders agreed, and 46 percent of Conservative leaders agreed. To the second question "Is your worship inspirational?"

58 percent of Reform synagogue leaders agreed, and 40 percent of Conservative leaders agreed.[7]

And so we must ask ourselves: When is the last time people cried in a synagogue? When do they laugh? Raise their voices in ecstatic prayer? When are they moved to dance? … and I'm not talking about Simchat Torah. Can't we bring a little emotion into our sanctuaries? We are really good at the head; let's get better at the heart.

The Self as Symbol

Nahum Sarna, a biblical scholar, taught that *tzelem*, the word that describes the creation of human beings by God, has another meaning besides "image." For Sarna, *tzelem* means "symbol." In this reading, every human being is a symbol of God, each with a unique purpose authorized by the Creator.

Philosopher George Herbert Mead founded a school of thought known as "symbolic interactionism," an approach to understanding how human beings find meaning in relationship with others.[8] One of Mead's disciples, Herbert Blumer, identified the basic premises of symbolic interactionism in his book *Symbolic Interactionism: Perspective and Method*. As explained by Blumer, symbolic interactionism claims that individuals derive meaning by taking on the role of others in order to better see herself/himself. When I stand in your shoes, when I can see the world through your eyes, I can better understand the meaning you ascribe to actions.[9]

This is what Martin Buber taught. When I treat an Other as an "It," the "It" is an object to be used. When I treat an Other as a "Thou," the relationship is one of authentic, mutual encounter. An I–Thou relationship exists "in the between," without any objectification of the Other.[10]

When you see yourself—and others—and God—as a Thou, you open up yourself to the possibility that there is something beyond your self, to the understanding that meaning is found in the ability to experience life as a dialogue, not a monologue, to rejecting self-ishness as a limiting narcissism and embracing relationship as your guiding existential principle of being.

The sacred self is relational. The sacred self is unique. The sacred self is imbued with a sense of *kedushah*—a spirituality born of the realization that what I do in the world makes a difference, a unique contribution that only I can make.

The task of Jewish institutions is to inspire our individuated, privatized Jews to engage in a Relational Judaism that speaks to their lives, moves their hearts, and encourages their souls to break the bondage of insularity and prepare the self to bond with the other levels of relationship that define a fully engaged Jew. This is the goal of the first level of relationship—*bayn adam l'atzmo*.

The Second Level: *Bayn Adam l'Mishpachah*—Family

Rabbi Tony Bayfield, past president of the Movement for Reform Judaism in Great Britain, teaches that the key relational phrase in the Torah is *lo tov he'yot ha'adam l'vado*, "it is not good for human beings to be alone" (Genesis 2:18). He points out that in the promise and blessing made to Abraham by God—"all of the families of the earth will find a blessing in you" (Genesis 12:3)—the use of the term "families" is instructive. Family members are often called "relations," a word etymologically related to "relationships." Rabbi Bayfield underscores the idea that it is within our familial relationships that we often find the most significant experience of relating as social beings.[11]

Family is a powerful influence on Jewish identity formation according to Arnold M. Eisen and Steven M. Cohen in their book *The Jew Within: Self, Family, and Community in America*, including their surprising finding that grandparents have a significant impact on the Jewish identity of their descendants. Although the sovereign self retains the right to change and develop in her/his own way, the "negotiation with others, particularly other family members" has an influence on Jewish choices.[12]

Covenantal relationships are at the heart of family life. Whether gay or straight, a marriage or commitment ceremony represents the beginning of a family. When a child is born or adopted, the *brit milah* or *simchat bat* not only marks the covenant between individuals and God, but also bestows a name that links the familial generations. The education of children is incumbent upon their parents in Jewish tradition. In our liturgy the imperative for parents to "teach your children diligently" is recited immediately after the *Sh'ma*, the declaration of faith. Bringing a child to Bar/Bat Mitzvah, shepherding teenagers through the turbulence of adolescence, and launching them into young adulthood—all these require a deep understanding of the mutual obligations and responsibilities inherent in the parent-child relationship.

Children have a special relationship with God, as beautifully illustrated in this famous midrash:

> Rabbi Meir said: When the Israelites stood before Sinai to receive the Torah, God said to them, "I will not give you the Torah unless you provide worthy guarantors who will assure that you will maintain My covenant with you." The Israelites answered, "Master of the Universe, our ancestors will be our guarantors!" "Your guarantors themselves require guarantors!" God replied. "Master of the Universe," the Israelites exclaimed, "our prophets will guarantee the covenant." God answered, "I have problems with them, too. 'The shepherds transgressed against Me and the prophets prophesized to Ba'al' (Jeremiah 2:8). Bring proper guarantors ... and only then will I give you the Torah." As a last resort, the Israelites declared, "Our children will be our guarantors." God replied, "They truly are worthy guarantors. Because of them, I will give you the Torah."
>
> *MIDRASH RABBAH*, SONG OF SONGS 1:4

The Jewish understanding of the relationship between parents and children is counterintuitive. It is codified in the fourth of the Ten Commandments:

> Honor your father and your mother.
>
> EXODUS 20:12

We might expect the imperative to be not to honor parents, but to love them. But the Torah's choice of words reveals an important truth: for some children, it is difficult to love their parents. Relationships between parents and children can be filled with challenges, disappointments, hurts. Interestingly, the Torah has no problem commanding "Love Adonai your God" (Deuteronomy 6:5) and "Love your neighbor as yourself" (Leviticus 19:18). But, when it comes to parent-child relationships, even if love is not possible, honor and respect are always expected.

Love plays a more essential role in marriage, of course. Marriage is such a powerful relationship that the Jewish tradition uses it as a metaphor for the relationship between the people Israel and God. As noted below, the entire book of *Shir ha-Shirim*, the Song of Songs, is viewed by the sages as a metaphor for the loving relationship between God and God's covenantal partner. A great marriage has all the hallmarks of a great relationship—the recognition of the individuality of each partner, along with the acceptance of mutual obligation and responsibility. It is a covenantal relationship based on mutual agreements, publicly recorded and recited in the marriage contract, the *ketubah*. But, as in all relationships, there is constant renegotiation of the terms of agreement, as well as the terms of endearment. It is not an easy process; there is a reason that nearly 50 percent of marriages in North America end in divorce, a severing of the covenant.

There are other challenges and opportunities in Jewish families today. Significant rates of intermarriage have spurred efforts at *keiruv*—"bringing closer" those who are not Jewish. Lesbian/gay/bisexual/transgender (LGBT) individuals create new forms of family while seeking acceptance among their families-of-origin. A substantial percentage of couples cannot conceive children; surrogate parenting, in vitro fertilization, and adoption are real issues that impact relationships throughout the family dynamic. Delayed marriage has actually improved the relationship between many young adults and their parents. Professors Karen L. Fingerman and Frank F. Furstenberg have written, "In this new century with delays in marriage, more Americans choosing to remain single and high divorce rates, a tie to a parent may be the most important bond in a young adult's life."[13] As the baby-boom generation ages, caring for elderly parents and grandparents will take a toll on families and Jewish institutions.

It is the mission of Jewish social service agencies, Jewish educational settings, Jewish educators, and clergy to embrace the challenge of deepening relationships in the family. Jewish family education, a field of practice with a nearly thirty-year history in North America, is devoted to the mission of strengthening both the Jewishness and the "family-ness" of Jewish families. The task of Jewish family education is to provide the inspiration, the motivation, and a set of specific strategies designed to deepen relationships among family members and between individuals in the family with the other levels of Relational Judaism, *bayn adam l'mishpachah*.

The Third Level: *Bayn Adam l'Haveiro*—Friends

The third level of relationship is between the individual and his or her friends. The traditional meaning of the phrase *bayn adam l'haveiro* refers to the relationship "between humans and fellow humans." Permit me to be more specific: in a Relational Judaism, an essential foundation of the Jewish community will rest on the relationships between friends.

In their study of American religion, Putnam and Campbell assert the number one reason people remain members of congregations is because of their friends:

> Americans may select their congregations primarily because of
> theology and worship, but the social investment made within
> that congregation appears to be what keeps them there.[14]

In my own work with Jewish institutions, I hear the same answer when I ask why people stay involved in the organization: relationships with others. In synagogues, the friends with whom you raised your kids, the friends with whom you work on projects, the friends with whom you study and worship, the friends who are there to support you in good times and bad—these are the people who, besides family, are your closest relations. In JCC, the friends I work out with, the friends with whom I play cards, or basketball, or swim, the parents of the preschool kids—these are the people who keep me coming back. This is true of any number of other Jewish groups: it is my friends who volunteer with me to raise funds for a cause, who travel together on missions, who meet together to debate issues or engage in social justice work. These are the people who share my interests and my life.

So, what makes people friends?

In my experience, there are five ways we create relationships with friends:

1. When you tell your story to each other
2. When you find commonalities—affinities, life stages, professions, interests

3. When you share experiences together—worship, sing, study, celebrate, travel

4. When you care for each other and are there for each other

5. When you act together—when you volunteer together, when you forward an agenda together

The power of small groups to engage people rests on this fact: the best groups foster friendships. Rick Warren famously teaches that the only way for a large congregation to feel "small" is to ensure that every new member connects with five to seven other friends. Small groups are the hallmark of Saddleback Church; there are more than three thousand of them, most meeting weekly in people's homes. You might think, "That sounds like a *havurah*." Yes, but their small groups are different. Synagogue *havurot* are usually built on a social dynamic; if the chemistry is not just right, the group can easily fall apart. The Saddleback groups are built on affinity and purpose— people who like to do the same thing or have the same interest: car guys who come to the church parking lot once a week to help people needing work on their cars, Bible study groups, addicts in recovery, social justice teams. Some groups are built around a shared identity: preschool parents, health care professionals, lawyers. Other groups are targeted for specific transition moments in life. From the moment a person joins Saddleback as a member, the church does everything in its power to connect her or him to a small group as soon as possible.

My wife, Susie, and I belong to two *havurot* in Los Angeles. We were invited into an existing group when our kids were quite young. For twenty-five years, we have gathered to celebrate life-cycle moments and holidays. The other group we helped form. Once our kids left for college, we sat alone on Friday nights, looking at each other across the table. Boring. We realized there were another five couples at the same stage of life in our neighborhood. So, the idea emerged of gathering together to share a potluck Shabbat dinner once a month, rotating to each other's homes. Our synagogue didn't put us together; we did it ourselves. We call ourselves the Empty Nester Shabbat Group. And we are still meeting to this day.

Noah Farkas, rabbi at Valley Beth Shalom in Encino, California, and a talented community organizer, teaches that *connection comes before commitment*. The task of this level of relationship is to create connection between as many individuals and families as possible. This is not about another "program"; this is about building relationships—friend to friend, *bayn adam l'haveiro*.

The Fourth Level: *Bayn Adam l'Yahadut—* Jewish Living

The fourth level of relationship is between the individual and Jewish living. I translate *Yahadut* not as "Judaism," but as "Jewish living" in order to emphasize the actions that demonstrate engagement with the Jewish experience.

How are our organizations empowering people to engage with Jewish living?

I have always taught that institutions should think of themselves as the American Automobile Association centers for the Jewish journey. Just as many of us belong as members to local AAA (CAA in Canada) groups in order to access their unparalleled expertise and assistance, we can imagine a synagogue, a JCC, a communal organization providing similar guidance and support as we travel life's hills and valleys, on-ramps and speed bumps. Yes, it is true that today I can order a travel planner online and depend (at my peril) on the GPS device in my car or smartphone, but there is something quite reassuring in knowing that I can walk into my local AAA office and sit face-to-face with an empathetic and knowledgeable counselor who will act as a personal concierge for my journey.

The same is true today for those seeking to build a relationship with Jewish living. Parents of young children can access kveller.com; interested web surfers can find hundreds of websites containing Jewish content—from MyJewishLearning.com to the most visited Jewish content website in the world, Chabad.org. Most Jewish institutions have websites, Facebook pages, even apps for smartphones and tablets. You can watch live streaming of Shabbat services; view funerals televised on Skype; read hundreds of blogs (which we might think of as modern midrash on all things Jewish); and participate in online forums, discussion groups, and communities of practice.

And yet, something very deep draws me to an in-the-flesh teacher, rabbi, counselor, therapist, youth educator, cantor, communal professional—someone I can meet face-to-face, someone with whom I can break bread, share a cup of coffee, shake a hand, lean on a shoulder, embrace in a warm hug.

The task of such a "concierge" for Judaism is to build a relationship between individuals and the Jewish experience. To circle back to our first level of relationship, the approach needs to focus on how Jewish practice can be a path to meaning and purpose, belonging and blessing. Jewish life-cycle and holiday rituals, liturgy, and study are all means to a goal—to self-discovery, celebrating relationships, and fulfilling communal obligations.

Jewish living regulates relationships to those who are sick and those who mourn, to animals and food, to the environment, sustainable agriculture, green buildings, and time. There is a profound lesson in the Torah's prohibition "Do not cook a kid in its mother's milk" (Exodus 23:19). The power to nurture, symbolized by milk, is perverted in such an act. The primary relationship between parent and child, albeit in the animal kingdom, is at risk. The term for Jewish law, *halakhah*, means the "way," the "path" to living a more fully realized life imbued with sensitivity and awe.

Shabbat, another central practice of Jewish living, is a covenant in time. Shabbat becomes the sign of the reciprocal relationship between God and creation, between God and Israel.

> The people Israel shall observe the Shabbat, to maintain it as an everlasting covenant through all generations. It is a sign between Me and the people Israel for all time, that in six days Adonai created the heavens and earth, and on the seventh day God ceased from work and rested.
>
> EXODUS 31:16–17

The midrash teaches a relational insight:

> When the Shabbat (the seventh day) complained, "All the days of the week are paired, I alone am an odd number,

without a mate," the Holy One replied, "The congregation of Israel is your mate."

P'SIKTA RABBATI 117B

A congregational leader once said, "We thought Shabbat would be a doorway to relationships. We learned that relationships are a doorway to Shabbat."

The prayer experience is also a relational act, enacted primarily in a minyan of ten others, but allowing for a personal relationship with God:

> God says to Israel: I asked you to pray in the synagogue in your city, but if you cannot pray there, pray in your field, and if you cannot pray there, pray on your bed, and if you cannot pray there, then meditate in your heart ... and be still.

P'SIKTA D'RAV KAHANA 158A

The primary vehicle for learning how to engage with Judaism is study. We read the best-selling book the world has ever known—the Torah—out loud four times a week. We are a people that highly values education. We excel at all types of adult Jewish learning. We publish excellent volumes of commentary. And yet, we fail to engage a significant number of our people (some like me, post–Bar/Bat Mitzvah Hebrew school dropouts) who will never pick up a book, never venture into the lecture hall, never enjoy the thrill of discovery that accompanies serious Jewish learning with a superb teacher. In an address to the Jewish Federations of North America's General Assembly in 2011, Rabbi Elie Kaunfer, executive director of Mechon Hadar, said:

> Why does Judaism need a future? Because Judaism offers a system, a covenantal language, a heritage and tradition that responds to the human need for meaning, substance and connection.... It is called Torah ... the sum total of Jewish sources and texts—the wisdom stored up in our textual heritage. Torah has the power to draw us into the conversation ... the power to push us to ask bold questions and to transform our relationships. We have to make Torah accessible to all.

Can the people you serve say that because of their encounter with your institution, they are more informed, better equipped Jews? Do they have a deeper relationship with Judaism ... *bayn adam l'Yahadut*?

These first four levels of relationship—self, family, friends, and Jewish living—are personal in nature. The next four explore how the individual relates to the community.

The Fifth Level: *Bayn Adam l'Kehillah*—Community

Engagement with community is the next level of relationship in a Relational Judaism. It is true, you can make decisions on your own about how to be Jewish, but then a truly engaged Jew feels a responsibility beyond the self. How to teach people that sense of responsibility is the challenge of the next four levels of Relational Judaism.

By "community," I refer to two fundamental elements of the Jewish experience: the synagogue and the local Jewish community. Both are called *kehillah* in Hebrew. The synagogue is a *kehillah kedoshah*, a "sacred community," and the Jewish community is simply called *kehillah*. The names themselves indicate the traditional roles each plays in Jewish life; the synagogue is the place for religious expression—in North American terms, the "church"—while the "secular" community serves the central organizing function—the "state," if you will.

Throughout the twentieth century, each of these communities served distinct functions. Synagogue was the place for worship services, Jewish education, pastoral counseling, and holiday celebration. The local community, headed in most cases by the Federation, raised funds to support local needs such as immigrant resettlement, vocational services, free loan assistance, homes for the elderly, central agencies for Jewish education, Jewish Community Centers, and of course, the needs of Jewish communities around the world, primarily in the State of Israel.

Yet, in the past thirty years, the turf boundaries between the sacred and the secular have steadily blurred. Building on Kaplan's vision of a "synagogue center," many congregations broadened their traditional offerings to become full-service institutions with programming that looked a lot like those offered in the secular community, including a few synagogues that built swimming pools and basketball courts.

Similarly, Jewish Community Centers began hiring rabbis and Jewish educators, established preschools, and even offered Shabbat dinners and holiday celebrations for unaffiliated Jews. Meanwhile, the emergence of donor-designated giving wherein individuals decide where their financial contributions should go rather than leave it to a committee of communal leaders; the economic success of the State of Israel, which reduced the impact of donations from the American Jewish community; and the simultaneous economic downturn of the Great Recession, which ratcheted up the need for local allocations—all of these factors put pressure on the centralized Federation fundraising model. As a result, many of the community institutions that depended almost exclusively on Federation funding necessarily began fundraising for themselves, further diminishing the influence of the "central address" of the secular Jewish community.

Moreover, when sociologists conducted demographic studies of the Jewish population, they discovered that the most engaged Jews in a community almost always participated in and supported *both* the sacred and the secular institutions. This influenced a newer crop of communal leaders to understand that synagogue affiliation is one of the top predictors of whether individuals will make a contribution to Federation. Even so, the turf tensions in many Jewish communities flare up when JCCs offer programming on Shabbat and holidays and synagogues sponsor sports leagues. Even among synagogues, there is a competition born of a belief that each must have its own schools and programming, a separation that limits interaction among members of other congregations. Unfortunately, all the institutions of the community are trying to appeal to what appears to be an ever-shrinking number of "affiliated" individuals and households rather than focusing on how to reach the ever-increasing number of disengaged or under-engaged people who could have a relationship with the organized Jewish community.

In the most recent demographic study (2011) of New York City, the results of questions seeking to identify "Indicators of Jewish Engagement" are quite revealing. Between 2002 and 2011, the number of "very low Jewish engagement" rose from 13 percent to 18 percent. More than twice as many respondents said they never attend a Passover Seder or light Hanukkah candles. Another 20 percent answered affirmatively to only two or three questions, resulting in a whopping 38 percent reporting little or virtually no connection to the Jewish experience. An identical number—38 percent—score "very high" or "high." Thus, we see the pattern of Jewish engagement at the end of the first decade in the twenty-first century: large numbers of highly engaged Jews and large numbers of barely engaged Jews, with 24 percent moderately engaged.[15]

The challenge, then, for Jewish community leaders is how to engage the least-engaged and moderately engaged Jews. When the sociologists looked at how the "least-engaged" engage along all twenty-four items on the "Indicators of Jewish Engagement," they observed the following indicators in descending order: "went to Jewish cultural event/museum," "have been to Israel," "fast on Yom Kippur," "study with teacher," and "access Jewish websites." Their conclusion: all of these behaviors can be done individually or with friends and family; they do not require formal affiliation or collective action. This finding is consistent with the DIY, don't-need-an-institution nature of life in the twenty-first century.

All this presents a daunting task for community institutions in both the secular and the sacred arenas that operate on an "affiliation" model. With a shrinking population base from which to draw members, volunteers, and contributors, they must work on two fronts simultaneously: (1) deepening the engagement of those who are already signed up and (2) finding new ways to attract and engage those who are moderately or least Jewishly connected.

Permit me a word about the differences between large and small centers of Jewish population and the role geography plays. I live in Los Angeles, a community of some five hundred thousand Jews, but I was raised in Omaha, Nebraska, a community of some five thousand. In Omaha, as in many Jewish communities of its size, the affiliation rate is in the 80 percent range, while in Los Angeles, the affiliation rate is 46 percent. Although the challenges of sustaining Jewish engagement are considerably more difficult in smaller population centers, the pressures to engage in Jewish communal life lead to much greater affiliation with synagogues, JCCs, and other organizations. Similarly, the further one travels from the Northeast Seaboard region of the United States, the lower the affiliation rate. In fact, the three lowest-scoring communities are San Francisco, Seattle, and Las Vegas. The Institute of Southern Jewish Life, led by the indefatigable Macy B. Hart, has developed an array of resources and people who support Jewish communities in the South. In every Jewish population center, whatever its size, the task of building relationships with the community remains formidable.

Some will argue that the "affiliation" or "membership" model is a thing of the past. People today prefer a "pay-as-you-go" model, a "fee-for-service" relationship with institutions. Their needs change over the life cycle, and we can expect them to "belong" to synagogues when their children are being raised, to join a JCC when synagogues feel too intimidating, to support Jewish organizations like the Anti-Defamation League, AIPAC, and Jewish homes for the aging when the cause hits a nerve, and to give to the centralized Jewish Federation system when there is a crisis in Israel or among world Jewry.

I am not a champion of abandoning the membership or affiliation model, because without it, Jewish institutions as we know them would be unsustainable. I believe that if we wiped the slate clean, sunsetted all Jewish institutions, we would quite quickly reinvent them or create new ones. Societies need organizations to do the work that needs doing, especially to provide social safety nets for those requiring communal support. In the Jewish community, our basic institutions have evolved over time depending on the needs of the people. After World War II, synagogues were ascendant as families with young children flooded the suburbs. Hillel Foundations were moribund until they received a jolt of renewed energy and purpose when leaders began to focus on reaching out to Jewish students in the dorms and the Greek houses rather than waiting for them to wander into their buildings. New organizations to memorialize the Holocaust found support, while formerly Jewish hospitals and Jewish country clubs have all but disappeared as Jews have integrated into the general society. Young Jewish adults are busy inventing new start-up organizations and communities, some of which look very different from existing groups, while others appear quite similar, albeit with different strategies for engagement.

It is clear that engaging more Jews, as well as non-Jews living with Jews, is one of the most pressing challenges facing both sacred and secular community organizations. Whether organizations are membership based or not, attention must be paid to the three aspects of institutional engagement that will determine the health of Jewish organizations in the future: *recruitment*, *engagement*, and *retention*.

If we do well with these three things, we will succeed in creating relationships *bayn adam l'kehillah*.

The Sixth Level: *Bayn Adam l'Am*—Peoplehood

This sixth level of relationship is between the individual Jew and the Jewish people, known in Hebrew as *am*.

A story to illustrate: My late father-in-law, Abe Kukawka, survived World War II by fleeing into Russia from his small village of Slawaticze on the far eastern border of Poland. His mother insisted that he and his younger brother Gedalia (George), both young single men, escape from the onslaught of the Nazis, who had invaded from the west. Abe's mother and father were too old, too settled to move, and his three sisters were married with young children. It seemed much too difficult to uproot the entire family, even as they understood that an uncertain future awaited them under Nazi occupation. Ultimately, of course, they all perished—fifty-two relatives in the large extended family were murdered.

George was soon caught stealing potatoes from an open field and was sent to a Siberian labor camp. Abe was resourceful, finding work with the Russian army. After two years, though, he broke away from a benevolent Russian colonel to make his way in the forests of central Europe. It was a difficult and dangerous journey. While there were partisan groups hiding out among the trees, you were never sure about the identity of those you met along the way. When he encountered a stranger, the first communication was a one-word question: "*Amkha?*" The Yiddish word means "your people." Asked as a question, the meaning was clear: "Are you Jewish?" If the other person responded, "*Amkha!*" Abe knew that he had found a friend, a fellow Jew, a member of the tribe.

Jewish peoplehood is a worldwide phenomenon. Why is it that a Jew who never walks into a synagogue at home will travel to Rome and suddenly seek out the Jewish Quarter, eat in a kosher restaurant, and perk up when meeting Italian Jews wearing a Star of David? Why is it that a young Jewish climber on a trek up the Himalayan mountains can post a small notice on the bulletin board of a hostel, "Meet for Seder, 7 p.m., April 10, Café Europa, bring what you can," and nineteen Jews will show up, one with a box of matzah, another with a small bottle of kosher-for-Passover wine, a third with a can of macaroons? Why is it when a professor with a Jewish-sounding name is proclaimed the latest winner of a Nobel Prize, a rush of pride envelops the heart of just about anyone who claims to belong to the Jewish people?

This is the palpable sense of Jewish peoplehood, a relationship to Jews throughout the world, no matter where they live, no matter what color their skin, no matter their ideology, no matter their politics, no matter their ethnicity, no matter their country.

This phenomenon notwithstanding, historian Jack Wertheimer laments the decline of Jewish peoplehood:

> It is not just that, at the moment, no large-scale crisis seems to engage the American Jewish psyche. Rather, something vital in that psyche has changed. Mounting evidence now attests to a weakened identification among American Jews with their fellow Jews abroad, as well as a waning sense of communal responsibility at home. The once-forceful claims of Jewish "peoplehood" have lost their power to compel.[16]

The truth is that belonging to the Jewish people requires a reciprocal relationship between individuals and the collective. There are responsibilities that come with community, an antidote to what Wertheimer calls "unbridled individualism." Among these are "seeing Jews as a global extended family, exhibiting concern on these grounds for one's fellow Jews ... to see oneself as part of a larger collective entity [situating] oneself in a history of 3,200 years and more, imparting a sense of transcendent connection, purpose, and destiny. [Peoplehood] buttresses faith, enhances religious activity, lends significance to communal affiliation."[17]

Moreover, Jewish peoplehood is inseparable from Jewish religious ideas. Wertheimer, a Conservative Jew, professor of American Jewish history, quotes Eugene B. Borowitz, a leading Reform theologian (1965):

> Jewish peoplehood is an indispensable part of Jewish religious thought and Jewish religious practice. A specifically Jewish religious life … means, therefore, life in and with the Jewish people, the Covenant community…. When at least ten Jews congregate to pray, they … represent all Israel, past and present, here and everywhere.[18]

The challenge to create a sense of peoplehood is a formidable one indeed. It will require teaching the basic Jewish value of obligation to fellow Jews, responsibility for one another's welfare—*kol Yisrael areivim zeh ba-zeh*—and acting to support and connect with Jews throughout the world who share in a relationship born of history, experience, and destiny—*bayn adam l'am*.

The Seventh Level: *Bayn Adam l'Yisrael*—Israel

The seventh level of relationship is between the individual Jew and the State of Israel—*bayn adam l'Yisrael*.

The dream of a homeland in Israel sustained the Jews of the Diaspora for nearly two thousand years. They prayed daily for the realization of this dream. They ended the Passover Seder with the cry, "Next year in Jerusalem!" They endured centuries of persecution, ghettoization, and ultimately, attempted genocide. Yet out of the ashes of Auschwitz and Buchenwald, the modern State of Israel arose, miraculously, surrounded by hostile countries bent on pushing its small population of 650,000 Jews into the Mediterranean Sea. A short sixty-five years later, Israel has become a beacon of democracy in the Middle East, a "start-up nation" of nearly eight million enjoying unprecedented economic growth and prosperity. And yet Israel lives under what many regard as an existential threat to its very existence, publicly threatened by neighbors who regard it as anathema and are bent on its destruction.

There is no question that the passionate debate concerning how to resolve the Israeli-Palestinian conflict has taken a toll on the relationship between North American Jews and Israel, especially among young adults. Alarmed that the vast majority of young Jews had never visited Israel, major philanthropists joined with the Jewish Federation system and Israeli governmental agencies to launch Birthright Israel, an all-expenses-paid ten-day trip to entice them to make the journey. Despite doubters and critics, the Birthright Israel initiative has been a resounding success, sending three hundred thousand young Jews for a carefully articulated educational experience. One goal of Birthright Israel is to strengthen the Jewishness of participants; sociological studies indicate that a trip to Israel, along with summer camp and Jewish day school education, impacts personal Jewish identity. But clearly, another goal is to build a positive relationship between the young Jews and the State of Israel. Simply put, there is nothing quite like a trip to Israel to bring Jews face-to-face with their faith, with their people, and with their heritage.

My own experience as a Jewish educator testifies to the power of an Israel experience to influence Jewish identity formation. As a college student, I was privileged to lead a group of thirteen fifteen-year-olds from Congregation B'nai Amoona in St. Louis on a nine-week intensive living experience on a cooperative moshav in Israel in 1972. My PhD dissertation is a description and analysis of this pioneering experiment in building deep relationships between American Jewish teenagers and Israeli teenagers and their families.[19] Shaped by a brilliant congregational rabbi, Bernard Lipnick, and his mentor, Professor Moshe Davis of the Hebrew University, the idea of emulating the life of an Israeli teenager during two summer months in a modern Orthodox agricultural settlement captured the imagination of both the Israeli hosts and their partners in America. The students worked side by side with their Israeli sisters and brothers for four hours a day in the fields for four weeks, traveled the country in the back of pickup trucks, worshiped and celebrated in traditional modes, and lived with Israeli families. The impact on the American teenagers was extraordinary, but the biggest surprise was the nearly complete reversal of the previously held negative image many in the Israeli community had of American youth. Unlike other short-term visitors from abroad, the teens from B'nai Amoona earned the respect and affection of the Israelis by successfully adopting the norms of the quite idyllic authentic Jewish community of the Israeli moshav. Survey research conducted for the thirtieth anniversary reunion of more than three hundred participants in the program, which operated between B'nai Amoona and the moshav for more than a decade, confirmed that the living experience created a "reference relationship" with Israel that many respondents claimed was one of the most important influences in their lives, evidenced by many of the now-adult participants maintaining regular contact with their Israeli "families."

Yet, even with the availability of a variety of trips to Israel for teenagers and now for young Jewish adults, 59 percent of adult American Jews have never been to Israel. According to a 2012 survey conducted by the American Jewish Committee, among the 41 percent who have made the trip, 19 percent have only traveled once. Predictably, Orthodox Jews have visited the most (80.5 percent), while Conservative Jews (54 percent), Reform Jews (36 percent), and "Just Jewish" Jews (22 percent) lag behind. Thirty-one percent of American Jews say they have no interest in visiting Israel.[20]

And yet, 71 percent of survey respondents agree that "caring about Israel is a very important part of my being a Jew."[21] More than a few wags have suggested a Birthright Israel trip for everyone else, with special targeted experiences for families, intermarried couples, and the "Just Jewish." While the Conservative movement boasts of one hundred synagogue-based missions to Israel annually and a panoply of other Jewish organizations offer a wide variety of Israel experiences—from ecological tours to intensive study opportunities—there still appears to be a considerable challenge for Israeli tourism and educational authorities, along with Stateside sponsors, to tailor its marketing to the increasingly diverse population of North American Jews.

Short of a trip to Israel, Jewish institutions are challenged to create positive relationships between American Jews and Israel. Political advocacy groups like AIPAC—the American-Israel Political Action Committee—have found success by encouraging synagogues and other groups to bring delegations to Washington, D.C., for their annual conference, one of the largest gatherings of North American Jews. Local Federations sponsor annual Yom Ha'atzmaut Israeli Independence Day parades and celebrations. Major cities sponsor Israeli film festivals. Israel is often in the news, and the Israeli government sends young diplomats to Jewish population centers to represent the state. Stand-WithUs, the Israel on Campus Coalition, Hillel, and other campus-based organizations do their best to educate Jewish college students about the challenges facing Israel.

Ironically, the very word *Yisrael* has "wrestle" at its heart. Struggle or agree, defend or critique—what matters is to be in relationship with the Jewish homeland in all its complexities and glories—*bayn adam l'Yisrael*. So, whatever one's opinion about the direction Israel should take in solving its problems, whether hawk or dove, religious or secular, proponent or critic of Zionism, a relationship with Israel is an important plank of a Relational Judaism in the twenty-first century.

The Eighth Level: *Bayn Adam l'Olam*—World

The eighth level of relationship in Relational Judaism is *bayn adam l'olam*—between the individual and the world. The purpose of the Jewish people is to remind the world of God's existence, to be a "light unto the nations" (Isaiah 49:6). How are our institutions inspiring people to repair the world—the *whole* world?

Of the many well-known values in Judaism—*tzedakah* (righteous giving), monotheism, and ethical behavior—perhaps the most salient in recent years has been *tikkun olam*, "repair of the world." The idea can be traced to the kabbalistic mystics who imagined the world was shattered shortly after creation into countless "shards," and only intentional work can repair the brokenness. The term also appears in the second paragraph of the *Aleinu* prayer: *l'takein olam b'malkhut Shaddai*, "to repair the world in order to bring God's presence." In both references, notice that the term is not particularistic—it is not "repair the *Jewish* world." Rather, it is a universal call for repair of *the world*.

When the genocide occurring in Darfur became known, Rabbi Harold Schulweis gave a sermon to his congregation on the High Holy Days that I will never forget. He taught us that Judaism is not a parochial religion; we are a world religion. He taught us that the Jewish people must care for their own, but that we must also care for those who cannot fend for themselves. He reminded us that we, of all people, could not stand idly by while other human beings are being systematically massacred.

On that Rosh Hashanah day, Rabbi Schulweis called for the creation of a Jewish World Watch, an effort by synagogues to raise consciousness among its members—young and old alike—and to mobilize action to help those who are under siege, regardless of their race, color, religion, or ethnicity.

Two weeks later, Rabbi Schulweis called a meeting of his congregation to mobilize the community to action. The meeting was attended by my good friend and fellow *havurah* member Janice Kamenir-Reznik, a busy lawyer, mom, and community leader, who was moved to respond. She cofounded the organization that is called Jewish World Watch with Rabbi Schulweis, and they set about raising awareness and funds to help the women in Darfur. Jewish World Watch launched a solar cooker project to teach women how to cook without risking their lives to gather firewood, built a half-dozen medical clinics, and allocated funds to support refugees in the Congo. The organization has galvanized synagogues throughout Los Angeles across the denominations, with some seventy-seven synagogues signed on.

Closer to home, Jews have always been sensitive to the relationship between the Jewish community and the surrounding non-Jewish majority. Many Jewish Federations have "Jewish Community Relations" departments charged with the responsibility to nurture positive relationships with other religious groups and local governments. National organizations like the Anti-Defamation League and the American Jewish Committee work to build relationships with "the world" in which we live. Synagogues partner with neighboring churches and mosques in congregation-based social justice initiatives. In my hometown of Omaha, Nebraska, Rabbi Aryeh Azriel is leading the groundbreaking effort to create the first "tri-faith" campus in North America, a thirty-five-acre property featuring three houses of worship—a Reform synagogue, Temple Israel; a church, the Episcopal Diocese of Nebraska; and a mosque, the American Institute of Islamic Studies and Culture—along with a shared community and education center. Living as a distinct minority in a democracy, these relationships—both individual and communal—are important anchors to ensure our security and safety.

When we teach our people that being Jewish means to be in relationship with the world, to work for *tikkun olam*, we are creating a Relational Judaism that anyone would be proud to be a part of—*bayn adam l'olam*.

The Ninth Level: *Bayn Adam l'Makom*—God

The ninth level of relationship is *bayn adam l'Makom*—between the individual and God.

As I write these words, the headline on the home page of my computer and on the front page of my newspaper reads as follows: "Scientists Discover the God Particle."

It is July 4, 2012. For nearly fifty years, scientists have been searching for evidence of something called the Higgs boson, defined by scientist Dennis Overbye as "the only manifestation of an invisible force field, a cosmic molasses that permeates space and imbues elementary particles with mass."[22] It is the missing piece of a grand theory, the Standard Model, which seeks to explain how nature itself works. Over the past half-century, physicists have deciphered the mechanics of how protons, neutrons, and electrons, the particles that make up atoms, interact. All matter has mass, yet the particles themselves appear to be massless. So the question bedeviling scientists is, how do these particles gain mass? Particles with no mass move quickly at the speed of light; other particles move more slowly, like tennis balls in molasses. The theory is that a then-as-yet unobserved particle—the Higgs boson—attaches itself to some particles to, in effect, create matter. This, then, would explain how everything in the universe exists, ergo "the God particle."

This is how science works: there are phenomena we cannot explain. Scientists theorize what might be happening based on previous knowledge. Stars disappear from the universe; astronomers think the body was sucked into a black hole. But until recently, they could not "see" it happening. Technology—high-performing telescopes sent into space—allowed us glimpses into the vast universe that previous generations of astronomers could only imagine. Likewise, doctors encountered symptoms they could not explain and, so, developed hypotheses about what was happening in the body. Then in 1953, James Watson and Francis Crick discovered the double helical structure of DNA, and medical research was forever changed. My father, Alan, liked to say M.D. stands for "Medical Detective."

In the case of the search for the Higgs boson, physicists created the Large Hadron Collider, a $10 billion particle accelerator to smash trillions of protons together, hoping that the resulting fragments might be physical evidence to prove their theory. In December 2011, scientists cautiously admitted that they had seen "hints" of the existence of the Higgs boson, but they couldn't say for sure. Then, in the early morning of July 4, 2012, elated physicists, including Peter Higgs, who initially proposed the idea, gathered in Geneva to view the data that confirmed their discovery.

VOICES FROM THE COMMUNITY

Rabbi David Wolpe marked the discovery of the "God particle" with this poem, published in the *Washington Post*, July 18, 2012:

> *No doubt you have all read about*
> *The stunning confirmation*
> *That the collider replaced Mount Sinai*
> *As the site for revelation.*

> *God is out, Higgs Boson in,*
> *Invisible, unseen*
> *Particulate angels on a pinhead*
> *From absences, we glean.*

> *But who can help but wonder if*
> *At the dawn of dark and bright*
> *A voice pronounced "Let Boson be"*
> *And we've just seen the light.*

There are many things in life that cannot be seen, yet there is evidence of their existence. So it is with God. To quote my favorite children's book, *Let's Talk about God* by Dorothy Kripke:

> We cannot see God … we cannot see many things. We cannot
> see the wind. But we see autumn leaves flying and dancing,
> all orange and gold. We see a bright green kite sailing in the
> sky. Then we know the wind is there. We see what the wind
> does, even though we cannot see the wind itself.
>
> We cannot see love, but we know when someone loves us.
> We feel love in a hug or a smile or a friendly look or a warm
> touch. We feel love in many ways, but we never see love. We
> know it by what it does to us.
>
> We cannot see God. But we do see what God does in the
> world.… We cannot see God, but we know that God is there.[23]

For centuries, Jewish philosophers have sought proof of God's existence. Maimonides gave up. A scientist himself, he famously taught that all we can say about God is what God is not. Others have denied God's existence altogether; an influential book published while I was a college student was Richard Rubenstein's *After Auschwitz*. Rubinstein essentially declared God dead, arguing that a God who works in history would never have allowed the genocide of six million Jews and millions of others during World War II.[24] Teachers such as Rabbi Harold Kushner popularized a Kaplanian view of God, effectively taking God off the hook for evil, claiming that the free choice given to human beings to do good or bad means that when bad things happen to good people, we should not blame God. The world is not perfect; illness, death, and accidents happen, and all we can do is cope with their inevitability.[25]

My own view is that the search for evidence of God's existence should not focus on the heavens, but here on earth. We should look to our hearts, not to the stars. Yes, I believe that the order of the universe, creation itself, and inexplicable happenings in our lives can be attributable to some force, some Thing beyond our comprehension, evidence of something that we cannot see yet, though we can feel its effects. For some, the search will lead to discovery, perhaps a discovery as monumental as that of the Higgs boson. For others, a lack of proof will lead to doubt and disbelief. Amazingly, hard scientists continue their search for answers to the mysteries of life, even as their experiments fail and the inevitable disappointments unfold. Yet, their passion for discovery, their thrill of the search, is as motivating as the discoveries themselves. It is the search that gives meaning and purpose to their lives.

The charge of Jewish institutions is to guide people in this search for a personal relationship with God. This is a daunting task for institutional leaders, many of whom are baby boomers who grew up in a generation where talk of God from pulpits and lecterns was scarce, indeed.

When I lecture about my book *God's To-Do List: 103 Ways to Be an Angel and Do God's Work on Earth*, I say something that shocks most of the audience. I tell them that when I was in my teenage youth group, United Synagogue Youth, I was asked to read Abraham Joshua Heschel's masterpiece *God in Search of Man*. Even before I opened the book, I thought Heschel had it backwards. Aren't we always looking for God? Isn't that what religion is all about—our search for God? No, Heschel taught, God is looking for us. God needs us to be God's eyes and ears, hands and feet, heart and soul. Judaism's answer to the question "What on earth am I here for?" is simple, but profound: we are here to be God's partners, to do the big and small things that God needs done to continue the work of creation and to work on perfecting the world.

I have written two books about God—one for adults (*God's To-Do List*) and one for children (*Be Like God*). In spite of their titles, these books are not really about God. The purpose of the books is to teach what Judaism says about the purpose of human existence. God is the model for what we are to do on earth. In the end, it's about each of us and what we do with our God-given powers and gifts to make a difference in the world. The spark of divinity is within each and every human being. It is God who provides the spark, who ignites the spark, but it is up to us to keep the flames going.

The question, of course, is how? Since the time of Moses, Jewish leaders have faced a similar challenge: how can we guide a sometimes skeptical people in a spiritual direction that leads to a relationship with God?

A helpful beginning is the school of thought called "process theology," defined by my colleague Rabbi Bradley Shavit Artson, dean of the Ziegler School of Rabbinic Studies at the American Jewish University, as a "constellation of ideas sharing the common assertion that the world and God are in continuous, dynamic change, of *related* interaction and becoming" (italics mine). In his seminal monograph "On the

Way: A Presentation of Process Theology," Rabbi Artson skillfully peels away layers of Greek/Western philosophical categories of omnipotent, omniscient, and omnibenevolent "God" to reveal the God of the Torah, Talmud, Midrash, and Kabbalah.[26] This Jewish God gets angry, argues, loves, gets frustrated and surprised, gives in, asks forgiveness, and grieves. Artson quotes the Talmud:

> When the blessed Holy One recalls God's children, who are plunged into suffering among the nations of the world, God lets fall two tears into the ocean and the sound is heard from one end of the world to the other—and that is the rumbling of the earth.
>
> TALMUD, *BERAKHOT* 59A

As Artson observes, the God of the Torah is emotional. Almost immediately after God creates human beings, we read, "The Holy One regretted having made people on earth, and God's heart was saddened" (Genesis 6:6). Artson comments:

> What does it mean for God to regret and feel sorrow? A timeless, unchanging God cannot regret. Regret means being different than you were a moment ago. So the Torah itself asserts God's dynamism in the context of relationship. Over and over again the Torah emphasizes a God who expresses emotion, a God who is always meeting people in relationship, and changing because of that relationship.

If God changes because of the relationship with human beings, certainly human beings can change when in relationship with this dynamic, emotional, personal God.

Rabbi Artson titles a key piece of his thinking "Not by Might, Not by Power, but by My Breath," his translation of Zechariah 4:6. Though the term *ruach* is more commonly translated as "spirit" than as "breath," Artson understands *ruach* as God's influence, God's persuasive power. It is a total rejection of the most common image of God in the minds of most people—"a bully in the sky." In process thinking, God "does not work through coercion; God works through persuasion and invitation, through persistently inviting us to make the best possible choice, and then leaving us free to make the wrong choice." This is the notion of free will. In the face of human beings making wrong choices quite often (read: sin, missing the mark), Artson reminds us, "But then, the instant we have made our choice, God persistently lures us toward making the best possible subsequent choice." This is the notion of *teshuvah*, the God-empowered ability to right a wrong.

This is a God that "lures" us into doing the best we can do, "despite our drives, selfishness, desires or laziness." This is the "still, small voice" (1 Kings 19:12) that encourages us to do the right thing. This is the relational partner who loves us. The Bible recognizes love as the very heart of the relationship between human beings and God. In the *V'ahavta* prayer, the language is imperative: "You shall love Adonai your God with all your heart, with all your soul, and with all your power." In the weekday morning service, the tefillin straps bind ourselves to God in relationship. In fact, as the straps are wrapped around the finger as a ring, we recite the same words from the prophet Hosea (2:21–22) that are often recited during the wedding ceremony:

> *V'eirastikh li l'olam, v'eirastikh li b'tzedek, uv'mishpat, uv'chesed, uv'rachamim. V'eirastikh li be'emunah, v'yada-at et Adonai.*

> I will betroth you to me forever; I will betroth you in righteousness, with justice, with love, and with compassion. I will betroth you to me with faithfulness … and you shall know the Holy One.

In a fundamental way, the relationship of human beings with God is very much like a marriage, a good marriage in which it is possible "to feel another's pain, to exalt in the lover's triumph."

Building a relationship with a potential marriage partner is a deliberate process. We meet someone, we hear his or her story, we date. Sharing experiences, we create memories and share mementos of our time together. We build trust, we may even squabble occasionally, and ultimately we say the words "I love you." The relationship grows until it is absolutely obvious that the partnership, the match, is "made in heaven," we become engaged, and then, in the Jewish wedding ceremony, we concretize our commitment to each other in a wedding ceremony called *kiddushin*, the process of elevating the relationship to the sacred. Can we do the same with a personal God? I believe we can.

How, then, shall Jewish institutions and its professionals guide people to a relationship with God? If process theology resonates as a way to understand God, then teach that God is looking for us as much as we are looking for God. Celebrate and remember the experiences we shared/share with God; begin with the Passover Seder, the climax of which is a single sentence: *B'khol dor va-dor chayav adam lirot et atzmo k'ilu hu yatza mi'Mitzrayim*, "In every generation, each person should see her/himself as if she/he were redeemed from Egypt." There is a palpable power in placing today's Jews at the foot of Mount Sinai. Live in hope, not fear; encourage a trust that God will be there in the good times and the bad. Do not shy away from the inevitable wrestling matches with God. But, above all, remain committed to the relationship, stay faithful to the divine partner.

As with our relationships with other human beings, building a relationship with God begins with listening. *Sh'ma Yisrael!* "Listen up, people of Israel, Adonai our God, Adonai is One." How does one really hear the voice of God? Louis Finkelstein, longtime chancellor of The Jewish Theological Seminary of America, famously quipped, "Prayer is the way we talk to God; study is the way we hear God's voice." This is the crucial importance of Torah study. Whether you believe the Torah was written by God or interpreted by human beings, the Jewish tradition views Torah, broadly defined, as God's little instruction book for how to lead a life of meaning and purpose, belonging and blessing. Torah reveals God's face. When we encounter God's word, we come face-to-face with God. When we adopt Jewish practices, rituals, and *mitzvot*, we walk in God's ways. When we build relationships with other human beings—our family, our friends, our community, our neighbors, our fellow Jews, our world—encountering each person "made in the divine image," we are relating to God, to the godliness in each and every human.

The Hebrew word for "face" is *panim*, which has the connotation of inner essence. In contrast, "personality" comes from the Greek word *persona*, which means "mask." *Persona* is the outer face that blocks or hides the inner essence. But, God meets Moses *panim el panim*, "face-to-face" (Deuteronomy 34:10). That is the ultimate expression of relationship.

Looking into the face of another is looking into the face of God. The word *panim* is plural, not singular. Rabbi David Wolpe writes, "The human face is capable of almost infinite shades of meaning— joy, sorrow, skepticism, laughter, love. The truest image of God in this world shines through each."[27]

The question is often asked, "Where is God?" The Kotzker Rebbe, a great Hasidic master of the nineteenth century, answered, "God is wherever we let God in." Rabbi Harold Schulweis changes the question. He advises, "Don't ask: '*Where* is God?' Ask: '*When* is God?'" God is to be found *in the between*, when human beings encounter each other, when we are in relationship. The task of Relational Judaism is to create a face-to-face relationship with God—*panim el panim, bayn adam l'Makom*.

Re-viewing the Nine Levels of Relationship

Here, then, is a list of the Nine Levels of Relationships in a Relational Judaism:

Self

Family

Friends

Jewish Living

Community

Peoplehood

Israel

World

God

This is the vertical view. Here is the horizontal view:

World Israel Peoplehood Community God Jewish Living Friends Family Self

Communal   Personal

Turned on its axis ninety degrees, the Nine Levels become the nine "lights" of the *hanukkiyah*, the nine-branched menorah that holds the candles celebrating Hanukkah. The lights remind us of the meaning and purpose and blessing of Hanukkah—the rededication of Judaism in the time of the Maccabees.

In a ritual familiar to a vast majority of the Jewish people, the flames are ignited in ascending order, ever increasing the light of the holiday. On the first night and every other night, the *shamash*, the servant candle, is the first to be lit. It then is used to light the first night's candle. On the second night, the *shamash* and candles one and two are lit ... and so on, until the eighth night of Hanukkah, when the *shamash* and all eight of the other candles—nine in total—are aflame.

According to traditional practice, the placeholders for the candles are to be in a straight line so that when totally lit, the *hanukkiyah* does not appear to be a torch, probably because the sages wanted to avoid any hint of pagan winter solstice festivals, in which torches were prominent symbols. On most *hanukkiyot*, the placeholder for the *shamash* is higher than the other eight candles, a recognition of its role as the igniter of the flames. Moreover, the *shamash* is most commonly found in the center of the *hanukkiyah*, although it could be placed on either end of the candelabrum.

For me, God is at the center—the *shamash* of Relational Judaism. However one defines God—something beyond the self, a force, an internal compass, the Sovereign of the Universe—it is that relationship that kindles the spark of divinity within the self.

One of my favorite *hanukkiyot* is fashioned as a nine-branched "tree of life" candelabrum. The branches overlap each other, much as the arms of a fully grown tree do. This is an apt metaphor for the Nine Levels of Relationship in Relational Judaism. At different points in our lives, one of the "branches" (levels) may have more resonance in our expression of Jewishness, but as in a magnificent, mature plant, their intersection provides the stability and beauty of the living tree. *Etz hayim hi lamachazikim bah*, "It is a tree of life to one who takes hold of it" (Proverbs 3:18). Like a broad tree, Torah broadly conceived can lead to a life shaped by the Nine Levels of Relationship, a life of dedication and rededication.

When I shared this conception with my revered teacher and rabbi, Harold Schulweis, he offered a creative ritual innovation: "Teach people to dedicate each night of Hanukkah to one of the relationships, but remind them that it is the ninth—God the *shamash*—that ignites them all." Each light, each relationship, deserves attention. Each light, each relationship, illuminates our lives. But it is the cumulative effect of the Nine Relationships that ignites our passion, our search for meaning, our drive for purpose, our desire for belonging, our commitment to justice, our gratitude for blessings. We are "on fire" for a Relational Judaism.

4

Transforming Programmatic Institutions into Relational Communities
Six Case Studies

AS AN EDUCATOR AND CONSULTANT who travels the Jewish world, I am eyewitness to what I believe to be a developing tipping point that will hasten the transformation of program-centric institutions into relational communities. I have been on the search for those organizations and their leaders who "get it," those who are working on the cutting edge of a new model of engagement that will be the calling card of Relational Judaism. They are:

Chabad

Hillel

Congregation-based community organizing

Next-generation engagement initiatives

Social media

Fundraisers' wisdom

To be sure, there are other instances of individuals and communities who shape their work on the core principles of relationship building, but these six stand out for their absolute commitment to put people first. As we unpack their strategies, we will meet some of the personalities leading the way, discover specific techniques, and develop a template for other organizations interested in joining the move toward a Relational Judaism.

Chabad

I remember the reaction of significant leaders of the liberal movements when I pointed out the seemingly ubiquitous presence of Chabad in the mid-1970s. Chabad *shluchim*—emissaries—had begun branching out from their first storefront locations near college campuses, setting up what looked like synagogues in neighborhoods usually dominated by Reform, Conservative, and mainstream Orthodox (not Hasidic) congregations. My colleagues reacted with disdain and/or laughter. "Chabad is a cult," "they are an anachronism," "they are embarrassing," "dancing rabbis—they'll never amount to anything." These leaders scoffed at Chabad, regarding them as unsophisticated throwbacks to a nineteenth-century Eastern European shtetl Judaism that would have little or no resonance with modern Jews.

Today, Chabad (www.chabad.org)—the name is an acronym for *chokhmah, bina,* and *da'at,* Hebrew words for "wisdom," "understanding," "knowledge"—has sent more than four thousand *shluchim* to virtually every country in the world. They are the Starbucks of Jewish outreach—a Chabad rabbi on every corner. Eschewing the dominant dues model of affiliation, each Chabad rabbi is responsible for developing their own supporters, so they are relentless fundraisers. Estimates suggest that Chabad collects in excess of one billion dollars annually, ranking it among the most financially successful Jewish organizations on the planet. While some liberal synagogues are merging or selling their aging facilities, Chabad is building some of the most magnificent Jewish "centers" in the world.

Who's laughing now?

The first Chabad *shluchim* were sent to their posts in the 1950s. At first, there were only a handful, mostly serving college campuses. The first *Kinus* (conference) of *shluchim* was held in 1984, with roughly sixty-five attendees. In November 2011, five thousand Chabad rabbis and lay supporters gathered for their annual conference of Chabad rabbis (wives have their own conference in the spring), culminating in a gala banquet, as slick an event as any AIPAC conference, General Assembly convention, or biennial of a synagogue movement. It was amazing. I know. I was there.

During the October 2010 launch of Next *Dor*, the Synagogue 3000–sponsored initiative to encourage synagogues to engage young Jewish adults, I told the 180 people from fifty-three congregations across the denominations who had come to the meeting, "I am *plotzing* [a technical term meaning 'dying'] to go to the annual Chabad *shluchim* conference." Unbeknownst to me, Rabbi Daniel Brenner, then director of Birthright Next, was texting Rabbi Hershey Novack, the Chabad campus rabbi at Washington University, while I was still in the middle of my speech: "Wolfson says he wants to attend the *shluchim* conference." Rabbi Novack texted back immediately: "I'll invite him." At the conclusion of my presentation, Rabbi Brenner made a beeline to me to relay the news that he had arranged an invitation and asked for my cell phone number. Later that day, Rabbi Novack called to give me the details of how to register and where to meet him.

Three weeks later, I found myself in a taxi heading for the Brooklyn Cruise Terminal, where the QE2 disembarks. Serviced by one narrow two-lane road, the traffic was backed up for blocks with the thousands of people jamming into the largest sit-down dinner of the year in New York City. I was late, so I called Rabbi Novack on his cell phone to tell him.

"No worries, Ron," he said. "I will leave the event and meet you at the entrance."

"But Rabbi," I asked, "how will I know it's you?"

With the timing of an expert comedian, he replied, "I'm the guy in the black hat and the beard."

Of course, Rabbi Novack left the hall, met my taxi at the entrance, welcomed me warmly, handed me my credentials, escorted me through security, and led me to a prime table in the massive hall. At one end of the room, the dais was an exact replica of the Lubavitcher Rebbe's study. At the other end was a huge bank of tables laden with sophisticated electronics beaming the program onto some twenty large video screens ringing the room, as well as a live streaming feed onto the Internet. Fortunately for my research interests, Rabbi Novack knew the vast majority of the *shluchim* and all of the key leaders of Chabad International based at the organization's headquarters in Crown Heights. We had hardly been served dinner when Rabbi Novack motioned for me to join him as we "worked the room," moving from table to table as I met and chatted with the chairman of Chabad, the chairman of the *Kinus*, the head of Chabad.org, and leading Chabad rabbis from major cities. I reviewed the thick program describing a wide variety of workshops offered to the participants during the professional development days of the conference. I was not at all surprised to find cutting-edge issues addressed: social networking, engagement strategies, media relations, and development techniques, led by both colleagues and expert consultants outside the Chabad community. After a number of inspiring speeches to the troops, the evening crescendo hit its peak with the annual "Roll Call of the *Shluchim*," a public naming of every country around the world where a Chabad rabbi serves. When the "United States of America" was announced, the hall exploded into a *hora* (dance) the likes of which I had never experienced. It was breathtaking.

What is the secret of this enormous success? In a nutshell, the Chabad rabbi knows how to build warm, personal relationships, beginning with a nonjudgmental welcome and a personal invitation to share a meal in his home. And, once you're in a relationship with a Chabad rabbi, he knows your name, he is at your side when stuff happens in your life, he is usually a good teacher, and he empowers you Jewishly. Yes, he is an aggressive fundraiser, but people give because they are grateful for the relationship.

Let's go deeper and unpack the principles and strategies of Chabad that could be emulated by other groups seeking to build a relationship-based community. I have discussed the phenomenon of Chabad with noted observers of the American Jewish community— Steven M. Cohen, Sue Fishkoff (author of *The Rebbe's Army: Inside the World of Chabad-Lubavitch*), Rabbi Joseph Telushkin, and Gary Wexler, marketing consultant extraordinaire, who has worked extensively with Chabad International.

I have also had the opportunity to get to know two outstanding Chabad rabbis in Southern California—Rabbi Moshe Bryski and Rabbi Dovid Eliezrie. I regularly invite them to teach my Ziegler School of Rabbinic Studies students in a course titled "Creating Sacred Communities" at American Jewish University. Twenty years ago, I doubt Chabad rabbis would step foot inside a Conservative movement rabbinical school, a significant indication of both the acceptance of Chabad on the communal landscape and their willingness to engage with non-Orthodox Jewish leaders.

Listen as Rabbi Dovid Eliezrie begins to identify the principles that have fueled Chabad's success:

> *The Rebbe taught: The Torah teaches us of three loves:* ahavas ha-Hashem—*love of God,* ahavas Torah—*love of Torah, and* ahavas Yisroel—*the love of Jews. If you have the love of God and the love of Torah, but not the love of fellow Jews, then your love of God and love of Torah is deficient. What's the Rebbe doing here? Something important: he is telling the Orthodox world, we don't need fortress Judaism. We don't need you to sit in yeshivas all day. We need to reach every single Jew. Every single Jew, not just my "members." The lines between religious and nonreligious won't be the same anymore. We tell the* shluchim, *"Build relationships first, then you'll figure out the programs."*

This first "secret" of Chabad sets the stage for everything they do. The goal of reaching "every Jew" is a refusal to rely on the membership model that has been the social and financial structure of synagogues and Jewish Community Centers. Moreover, the value of loving every Jew supersedes, on the surface at least, a narrow orthodoxy that hinders the development of relationships with those who do not share your theology and practice. Some Orthodox rabbis refuse to recognize or engage with anyone who is not Orthodox. As true "Jewish evangelicals," most Chabad rabbis view the non-Orthodox as their prime targets, hoping their personal relationship will encourage them to "do more *mitzvos* (commandments)" and become more observant of Jewish law and practice.

The engagement strategies of Chabad have evolved over time. Rabbi Eliezrie claims that the days when Chabad rabbis would commandeer public spaces or drive around in "Mitzvah Tanks," looking for Jews to put on tefillin or stand in a sukkah as a first step into a relationship, are all but over.

Rabbi Eliezrie tells my students:

> I'm not standing on a street corner anymore. People are coming to me ... to put their kid in our Hebrew school. Or, I go to them; I know who they are and where they are. We've changed. A tefillin campaign is for yeshiva bochers [boys]. We rabbis are too busy meeting with people, visiting hospitals, teaching adult education courses, raising money, building buildings.

This shift in approach is quite revealing. Chabad rabbis used to start with getting people to do a *mitzvah*. Today, they begin with relationships first, then *mitzvot*. The candidates for *shluchim* are selected based on their ability to relate to others.

Chabad employs the most important engagement strategy I know; I have called it "radical hospitality." Encounter a Chabad rabbi and you are certain to receive a personal invitation for a Shabbat or holiday meal, often in the rabbi's home. At the table, there is more than breaking bread; there is breaking the ice, breaking down the obvious differences that would appear to prevent a relationship between a Hasidic Orthodox rabbi and a modern secular Jew. The warmth of the home, the generosity of spirit, the patently nonjudgmental acceptance of each person—no matter his or her personal observance—the passionate singing of *zemiros* (songs), all have their effect on the guests.

Rabbi Eliezrie continues:

> *Then we care about them. We find out what they care*
> *about, what they are interested in. I teach doctors once a*
> *month. I build a connection with them and between them*
> *and Torah. I find a mitzvah that they will find important*
> *and meaningful. Yes, we bring them shmurah matzah and*
> *Hanukkah candles. But, mainly we're there for them when*
> *they need someone to be at a bedside, to celebrate a sim-*
> *cha, to say Kaddish at a shiva. We connect in a profound*
> *spiritual way.*

A second engagement strategy is the continuity of relationship. The Chabad rabbi who accepts an assignment to go to Siberia knows that he will be there for life. "What's behind this?" I ask Rabbi Eliezrie. "That's the way the Rebbe wanted it. He wanted us to build relationships within the communities. He wanted the people to know that their rabbi is there forever." There is no question that much of the success of Chabad is due to this remarkable commitment to a specific community. Unless something really bad happens or he cannot raise sufficient funds to support the operation, the Chabad rabbi and his family are in the community for the long term. For instance, Rabbi Mendel Katzman, the Chabad rabbi in my hometown of Omaha, Nebraska, has been there for twenty-six years. He knows every Jew in the community. He seems to show up everywhere, whether you support him financially or not. He works on projects with the Federation. His wife is a beloved teacher. Together, they have built a web of relationships that are solid and enduring. Think of non-Chabad rabbis who have served a community for many years; they, too, enjoy relationships with many of their congregants and their families, often for multiple generations. With more Chabad rabbis than *shluchim* positions, the organization is in the envious position of carefully selecting the right match for a community.

Rabbi Eliezrie concludes:

> *When people know you're committed to be there for life, it*
> *changes their attitude toward you. They realize you're not*
> *a "come and go" guy. You're fully committed to them as a*
> *community. You get to know them.*

Rabbi Eliezrie points out a third engagement strategy: Torah study.

> *Our Jewish Learning Institute produces outstanding adult education courses that are offered in over three hundred and fifty locations worldwide offered in English, Spanish, Russian, Hebrew, and other languages. There are non-Orthodox Jews who may not want to pray with a mechitzah (separation between men and women), but welcome the opportunity to study with a Chabad rabbi, either in class or sometimes one on one.*

A fourth engagement strategy is to lower the economic barriers of participation. Free Hebrew schools and Bar Mitzvah training, free adult education classes, free High Holy Day services, free giveaways of candles, matzah, and meals. Contrast this with the model most membership-based institutions use: pay up-front dues and then you can engage. To be fair, Chabad programming is not really "free"; the Chabad rabbi is a tireless fundraiser. Engage a Chabad rabbi or attend a program and you will inevitably receive a direct mail and/or a direct personal appeal for funds. Yet, many of those who are engaged by these "free" offerings and many who are grateful for the relationship with the rabbi willingly respond, sometimes at levels that exceed what "fair share" and other dues structures would collect. Moreover, the vast majority of the money raised by Chabad comes from Jews who are not Orthodox in practice.

The use of television, advertising brochures, the Internet, and social media is a fifth engagement strategy of Chabad. In Los Angeles, Rabbi Baruch Cunin pioneered the annual Chabad telethon, a multi-hour celebration of Chabad that raises millions of dollars. Intercontinental streaming video, a "Chanukah Live" spectacular, and local advertising of *farbrengen* (celebrations) create a palpable presence in the community. Furthermore, Chabad.org is the largest Jewish presence on the Internet, with some three hundred Chabadniks working full-time on the site. Every Chabad outpost has its own Internet site, often linked to and/or hosted by Chabad.org (for a monthly fee paid to 770 Eastern Parkway). At the Chabad *Kinus*, nearly every rabbi had a smartphone, a Twitter following, an easy facility with texting. The brochures advertising adult education, preschools, High Holy Day "retreats," and other experiences are as slick as anything produced by Madison Avenue. An entire cottage industry of Chabadniks offer their design templates and customized production services via a password-protected Internet site to *shluchim* on a "pay-as-you-go" basis. Compare these rich resources with those offered by other national organizations to their local constituents—frankly, it's no contest.

This leads to the sixth engagement strategy: take Judaism unapologetically to the people, rather than wait for the people to come to you. As Professor Steven Windmueller points out in his review of *The Visual Culture of Chabad* by Maya Balakisky Katz, "While the rest of North American Judaism would claim the private space of the sanctuary, Chabad would capture the public square."[1] Using art, music, and public displays of Hanukkah menorahs in parks and malls, Chabad effectively creates a brand recognition that serves its core mission of *keiruv*, bringing Jews close to Judaism. Only recently have the liberal movements and outreach organizations promoted the idea of "public-space Judaism"; Chabad invented it.

A seventh strategy rests on a basic principle articulated by the Rebbe when he began sending his Hasidim out from Brooklyn: *shluchim* are never sent alone to a community; only married couples are given a position. A Chabad operation is almost always a family affair. The rabbi's wife teaches, the children are taught that being chosen for *shlichus* (emissary outreach) is a coveted goal, and the larger Chabad territories are often served by extended family members. As noted earlier, a separate conference for *rebbetzins* is held annually, attracting some three thousand women. According to Rabbi Eliezrie:

> *Women have always been considered equal partners in running the institutions. We may have a mechitzah during davening, but our women take a tremendous leadership role. Whose idea was it to have a conference for the women? Not the women. It was the Rebbe's idea; it was a revolution in the Haredi (ultra-Orthodox) world. Our women are empowered, they take charge, they are crucial to the whole enterprise.*

There is little doubt that the Chabad family makes a total commitment to their mission.

Finally, Chabad has invested heavily in an educational system for their young people. There are yeshivot, rabbinical seminaries, and extensive opportunities to learn engagement work in the field. Like the Mormons, Chabad sends nineteen- and twenty-year-olds all over the world as emissaries, to serve as teachers, run Passover Seder experiences, help out every Shabbat in Chabad Houses, organize relief efforts, and counsel kids in summer camps.

The mastermind behind the incredible growth of Chabad was, of course, the Lubavitcher Rebbe, Menachem Mendel Schneerson (1902–1994). Although he was one of the most influential Jewish personalities of the twentieth century, his death did not slow the movement. Author Joseph Telushkin, who is writing a biography of the man simply known worldwide as "the Rebbe," observes:

> If it was the Rebbe's personality alone that dominated the movement, then the movement should have disintegrated, or greatly weakened, with his passing. But it hasn't. In fact, it has increased substantially. There are now three times as many *shluchim* as there were when the Rebbe died in 1994, and Chabad Houses can now be found in 47 states and in over 75 countries. Eighteen years ago, there were Chabad Houses in only 38 countries. How does one account for this?… It strikes me that the primary and most precious commodity he bequeathed his followers—one he urged the whole Jewish world to accept—was an unconditional love and respect for every Jew, even for those Jews whose lifestyles and religious practices were very different from his own.[2]

While the organization is widely admired, there are points of tension between Chabad and a variety of organizations and individuals in the Jewish community. Most Chabad rabbis have no lay board of directors, and a few rabbis have run into serious financial difficulties. Suspicions abound regarding the political aspirations of Chabad in Israel. Some Chabad rabbis build relationships with colleagues on the local boards of rabbis, with local Federations, with other college-based groups;

others do not. When I lecture about Chabad, inevitably some leader will tell me a horror story about what a Chabad rabbi did or said ... while others will shake their heads knowingly that despite any misgivings, there is little doubt that Chabad has invented and perfected the modern practice of engagement outreach.

At the Chabad *Kinus* in November 2011, the chief rabbi of Great Britain, Jonathan Sacks, gave a stirring keynote address to the *shluchim*, recalling the influence of the Rebbe on his own life. At key moments of decision on his career path, Rabbi Sacks, like thousands of others, turned to the Rebbe for advice. Invariably, the good counsel he received led Rabbi Sacks to a distinguished career as a pulpit rabbi and ultimately as the leader of the Orthodox community in England. In his speech, he perfectly captures the organizing principle of Chabad, indeed of any organization that seeks to *move* people toward a greater sense of connection:

> Most people look at others and see what they seem. Great people look at others and see what they are. The greatest of the great—and the Rebbe was greatest of the great—see others and see what they could become.

This ability to see the potential in every person to "become" more engaged with *Yiddishkeit* is what drives the Chabad emissary.

In the climax of his speech, Rabbi Sacks makes a sharp distinction between religious Jews who are content to remain in their communities, satisfied that their own commitment to an observant life is enough, and those who reach out beyond their comfort zone in the effort to bring Judaism to others. He cites the debate in the Talmud between Rav and Shmuel regarding whether a Hanukkah candle can be used to light another Hanukkah candle. Rav argues no, lest a tiny bit of wax or oil be lost in the process and diminish the first light. Shmuel does not worry about this and says, yes, one candle can be used to light another. Rabbi Sacks points out that *halakhah* (the law) almost always follows Rav, except in three instances. This is one of them. Rabbi Sacks asks, "Why?"

> The answer, you will find in today's Jewish world, you will take two *Yidden*, two Jews, both religious, both *frum* [religious] ...

both keeping all the *mitzvos* [commandments]. But there's a big difference between them; one of them says I have to look after my light, and if I get involved with Jews who are not *frum*, not religious, who are not committed, *ko machish mitzvah*—my *Yiddishkeit* will be diminished. That is the view of Rav, and Rav was a spiritual giant. But Shmuel dared to say otherwise. He said when I take my light to set another Jewish soul on fire, I don't have less light, I have more! Because while there was once one light, now there are two, and maybe from those two more will come! And on this, the *halakhah* is like Shmuel. Friends, that is what it is to be a Hasid, to *paskin* [decide] like Shmuel, to know that when we go out to Jews who are less committed than we are, our light is not diminished; the result is we create more light in the world.[3]

Rabbi Sacks was not only giving a not-so-subtle *shtuch*—a jab in the ribs to his own (and by implication to North American) modern Orthodox constituencies for being too insular; he was also validating the value of *shlichut*, of outreach to those who are not (yet) "Jewish souls on fire," the practice of which no one is better at than Chabad.

Hillel

When I enrolled as a freshman at Washington University in St. Louis, Missouri, a school with a large Jewish student population among the four thousand undergraduates, I received an invitation for a "Lox and Bagel Brunch" during "Welcome Week" at the Hillel House on Forsyth Boulevard, directly across the street from the main campus. On a bright fall Sunday morning, I joined with hundreds of hungry Jewish college kids who descended on the lovely three-story brick home with newly built attached social hall and kitchen to enjoy the food. For the vast majority of those students, it was the first—and last—time they set foot in the building. Not for lack of a warm welcome from the Hillel rabbi and staff; rather, in those days, the message of Hillel (Hillel.org) was like most Jewish institutions: "You come to us; we don't come to you."

Greeting me in the lobby of the Hillel House that morning was Rabbi Robert Jacobs, a kindly short man with a broad smile and a deep baritone voice. "Shalom, welcome to Hillel," he bellowed and offered a used-car salesman handshake. "My name is Rabbi Jacobs; what's yours?" I introduced myself, but before I could tell him anything substantive about me or my experiences as a youth group leader, Rabbi Jacobs surprised me with his next question: "Well, Ron, tell me. What would you like to see us do here at Hillel?" "What do you mean exactly, Rabbi Jacobs?" I asked. "Well, Ron [his drawl made "Ron" into three syllables], what I mean is what kind of programs would attract you to the Hillel House? For example, is there someone we could invite to speak at Hillel who would entice you to come?" My mind raced to find the name of a major Jewish figure, someone I doubted a Hillel rabbi would be able to contact, let alone attract. "How about Rabbi Abraham Joshua Heschel?" I suggested, fully expecting Rabbi Jacobs to say there was no way he could get the famous Rabbi Heschel, the leading theologian and social activist in the Jewish community at the time. Heschel had not only written some of the most influential books I had read as a teenager (*The Sabbath, God in Search of Man*), but he also had forever earned the respect of the young Jews who emerged during the turbulent sixties and early seventies by walking arm-in-arm with Reverend Dr. Martin Luther King in the March on Selma demonstration for civil rights. No way a Hillel rabbi in St. Louis, Missouri, was going to get Heschel to meet Jewish students at a small Midwestern university!

What happened next stunned me. Rabbi Jacobs grabbed me under the elbow and began to escort me to his office. "Let's call him now!" he drawled. We walked to his desk, he picked up the phone, and he dialed The Jewish Theological Seminary in New York City. "May I speak to Rabbi Heschel, please," he confidently said to the operator. "Oh, I see," he murmured, clearly disappointed. "I'm sorry he is not in. Please ask Rabbi Heschel to call me as soon as possible." Although this was indisputably impressive, it nevertheless fit within the engagement strategy of the times—"get the Jewish college kids into the building"— a strategy that led to the gradual decline of Hillel as a force on campuses nationally.

I was an easy catch for Hillel. Coming off my year as regional president of EMTZA USY, a region that included St. Louis in its territory, I was eager to find a Jewish home on campus. So were a small number of other students from various parts of the country who were already hooked on Judaism. I quickly found a *hevre*, a group of friends, mostly lovely but nerdy kids who avoided the Greek houses in favor of the familiar comfort of Shabbat dinners, holidays, and the occasional lunch-and-learn, in which the main attraction was most definitely the kosher deli lunch, not necessarily the learning. It was great, a kind of synagogue on campus.

During my sophomore year, I accepted the role of student president of the Hillel House. I had quickly ascertained that Jewish students were not showing up for a number of reasons, among them the fact that they had to pay dues to "belong." I felt we were missing the boat. So, I rocked the boat. At my first board meeting of local lay leaders and Jewish professors from Washington University, among them the well-known philosopher Steven S. Schwarzschild, I suggested we eliminate dues and declare every Jewish student on campus a "member" of Hillel automatically. Rabbi Jacobs almost fell off his chair. To my surprise, the board approved the idea, and it had some effect on attendance. And, when I learned that Rabbi Heschel had indeed accepted an invitation to come to campus to deliver a speech in a lecture series sponsored by the university, I managed to find a way to get him to the Hillel House. Through the student grapevine, I learned that if a group of Jewish students invited Rabbi Heschel to help make a minyan while he was on any campus, he would show up. So, I wrote him a letter inviting him to do just that … and he graciously accepted. It was the first and only standing-room-only daily minyan in the history of Washington University Hillel. Nevertheless, with the exception of the annual free lox and bagel brunch and High Holy Day services, attendance at Hillel events in that big, beautiful building was meager, at best.

Years later, it was the leadership of Richard Joel, a charismatic director of International Hillel, who began the process of resuscitating a moribund Hillel model. Working with deep-pocket funders who bought into his vision of a "Jewish renaissance" on campus, Joel and his team, led by Rhoda Weisman, invented the Jewish Campus Service Corps, the first attempt to bring the work of Jewish student engagement out of the Hillel House and into the dorms. Recent college graduates were trained in a new approach to meeting generation-X students on their turf and their terms. The project brought renewed excitement and effectiveness to Hillel, proving that, indeed, there was plenty of opportunity to "maximize the number of Jews doing Jewish with other Jews," not just in the Hillel House.

Yet, by the middle of the first decade of the current century, it became increasingly clear that a new generation of students required a different approach. Understanding that the engagement of millennials on campus would depend on offering each individual a way to discover his or her own Jewish path, a new strategy was envisioned to introduce students to "meaningful Jewish experiences" that would develop "Jewish ownership"—increased Jewish knowledge, positive Jewish feelings and memories, and a sense of Jewish community and peoplehood. This sense of Jewish ownership would then lead students to make Jewish decisions, undertake Jewish behaviors of their own choosing, and even create initiatives on campus to further Jewish life.

Under the direction of Wayne Firestone, the leadership embraced a new, audacious goal in 2008: "Doubling the number of students having meaningful Jewish experiences and involved in Jewish life." To accomplish this formidable task, a creative team developed several "engagement" initiatives. The most interesting is a two-pronged model called the Senior Jewish Educator / Campus Entrepreneur Initiative (SJE/CEI). The project is built on the presence of a Jewish role model and the power of peer-to-peer social networking. The Senior Jewish Educator (SJE), a new full-time position, is relieved of the usual operational duties in order to focus on relationship building, crafting Jewish learning experiences, and creating opportunities to introduce students to Jewish ideas, social justice projects, and other engagement points. Unlike the Jewish Campus Service Corps' use of recent college graduates as engagement workers, the Campus Entrepreneur Initiative (CEI) offers college sophomores and juniors an annual stipend of $1,000 to $2,000, plus $600 in "coffee money," to build relationships with sixty friends and friends of friends. Working under the tutelage of an SJE who her- or himself accepts a target of contacting 180 students, CEI interns deploy across the campus, asking friends or students to meet for a "coffee date"—a one-on-one conversation, all in the effort to get to know them and eventually connect them to something Jewish.

Every new cohort of SJE staff and CEI interns meets for extensive training in August, just before the start of a new academic year. While researching this book, I accepted the invitation of Graham Hoffman, associate vice president of strategy at Hillel's Charles and Lynn Schusterman International Center, to attend the 2012 Hillel Institute, which met on the campus of my alma mater, Washington University in St. Louis. In a word, the gathering was stunning. Some 450 Jewish college students joined with nearly 450 Hillel staff from 153 campuses across North America, Israel, and Germany for a multilayered, well-articulated, and very intensive full week of workshops, trainings, simulations, and conversations, capped by an "immersive" Shabbat experience. I was particularly interested in observing the teams of CEI interns, college students who had signed on to learn how to build relationships with their peers.

Before my site visit, I was briefed by Hoffman and I conducted interviews with key frontline staff from International Hillel and several of the local Hillel professionals. With the support of a $10.7 million five-year grant from the Jim Joseph Foundation, twelve Hillel campuses across the country launched the joint SJE/CEI initiative in 2008. According to a formative evaluation conducted by sociologists Steven M. Cohen, Ezra Kopelowitz, Jack Ukeles, and Minna Wolf, during the first two-year rollout the SJEs and CEI interns together reached 13,883 students, about 60 percent of whom had had little or no contact with Hillel in the previous year. The contacts made a measurable difference in many forms of Jewish growth. The student entrepreneurs themselves experienced growth in the number of Jewish friendships made, while the SJEs were particularly effective in promoting Jewish learning activities and initiating "Jewish talk," particularly among the uninvolved.[4]

Of the sixty relationships CEIers build, ten are expected to be in their "inner circle," twenty are "regular contacts," and thirty are "friends of friends." There are targets for how frequently CEI interns interact with students in each of these "circles," but a "relationship" only counts if there are at least two documented interactions during the academic year for the outer circle of "friends of friends," and eight to twenty interactions for the inner circle and regular contacts.

"Interactions" may include an event they facilitate for the students or participate in together, a conversation/meet/coffee date, or an immersive experience such as a Birthright trip or an Alternative Spring Break.

On the morning of a full-day of "engagement training" at the Hillel Institute, groups of CEI interns, Peer Network fellows, Student Leadership interns, and MASA interns representing more than sixty campuses gathered in small groups to learn the art of building relationships. The first exercise, a get-to-know-you icebreaker called "Be Interested, Not Interesting," featured two circles of students taking turns asking questions of peers from different campuses. The twist: by only asking questions and not responding, the students practiced "active listening," a critical skill for effective one-on-one conversation. After a brief debrief of that experience, a "simulation" of a "Welcome Week" activities fair on campus found each Hillel group taking on different roles: University of Southern California played "Incoming Freshmen," University of California, Los Angeles played "Student Government," George Washington University played "Greeks," Ohio State University played "Hillel Student Leaders," and Columbia/Barnard played "Engagement Interns."

Later in the afternoon, each campus group learned a series of approaches for engaging peers and building deep and meaningful relationships. The key take-aways:

> The right relationship is everything. Building and developing relationships with others involve the fundamental skills that facilitate success in nearly every people-focused venture. Engagement predicated on the foundation of a strong one-on-one relationship can serve a number of purposes in facilitating growth for ourselves and others.
>
> The key skills involved in engagement include:
>
> *Establishing Rapport*
> Create a personal connection and finding common ground in order to follow up and build a stronger relationship in the future. Be interested, not interesting!
>
> *Demonstrating Empathy*
> Accept and value others' perspective and show a genuine interest in understanding them.

Asking Questions
Use clarifying, developing, and suggestive questions to help others think through an issue or make a decision, enabling them to solve the problem on their own.

Demonstrating Commitment
Invest in the success of others through under-committing and over-delivering. Align actions and priorities with words and feelings.

Developing Self-Awareness
Articulate your own perspectives, reactions, and assumptions to better understand the "lenses" through which you view the world.[5]

Students were then asked to create a map of their social networks as a jump-start to identifying friends and friends of friends they might approach to reach their goal of sixty relationships. Further workshops dealt with "Using REACH to Track Relationships," "Boundary Breaking," "What's Your Story?" and a wide variety of Shabbat worship and learning experiences, before ending the weekend with "Bringing It Back to Campus."

A "coffee date" is only the beginning of the Hillel peer engagement strategy. CEI interns and SJEs are also trained to be "connectors," personal concierges who link individual students to relevant Jewish opportunities, based on the stories heard during the one-on-one conversation. For example, if someone reveals an interest in ecology, the SJE or CEI intern will encourage the student to connect with the Jewish National Fund internship program. A second goal is to create "microcommunities," small groups of peers who share a similar interest or social network. For instance, the CEI intern will organize a Shabbat dinner for a small group, using the "coffee money" to host the evening. A third area of engagement is the creation of entrepreneurial projects, an ongoing effort that fills an unmet need and further engages students in Jewish life. This strategy builds on the notion that millennials like to be part of "start-ups," projects that tap into their creative talents and organizational skills.

According to Rachel Gildiner, the SJE/CIE project director at Hillel International, the greatest challenge in training students to do relational work is their previous training.

> *They come to us out of high schools and youth groups trained to create programs: how much food do we need to order, who will set up the chairs? They are good at counting tushies in seats; they've been taught that is the measure of success. We ask totally different questions: "Who are you meeting?" not "What did you do?" What did you learn from their stories? What meaningful experiences can you lead them to? What's your own Jewish journey?*

Margo Sack of University of Texas Hillel acknowledges that the shift from a programmatic to a relationship-based culture has been huge. "We would get busy creating one program after another. The goal was to 'fill the calendar' rather than 'let's get to know our students and help them along their Jewish journeys.'"

Graham Hoffman, the Hillel senior staffer spearheading the project, reports that one of the most important elements in the success of the program is the quality of the SJE and the level of support offered by the executive director of the Hillel Foundation. At the most effective campuses, the culture of Hillel itself has been transformed, moving from a program-centric to a relational methodology of engagement.

Gildiner admits that they look for CEI interns who have a social network that reaches beyond the "usual suspects," the young people who would gravitate to Hillel in any case. Often, the CEI interns themselves have weak Jewish content and connection. The challenge is to teach them how to have deep Jewish conversations, how to be a Jewish resource. This is the role of the SJE—to equip and mentor the CEI interns. The SJEs meet with their CEI interns weekly to brainstorm ideas, refresh skills, and role-play conversation strategies. The evaluation research indicates that, not surprisingly, the greatest impact of the initiative is on the Jewish growth of the CEI interns themselves. Although not specifically billed as a "leadership development" program, the SJE/CEI model certainly has become an effective vehicle for identifying and engaging student leaders for Hillel.

The SJE/CEI is only one part of the transformation of Hillel into a relationship-based organization. Other relational projects include a Peer Network Engagement Initiative (similar to CEI, but students are not paid a stipend), Student Leadership interns, MASA interns, Tzedek interns, and Ask Big Questions—an initiative to "deepen the conversations" with college students. All of the "relationships" created by this formidable group of "engagers" are tracked through a sophisticated relationship management software database called REACH. By the summer of 2012, the numbers on an expanded cohort of seventeen campuses had swelled to very impressive figures: 862 staff and CEI interns had engaged nearly forty-five thousand students, thirty thousand of whom reported attending at least one Jewish "event."

One Hillel-affiliated campus, New York University, has developed what Rabbi Dan Smokler calls CEI 2.0. At the Bronfman Center for Jewish Life, Rabbi Smokler and his colleagues offer the Jewish Learning Fellowship (JFL), a ten-week series of twice-weekly two-and-a-half-hour sessions for groups of twenty-five freshmen and sophomores who gather to explore the "Big Questions" of life. He explains:

> Here's what I know. I know what students are thinking about when laying on their beds late at night: "Where is home? I have a room in the house I grew up in, but now I live in a dorm. How do I find true love? What should I do with the rest of my life?" These are deep questions ... and we create an experience to answer them. We discuss rootlessness. We study Jewish classic texts in English about a sukkah, a semi-permanent structure that is your home-away-from-home, kind of like a college dorm. We break for dinner every session. We go on a Shabbat retreat at a summer camp outside the city. We answer questions of meaning and build relationships.

Smokler—affectionately known as Rabbi Dan—reports that 1,150 NYU students have been through the Jewish Learning Fellowship experience since 2007. In addition to the "Big Questions" seminar, there is a more informal series for JLF alumni and one for graduate students and young professionals called The Torah Happy Hour. And, any

NYU Jewish student is welcome to e-mail one of the five staff to meet or study. Smokler's profile on the Jewish Learning Fellowship website reflects the tongue-in-cheek, yet serious invitation for engagement:

> You can always email him to set up a time to meet or study. Want to hear some interesting stories? Ask Rabbi Dan what he did before he was a Rabbi ... Rabbi Dan also thinks he is pretty serious about working out. He is always looking for someone to join him on a run. Just drop him a line.

In any one semester, the five staff at the Bronfman Center will work with some eight hundred students a month.

In a somewhat controversial move, the JLF program offers those whose applications are accepted a $300 stipend to participate. The stipend helps incentivize compliance with a number of norms: no missing sessions (college students are "terrible with commitments," according to Smokler), attending the weekend retreat, writing a mid-term reflection paper, and making a presentation at the conclusion of the seminar. Smokler concludes:

> *When the students come out the other end, they are in a radically different space. We want them to say, "The people really cared about me." CEI 1.0 gets you a social network; we want to go deeper. We want to get students engaged on six vectors. Three are social: Jewish friends, a Jewish mentor, and the experience of community that has a claim on you. Two are intellectual: we want you to live a Jewish calendar and love the discipline of studying Torah. One is spiritual: we want our students to live a life of avodah—service, not con-sumption. The JLF program moves students into a broader communal structure. The microcommunity works if someone in it is a link to a bigger community. We want students to know they can connect not just to an isolated havurah of five individuals; they can connect to the Jewish people.*

I asked a former SJE, Rabbi Joel Nickerson, to reflect on his experience at the University of Pennsylvania from 2009 to 2011 building relation-ships with Jewish students on campus:

Meeting me was the first time these eighteen- to twenty-one-year-olds were engaged in a conversation with a rabbi in a long time. Some had a relationship with the Jewish community when they were kids; some none at all. It's shocking, really, when you think about it, but most people never have the opportunity to be in a one-on-one relationship with a rabbi. Regardless of their background, there was no way they were going to go to Hillel. There was no way they were going to take Jewish studies classes. Unless there was some relationship, it wasn't going to happen.

I usually would start by sending students a carefully crafted e-mail introducing myself and inviting them for coffee and conversation "with no hidden agenda." I never met with them in my office. My study, a "rabbi's study," is not the place to meet someone. It's like going to the principal's office. They are defensive from the get-go because they think I'll judge them.

I would say that for 30 percent of the students, the one-on-one was a one-off; I didn't see them again. But, with 40 percent of them, I would maintain a relationship, I would stay in connection. And, with 30 percent, they would come learn with me, go on a Birthright trip with me, continue to meet me one-on-one. My goal was to get them to make a commitment to something—to learn, to do a project, to take a trip, to create an event … something.

I believe people want commitment. They yearn for commitment. They're lonely … and they are suffering for it. They want to connect to a community. They want meaning and commitment. Even young people. What better way to create that than to give it to them—to motivate them to be part of something. That's what they want. They don't want programs. Who wants programs? No one wants a speaker. No one wants a one-off thing. You go to the program … and then you go home. So what? Programs don't work. It's all about microcommunities and relationships and intimacy and commitment.

I asked Josh Miller, program officer of the Jim Joseph Foundation, himself a pioneer of engagement-based strategies, to name the most effective relational organizations working in North America today. His answer was quick and unequivocal: "Hillel and Chabad." While the Chabad *shluchim* seem to be born with a "relational gene," it is Hillel that has pioneered a sophisticated training model for teaching Jewish peers to build relationships and encourage connections to other peers, to a Jewish role model, and to Jewish living experiences.

Congregation-Based Community Organizing

Congregation-based community organizing, known as CBCO, is an initiative that grew out of the social justice world, a relational strategy that seeks to surface common concerns based on the self-interests of a community and then rally the people of that community to act. The CBCO approach comes directly out of the playbook of the Industrial Arts Foundation (IAF), pioneered by Saul Alinsky in Chicago, who taught that organized institutions acting together can have tremendous power for social good.

In the CBCO model, the synagogue invites a "leadership team" of diverse members of the congregation and clergy to meet with a skilled community organizer who trains the group in the art of conducting a "listening campaign." In synagogue settings, this campaign is often called "Face-to-Face," a reference to the *panim el panim* encounter between God and Moses. Individual members of the leadership team accept the responsibility of conducting a specific number of "one-on-one" meetings with members of the congregation, a systematic effort to bring them into "sacred conversation." (See the "Telling Stories" section below for a detailed description of the one-on-one technique.) These meetings often take place over coffee at a neutral location, not the synagogue building, although some congregations hold the conversations during worship services, during an *oneg*, or at other times. The goal of the hour-long meeting is twofold: two members share each other's stories and the surfacing of "justice concerns" by tackling probing questions such as "What keeps you up at night?"

At its heart, CBCO is a relational approach that has the potential to transform synagogues (and other institutions) into centers of Relational

Judaism. Virtually unknown a decade ago, the CBCO process has been initiated at more than 170 Reform congregations. Rabbis have been trained in community organizing skills, and nearly every start-up independent minyan considers the nexus of spirituality and social justice to be at the heart of the sacred community of the twenty-first century. (Lest one think that CBCO is only resonant in the liberal religious community, some in the evangelical megachurch world have embraced a form of social activism, as well. Pastor Rick Warren of Saddleback Church often cites the power that comes from churches acting together.)

Early evidence suggests that, when done well, CBCO meets three important goals, as identified by Rabbi Jonah Pesner, one of the pioneers of the approach: (1) to build power for social and economic justice, (2) to transform the synagogue into a congregation in which members are more deeply connected to one another, and (3) to shape synagogues into places where activists want to be.[6]

Rabbi Noah Farkas of Valley Beth Shalom in Encino, California, suggests that synagogues think of themselves as civic institutions—"machines that take people from their private lives and put them into public lives." How? In a four-step process: hear people's stories, build relationships, give them a voice in public discourse and plan together, and work for change through "actions," such as advocacy, legislative interventions, and social justice projects. "The same skills that community organizers use to bring private people into public space are the same skills we rabbis can use to get people from being private Jews to public Jews."

Stimulated by the creation of Just Congregations (www.urj.org/justcongregations), an arm of the Union for Reform Judaism, synagogues of all sizes have successfully "listened" to their congregants in hundreds of one-on-one meetings. The leadership team members bring the concerns they heard back to the group, and those issues that are mentioned over and over again form a "collective story" and rise to the surface for consideration as targets of "actions." Actions can range from collaborating with neighboring churches on a local issue to mounting a statewide initiative to change the law. For example, a synagogue in Chicago organized to shut down an arms merchant in a neighborhood, and a synagogue in Boston led the fight to change health care laws in Massachusetts.

Rabbi Stephanie Kolin, codirector of Just Congregations, summarizes the people-first approach of CBCO:

> *The key challenge is to get "inside the imaginations" of the congregants. This is a big paradigm shift: instead of just planning on the basis of what the professional staff wants, the conversations and house meetings should also reveal what the members want, what is in their self-interest.*

As important as the social actions that emanate from CBCO, the process itself has the potential to bring hundreds of members into conversation with each other, to share their stories, to sit in relationship, face-to-face in a relational, not programmatic, community.

I first learned about CBCO some half-dozen years ago when Rabbi Jonah Pesner and Lila Foldes presented their work at a Synagogue 3000–sponsored conference in Atlanta. It was clear from the outset that their approach was relational. As Rabbi Pesner says:

> *I have faith that once Jews are in deep relationship with each other, with Jewish community, and with Judaism itself, they will understand that the imperative for social justice is the heart and soul of our people; it's in our DNA. You cannot hear someone's story about losing a job or caring for a terminally ill relative and simply give her a hug. If you are truly in relationship with that person, you will go work for job equality, you will go work to rally the community to ensure that families of those who are ill have the support they need and deserve. I am convinced that the social justice agenda will not be lost in this critical work to build a different kind of Judaism.*

As Rabbi Jill Jacobs, a Conservative rabbi, teaches in her book *Where Justice Dwells*, the key verse in the Passover Haggadah is *lirot et atzmo*—to see yourself as having been a slave in Egypt. The beginning of social justice work is to "see oneself," to discover how each person understands her or his concerns and passions. But, the Sephardic Haggadah changes the grammar of the verse to *l'harot et atzmo*, "to show yourself." This demands action, not just introspection.[7] Building relationships internally and working on external actions are always related: one can lead to the other. Those who are engaged in the work of social justice often draw closer to the congregation, and those who discover the power of relationships in community can be inspired to work to repair the world. Both are essential to the Jewish experience.

The Jewish Funds for Justice and the Nathan Cummings Foundation were early supporters of this work, and their efforts have successfully engaged every major Jewish denomination in CBCO. In addition, rabbis and Jewish professionals are being trained in CBCO on nine Jewish seminary campuses across the United States. Rabbis Kolin and Farkas, along with colleagues Meir Lakein and Jeannie Appleman, are spearheading this groundbreaking Seminary Leadership Project. Some two hundred rabbis from across the denominations have been given basic training in relational organizing during the past seven years.

In April 2012, I attended the first national conference of CBCO leaders convened by JOIN for Justice—the Jewish Organizing Institute and Network (www.joinforjustice.org). Some 250 organizers and clergy gathered for a dynamic two-day exploration of how community organizing has impacted the community and which future actions might stimulate its growth. Each session modeled the basic principles of an organizing model of meeting: warm welcome, introductions (often a brief one-on-one conversation), agenda setting, consensus on agenda, presentation of a "big idea," a story from the facilitator about how the idea worked in a real-life situation, turn and talk (another one-on-one or small-group experience), recap, and check out. In addition to organizing training for both novices and veterans, much of the conference focused on how JOIN and Bend the Arc: A Jewish Partnership for Justice (the merger of Jewish Funds for Justice and the Progressive Jewish Alliance) could "move the needle" of influencing the broader Jewish community to embrace both the methodologies and the goals of social justice work. A concerted attempt was made to keep "politics" out of the public plenaries; the organizers of the conference were clearly aware of the reputation that "community organizing" has a left-wing, progressive agenda. While there was a palpable tension between those embracing the use of organizing strategies for internal community building and those whose ultimate goal is societal transformation, the excitement among the mostly young organizers and clergy was energizing and empowering.

Simon Greer, former president and CEO of Jewish Funds for Justice and currently president of the Nathan Cummings Foundation, offered a stirring keynote address, reviewing the history of Jewish justice organizing. Summarizing his message, Greer surprisingly showed the cover of Rick Warren's *The Purpose Driven Life* in his PowerPoint presentation and implored the crowd:

> We don't have a continuity crisis; we have a purpose crisis. What's our purpose? What are we here to do? Our purpose is to repair the world. To do that, we need to make a long-term investment in building real relationships. We need to give people something bigger than themselves to be part of. We need to find and welcome unusual allies; you don't have to give up your values to work with others who may disagree with you. Get the tools you need to organize. The problem is not commitment or passion; the challenge is: "Are we good enough and skilled enough at this craft to do it well over time?" What's our purpose? When my kids ask me why I'm going to a meeting, I tell them: "To make the world a better place for you." Let's make that true. Will you leave the world a better place for the next generation? Make friends, then grab your significant Jewish values, train, and make the world a better place.

In my conversations with Rabbi Pesner and Foldes, I suggested that the relational strategies could go far beyond the social justice agenda, as important as it is as a goal of synagogues. They agreed, yet there was hesitancy in their voices, born of the concern that the goal of CBCO—societal transformation—not be lost in the task of institutional transformation. Yet, there is ample evidence that the leadership of the organizing community has embraced the fact that some synagogues that have utilized CBCO strategies report significant impact in ways that both embrace the "action" agenda and change the culture of the congregation. Take the example of *Minyan Tzedek* at IKAR, which represents a new approach to engaging congregants as a result of a CBCO-initiated process.

Minyan Tzedek

No congregation is as committed to the nexus between social justice and spirituality as IKAR, a sacred community in Los Angeles, led by the dynamic Rabbi Sharon Brous. Sharing space in the Westside Jewish Community Center, IKAR is populated with substantial numbers of sophisticated young Jews, a West Coast mirror image of the Upper West Side of New York City. Many of the members of IKAR work in the entertainment industry or are professionals serving the Hollywood infrastructure. One would think CBCO would take root easily in such a community. Yet, when IKAR launched its campaign, it was a "miserable failure." Rabbi Brous explains:

> We put a lot of our cred on the line by promoting CBCO, but our people didn't get it; it wasn't working. People just weren't getting fired up by the one-on-ones, and weren't moved by the question "What keeps you up at night?" It was like pulling teeth. So, we pulled the plug on it and spent a year rethinking what had gone wrong and what we could do better.
>
> When we went back to the drawing board, we realized that as Jews we organize around minyanim, groups of ten, not one-on-one. Jews are a relational people within community. You need a minyan to daven, a minyan to have kedushah. It's the same with social justice. In a one-on-one, if you hit it off with the other person, great. If not, you're staring at your watch wondering how to get out of this. But, put ten Jews in a room, and you get fireworks!

IKAR developed *Minyan Tzedek*, literally "the Justice Minyan." Gathering ten to fifteen people for "house parties," the host invites a number of friends, and IKAR invites the others. After sharing snacks, drinks, and schmoozing, the rabbi leads a *hevruta* text study—itself a one-on-one model of learning—and then instead of "What keeps you up at night?" the participants are asked, "What gets you up in the morning?"—a question that comes from hope and possibility. This listening campaign leads to actions based on the stories, passions, and dreams that are surfaced during the house party conversations. As

Rabbi Brous observes, "CBCO is a great model; we just had to adapt it to our culture."

Rabbi Carla Fenves, a young Reform rabbi trained in CBCO, organized the listening campaign at Central Synagogue in New York City as a Just Congregations intern and now serves as rabbi at Temple Emanu-El in San Francisco. She observes:

> I see relational community as a lens for my entire rabbinate. I always ask about everything we do in the synagogue: "Are we doing this in a transactional way or a relational way?" There is a huge energy in a congregation to engage in a listening campaign, the first step in a CBCO process. It is more challenging to take the second step—implementing the action.

After all the one-on-one conversations, after all the house meetings, after all the sifting through the pressing issues demanding attention, the congregation agrees to use its power to advocate for change. Using the strategies of CBCO to build relational communities also has an "action" as its goal: to deepen relationships not just among people, but with each individual and the Nine Levels of Relationship with the Jewish experience: self, family, friends, Jewish living, community, peoplehood, Israel, the world, and God.

Next-Generation Engagement Initiatives

For me, this next example of relationship-based initiatives is extraordinarily personal. My son Michael is thirty-four, now living in Portland, Oregon, after seven years as a single young Jewish adult in New York City. My daughter Havi is thirty-six, living in San Jose, California, with her husband, Dave, and brilliant, darling, and delicious two-year-old daughter Ellie Brooklyn and newborn handsome Gabriel Elijah (I'm the *Zaydie!*).

They are homeless.

Oh, they live in nice dwellings … but they are homeless. Spiritually homeless. They are completely unconnected to a spiritual community. They have no ongoing relationship with a rabbi. They have no relationship to Jewish community organizations. Both Havi and Michael are Jewish day school graduates, summer campers, veteran travelers to

Israel, raised in a warm Jewish family … and their daddy and mommy are "in the business." They have warm Jewish feelings. They celebrate major holidays with their family and friends. But, they have no "third place" beyond home and work, no microcommunity of Jewish peers, no affiliation with a Jewish institution. Why? What's happening? Or, more accurately, what's *not* happening?

The transition from college to young Jewish adulthood is particularly challenging. In a previous era, when the time between college and marriage was a few short years, young Jews often joined synagogues or JCCs fairly soon after graduation. The average age of marriage was twenty-one. Today, the average age of marriage is well north of thirty. As sociologist Steven M. Cohen likes to say, the best predictor of synagogue affiliation is when someone gives birth to a seven-year-old Jewish child. Many parents are into their early forties when that blessed event occurs, and it is patently clear that institutions cannot count on them joining even then.

Until quite recently, Jewish institutions have been slow to understand this demographic reality. Even those organizations that tried to reach this growing population of "emerging adults" did so with old models: "Come to us, to our buildings, pay a reduced membership fee until you reach thirty-two (by then, you should be married with children), don't worry that you have no seat on our boards—we know what's best for you." It didn't work.

In Denver, Lisa Farber Miller and her colleagues at the Rose Community Foundation actually met with two hundred Jewish young adults in one-on-one conversations and at a retreat to find out what they themselves say they actually need. Miller says:

> *What we found is that young people do care—a lot. They have a strong and positive Jewish identity, and they are seeking meaning in their life, but they just never had anyone talk to them about it, especially after the age of thirteen. In many cases, they just didn't see the Jewish community as a safe or welcoming place, one where they could talk about the contemporary issues that concerned them.*

As a result of the study, the Rose Community Foundation created the Roots and Branches Foundation, an initiative to bring young Jews to the communal table and empower them to practice their own approach to community activism and philanthropy (www.rcfdenver.org/initiatives_roots.htm).

Fortunately, a few visionary leaders, foundations, and organizations began to take this challenge seriously; in the past decade there has been an explosion of effort to engage young Jewish adults (YJAs), from Birthright Israel (a free ten-day educational trip for those eighteen to twenty-six who have never been) to Moishe House (self-directed hangouts). The community has come to realize that much of the enormous investment in Jewish education could be lost if connections with young Jews evaporate in the teenage years or in the transition between the time when many young adults graduate college and when they marry, settle down, and begin their own families.

Several of the most interesting and effective YJA initiatives are focused on a relational approach. While there are programs aplenty that seek to attract young people, often with clever titles—a Pour-em Crawl, a progressive bar-hop to celebrate, you guessed it, Purim— once again these one-off events do little to build deep relationships among the participants, except perhaps in their not-so-hidden goal of encouraging Jewish dating and mating. Among those efforts that can shed light on strategies to emulate in building a Relational Judaism, we will look at five designed to engage postcollege YJAs—Jconnect, Moishe House, Synagogue 3000's Next *Dor* Network, Birthright NEXT, and Reboot—and two building relationships among teenagers—Jewish Student Connection and the URJ Campaign for Youth Engagement.

Jconnect

Jconnect (www.jconnectseattle.org) emerged in Seattle, Washington, as a project of the University of Washington Hillel Foundation. Rabbi Will Berkovitz and Josh Miller headed up the initiative in its early years. The current director is Josh Furman, twenty-eight, a native of Oregon, grandson of Holocaust survivors, who came to Jewish professional life after a social justice trip to El Salvador, where he met Berkovitz. In my interview with him, Furman reflected on the finely honed engagement strategies of Jconnect. In his own words:

My generation is transitory. We move in and out of jobs and cities with ease. So, it's difficult to create, and maintain, relationships and community. Our goal in Jconnect is to meet people, create microcommunities, and be a concierge for their Jewish experiences.

When we find someone new to Seattle, we send them an initial e-mail that says, "Welcome to Seattle, we'd love to meet you, how about a cup of coffee?" Sometimes people respond immediately, but often they won't respond right away. Three months later, we send a follow-up invitation: "We know it's challenging to move to a new city, you must be busy, but we're still on for that cup of coffee." The extra reminder sends the message that we're thinking of them.

The purpose of our events is to gather people together for us to meet them. It's not a program for program's sake. We troll the group for new people we can meet and follow up with. Success for us is to leave an event with a list of people who are willing to meet one-on-one so we can get to know them better and connect them to something Jewish.

We try to make every event a great experience. What are the elements of a great experience?

1. *There must be a warm welcome, a sense of genuine hospitality, "we're really glad to see you."*
2. *It must be inclusive; no one sitting by her/himself or wandering around a building not feeling part of anything.*
3. *There needs to be emotion; we want people to feel something.*
4. *There must be depth, content, a safe space to have thoughtful conversations, meaningful dialogue, a chance to grow.*
5. *We must challenge people to have a sense of responsibility, a sense of belonging to something beyond themselves.*

6. *Excellence—excellent marketing, excellent spaces, excellent food and drink, excellent lecturers, perform- ers, artists. We want to be proud of everything we do.*
7. *We want every experience to lead to the creation or expansion of microcommunities and networks; we are not connecting people to one large Jconnect com- munity—we are a community of communities.*

We track two thousand people a year. When people sign up online, much of what goes into the database are demo- graphic basics, but then we want to know about previous experiences and interests. We track "place in life"—are they single, settled with a partner, married with kids? When we meet someone at an event or in a one-on-one cof- fee, we immediately make notes in the database when we get back to the office. Then, for each person, we ask the key question: what's something he or she would value? I recently met someone who said she used to keep kosher, but now she doesn't because she can't get organic, sustain- able kosher meat. So, we had a Kosher Free-Range Turkey Shechting [slaughtering] experience.

The organized Jewish community expects young adults will come just because they are Jewish. They think every- one who says he or she is Jewish will automatically be attracted. But, that's not how my generation was raised. We were raised with the value that everyone is equal, to embrace diversity, to find your own path. We're looking for a "comfortable place" where you don't feel "differ- ent," where you can ask deep questions of meaning. We're trying to figure out answers to the question "Who am I? What's important to me?"

Young Jewish adults have a sense of entitlement. Much is given to them free—free Birthright Israel trips, stipends to study, etc. The message is: "Please, please, we beg you to come." My peers think, "If they are begging me to come, then either the event is no good ... or if it's free, they don't think it has any value." There is a thin line between incentivizing engagement and valuing it on its own terms.

The key to developing a sense of "peoplehood" is the staff. If the staff models and talks about the importance of connecting to the Jewish people, then it clicks. If they think Birthright is just a party trip to Israel—ten days of fun—and then you never hear from the leader again, it doesn't work. I only do Birthright trips where I can follow up on relationships I've created during the trip.

Many of my peers are social entrepreneurs. We live in Seattle—the home of Microsoft, Amazon, Starbucks, and a community of Internet entrepreneurs. My peers who work here do want to be part of something, and when they are part of something that has value to them, they want to give back. But this takes a long time to develop; it happens over many months or even years. Some people are talking about the extensive "delayed adolescence" among millennials. Our target age range is twenty-one to thirty-two, but we're talking about extending it to thirty-five. People don't like to "age out" … because it's like beginning the search for community all over again. But, when people get married, have kids—it's a different stage of life.

We're interested in real interactions, real relationships, real connection with community. Facebook is not a real community. Just because you have two thousand "friends" doesn't mean you really have friends. It may make you feel more confident … but it's a façade. You can't be friends with two thousand people. You're lucky to have a small group of real friends.

My parents grew up with the feeling of connection to a broader Jewish people. My peers do not. They don't see the value of being part of a people. We have to demonstrate it to them. When we see "value," then we respond and begin to see the possibility of connection to something beyond ourselves.

Moishe House

Moishe House (www.moishehouse.org) is a peer-driven initiative to engage postcollege YJAs in their twenties. Founded in 2006 by four friends who hosted Shabbat dinners in their rented house in Oakland, California, Moishe House (named for its first financial supporter) has grown to fifty-three "centers" in fourteen countries around the world, connecting with more than fifty thousand individuals annually.

The Moishe House model is remarkably simple, cost-effective, and, above all, relational. The "center" is actually an apartment or a home, staffed by three to five residents. These young Jews are selected based on their leadership abilities, welcoming personalities, and relational skills. They plan and host a diverse offering of low-barrier events for their peers, including Shabbat dinners, holiday celebrations, social gatherings, social justice projects, and learning experiences. Moishe House headquarters supports the residents with partial rent subsidy, funding for the events, and networking between the houses.

Several factors distinguish Moishe House as a unique relational initiative. First and foremost is the nearly total reliance on peer-to-peer relationship building. This is no top-down, staff-driven operation; the young Jewish residents plan their own events for their own networks. The residents represent a full array of Jewish backgrounds, ensuring the "post-denominational" feel of the place. Critics have wondered about the depth of Jewish knowledge among these young leaders. In response, the leadership of the organization has hired a director of Jewish learning and a director of immersive learning as well as encouraged house residents to partner with local rabbis, teachers, JCCs, synagogues, and other organizations in the Jewish community.

According to David Cygielman, chief executive officer, the success of each Moishe House rests on relational engagement:

> *A warm invitation to someone's home is totally different than recruiting them to participate in a program. We welcome people to share their lives. This generation gets lots of invitations to programs, but they don't go. When they receive a genuine invitation to our homes, they come. We don't have attendance problems. The key is peer-to-peer*

relationships, people of the same age, gathering together in community to celebrate and explore being Jewish.

Rachael Himovitz, twenty-five, is a resident at Moishe House West Los Angeles:

> *Once my three roommates and I felt like we were offering events that we could be proud of, we started attracting our friends and their friends in a way different than big-event programs. We don't have the budget for that, and frankly, we're not interested in that sort of thing. Here in the House, we can have more intimate gatherings and build relationships with people. Last week, we had fifteen people show up for a discussion with a rabbi on "Torah's Take on Taboo Topics" and fifty people for Shabbat dinner. When we plan the seven to nine events we do each month, we think, "What would we want to go to?" I'll probably do this for a year or two and then move on, but some of my best friends are people I've met through Moishe House.*

Synagogue 3000 / Next *Dor* Network (nextdoronline.org)

Following the Synagogue 3000 (S3K) Synagogue Studies Institute's two-year exploration of "Jewish emergent" communities, we learned lessons that had important implications for synagogues in the twenty-first century. Primarily, we discovered that the best of the emergent communities were successful in attracting previously unaffiliated Jews, many of them in the age range of twenty-three to forty. Several of these groups, such as independent minyanim, tended to attract mostly those with strong Jewish educational backgrounds and excellent experiences, such as day schools, summer camps, and youth groups. We concluded that these minyanim, especially those that were rabbinic led, with charismatic personalities driving the effort, did not especially need "help" and would likely thrive. Others tended to operate on the fringes of the Jewish community, far from the mainstream. We concluded that these groups would likely come and go, depending on a variety of factors such as leadership, funding, and stick-to-itiveness.

Yet, throughout the two-year study, we were impressed with the creativity and willingness to innovate among these groups … and their obvious attraction to YJAs, who saw in them an opportunity to "do Jewish" their way. We came away with two questions: "Why can't mainstream congregations learn from this?" and "Why aren't mainstream congregations investing resources to engage young Jewish adults?"

This led us to look for synagogues with demonstrated commitment to YJA engagement. In October 2008, S3K invited representatives of the handful of synagogues that we discovered were, in fact, doing this work. We heard reports of their efforts and the challenges they faced. And, everyone was amazed that this meeting was the very first gathering across denominations of synagogues working to engage YJAs. There was palpable excitement in this convening and a desire to continue in some way. S3K then proposed the broad outlines of what became known as the Next *Dor* Network (http://synagogue3000. org/next-dor-online) to gauge interest. Overwhelmingly, the attendees validated the idea of a continental, trans-denominational network of synagogues interested in what we had determined was the next cutting edge in congregational life.

S3K then brought a proposal to the Marcus Foundation to fund a first-year experiment (2009–10) with five synagogues interested in launching a Next *Dor* group. Each synagogue selected agreed to commit to raising the funds to hire an engagement outreach worker—a rabbi or communal professional—and to provide a budget for the activities of the group. The Marcus Foundation offered grants of up to $40,000 to each synagogue to assist in the effort, in addition to providing the funding for the beginnings of a continental infrastructure to serve the pilot sites: Temple Micah, Washington, D.C.; Central Reform Synagogue, St. Louis, Missouri; Rodef Sholom, Marin County, California; and Temple Beth Sholom, Miami Beach, Florida. In 2010–11, The Temple in Atlanta, Georgia, launched the Open Jewish Project, a community-wide effort to serve the YJAs in Atlanta, and Westchester Reform Temple sent a young rabbi as a *shaliach* (emissary) from the suburbs to reach out to the YJAs from synagogue families working and living in New York City. S3K National offered webinars, conference calls, on-site consultations by the S3K director of congregational engagement, Rabbi Jessica

Zimmerman, and an annual conference for the sponsoring congregations and their leadership to network, share successes and challenges, and learn essential skills in reaching out to engage YJAs. In October 2010, S3K sponsored a convening of synagogues interested in joining the Next *Dor* Network. Surprisingly, 180 participants representing fifty-three congregations attended; forty-two congregations have signed on, indicating a willingness to transform themselves into synagogues committed to engaging YJAs without requiring "membership" in the congregation.

The first four initiatives were the subject of an S3K report, "Different Growth for Different Folks: The ND Pilot Sites in Action."[8] Professors Steven M. Cohen and Lawrence A. Hoffman conducted survey research among the participants that indicated all groups attracted unaffiliated YJAs, but with different demographic and psychographic profiles. Regardless of profile, between 2009, when the initiatives began, and 2010, when this survey was taken, the YJAs all grew in significant Jewish ways.

As expected, some of the YJAs attracted to Next *Dor* were those already on an upward personal Jewish growth path. Hoffman calls these "loyalists." The question was, would Next *Dor* also attract "marginals," those with little or no Jewish educational background, those from intermarried families, those with non-Jewish friends? The answer was positive, but why?

Cohen and Hoffman believe it is due to the Next *Dor* philosophy of engagement. In their words:

> The field workers in all four sites took a genuine interest in the people they met, striking up relationships, and inviting participation personally. At the same time, members of specific circles of engagement had their own network of contacts, sometimes in adjacent circles farther out, whom they invited personally as well. Had the Next *Dor* Jewish offerings not been of the quality they were, and had the relationships not deepened as a result of quality time spent together, invitees would not have returned. But return they did. The more they returned, the more positive time they spent Jewishly, and the more positive time they spent Jewishly, the more they widened

their Jewish involvement, acquired still newer Jewish friends, learned of opportunities for Jewish engagement even outside of Next *Dor*, and then brought friends made there to Next *Dor* as an obvious next step.[9]

Another interesting finding during the first years of the Next *Dor* initiative was the discovery of three distinct phases of what sociologists are calling "emerging adulthood." In S3K, we call them "singles, settlers, and CHIPS (children in the picture)." "Singles" (roughly twenty-one to thirtysomething) are those YJAs who are right out of college, unattached, and untethered to either a career or a community. "Settlers" (thirtysomethings), on the other hand, are well entrenched in their career paths, more or less committed to a geographic location, and have "settled in" with a live-in partner or are married. "CHIPS" (thirty-two to forty-two) are singles or couples with young children ages newborn to five. Most are not yet affiliated with a community, but they are actively looking for friends in the same life stage with whom they can share the joys and oys of raising kids. For the most part, the three groups have little in common with each other: settlers don't want to hang out with singles, who are usually looking for mates; CHIPS have moved beyond the settler stage and are focused on child rearing. Each of the Next *Dor* sites attracts one or more of these populations, usually reflecting the life stage of the leadership.

Although all of the original Next *Dor* pilot sites share a common commitment to building relationships as their core mission, each one looks somewhat different. In St. Louis, Central Reform Synagogue renovated a ransacked house situated literally next door to the congregation into a center for Next *Dor* STL. The Marin experiment morphed into The Kitchen in downtown San Francisco, attracting mostly CHIPS, while Next *Dor* DC serves the large community of singles in the capital. The Open Jewish Project in Atlanta and The Tribe in Miami effectively created lay leadership teams among Jewish singles to partner with Next *Dor* rabbis. All of the sites have been extraordinarily creative in developing effective engagement strategies.

For the sponsoring synagogues, supporting a Next *Dor* initiative required a transformation in how the congregation viewed its relationship with YJAs. S3K leaders insisted that the synagogues not view the project as a vehicle to entice young Jews onto their membership rolls. "It's not about membership" has been an oft-cited rallying cry, a value reflecting all the research on how next-generation Jews operate. This challenged synagogue boards, which, naturally, concern themselves with how to raise the dollars to run the congregation. We appealed to their sense of responsibility: "Will you let your young people wander through a spiritual desert for twenty years until they show up with that seven-year-old newborn?" Our theory was that when the time comes to join, the young people will remember those synagogues that reached out to them. We bet that a young person who is welcomed into a personal relationship with an engagement rabbi or a community organizer will turn to that role model when the time comes to invest in a communal relationship. In the most effective Next *Dor* Network sites, evidence is emerging that this bet is already paying off: young people who otherwise would not be seen in the synagogue are showing up for High Holy Day services and asking Next *Dor* rabbis to officiate at their weddings. The likelihood of transitioning from engagement with Next *Dor* to engagement with a synagogue community is certainly heightened. With careful tracking, we will know whether the theory plays out as we expect.

For me, Next *Dor* is the beginning of what we have needed for a long time—a "non-Orthodox" Chabad. And we have the young rabbis who want to do this. Instead of scrambling around to find them shrinking numbers of pulpit jobs, let's create "engagement rabbi" positions in our mainstream congregations. In earlier times, synagogues created youth director jobs and program director jobs. Let's recruit, train, and hire a cadre of young rabbis and let them loose to build relationships, one-on-one. If we can engage young Jewish adults—inspire them, empower them, and invite them into a relationship with Judaism—through serious study, through music and prayer, through social justice work, and most important, through a personal relationship with a Jewish mentor—then I am convinced we will have a better shot at their eventually joining our congregations and our communal institutions.

VOICES FROM THE COMMUNITY

With three hundred thousand alumni of Birthright Israel trips, Taglit-Birthright Israel Foundation created NEXT, an effort to build on the impact of the Israel experience once the young Jewish adults come home. According to Morlie Levin, CEO of NEXT:

> *We take the spark ignited on a Birthright Israel trip and work with partners to fan it into a fire. We use choice and ownership as our guide, connecting young Jews to myriad events and opportunities that appeal to their individual interests and inclinations. But we are also cognizant of the fact that organized Jewish activities are not for everyone. For some, finding meaning and making community are not a function of attending organized activities run by others but happen rather within a circle of friends, at home. That insight galvanized NEXT to develop a do-it-yourself approach to holidays, Shabbat, and community building that enables young Jews to create authentic Jewish experiences on their own terms. We also provide all of the resources and funding necessary to help them along the way. More than twenty young Jews have received support to fund their own community projects through Natan/NEXT Grants for Social Entrepreneurs. Over sixty-four hundred Birthright alumni have hosted sixteen thousand Shabbat and holiday meals through NEXT Shabbat and holiday grant programs. With an average of ten people at the typical Shabbat meal or Seder powered by NEXT micro-grants and educational material, we now know that this approach truly resonates with Birthright alums and their peers.*

Reboot

Rachel Levin, executive director of Steven Spielberg's Righteous Persons Foundation, and her colleague Roger Bennett created Reboot (www.rebooters.net) in 2002 "to engage and inspire young, Jewishly unconnected cultural creatives, innovators, and thought leaders who, through their candid and introspective conversations and creativity, generate projects that impact both the Jewish and non-Jewish worlds." I asked Levin to reflect on how Reboot has influenced her own thinking about the role of relationships in the effort to engage these "creatives":

> It has to be an authentic relationship. If relationship building is just another gimmick or tool to get people to do what you want them to do anyway—join the organization, show up and work on a committee, give money—that's not really what it's about.
>
> In our work with Reboot, we've learned the building of relationships has to be based on open conversations. Like in community organizing, it has to flow from the grass roots, bottom-up. This is why we use Open Space technology as a key methodology during the Reboot summits. People get to talk about whatever is really on their minds, even if it's not the direction of Jewish life that the organizers think is a priority. This approach leads to a variety of issues being discussed—all stemming from personal interest. Our job as organizers is to help link these seemingly personal and individual issues to broader trends and questions.
>
> Reboot is based on a peer network that has sustained itself over ten years. We never expected that to be the case. We initially planned for a one-time event and were surprised by the interest among many of the participants to remain connected to each other and to continue the conversations they began at the Reboot summit—conversations they often did not find in other venues. Years later, the Reboot alumni network is very active; people do rituals together, support each other, learn together, continue to work on projects with other Rebooters.

Reboot started as a collaboration between Righteous Persons Foundation and the Andrea and Charles Bronfman Philanthropies to reach out to the next-generation creative community with the idea that if inspired, they would find ways to engage others like themselves. We started with thirty-five people at a summit in Park City, Utah. We now have key funding from numerous other foundations and individuals, including the Jim Joseph Foundation, and over four hundred people have been invited to participate in what has become an annual summit. To participate, they are nominated by their peers and then interviewed in a one-on-one conversation, where we are looking to hear the questions they are genuinely asking about Jewish life, identity, meaning, and community. These are people who have a certain edge; they ask probing questions about how Judaism can add meaning and purpose to their lives. Some really creative things have emerged from Reboot: the National Day of Unplugging—a campaign to disconnect on Shabbat (that includes a sleeping bag for your cell phone); Sukkah City—an international design contest and public exhibition of re-imagined sukkahs at New York City's Union Square Park, which reached close to two hundred thousand individuals; a 10Q project where people are asked ten questions about their lives every day on the ten days between Rosh Hashanah and Yom Kippur, the answers are sent to a vault, and a year later, people get their answers back as a way to review where they were the year before compared to where they are now. It's a profound experience. One Rebooter had a connection in New York City, and the 10Q questions went up on the Jumbotron in Times Square. Public figures as well as private individuals have all answered the questions. The people who participate in Reboot are often on the margins of Jewish life, yet at the center of American culture, activism, media, and the arts. We build relationships with them at intense gatherings: a summit conference and an alumni Reboot Camp. Local organizers help Rebooters make things happen in their communities; the peer network sustains the relationships.

Jewish Student Connection

While next-generation engagement is mostly focused on young Jewish adults ages twenty-one to forty-five, a number of initiatives are currently under way to engage Jewish teenagers in the critical years post–Bar/Bat Mitzvah. The Jewish Student Connection (www.myjsc.org; formerly the Jewish Student Union) takes advantage of a 1984 United States Supreme Court ruling that the Equal Access Act allows any organization to use public school facilities for affinity "clubs" to meet during noninstructional hours. Beginning ten years ago in Los Angeles under the sponsorship of NCSY, the National Conference of Synagogue Youth, a modern Orthodox movement affiliated with the Orthodox Union (OU), Jewish teenagers of all denominations were invited to meet together for conversations about topics of Jewish interest with a Jewish teacher/sponsor or outside professional. Attracting the kids with free pizza, the idea grew rapidly. In 2012, the organization spun off into its own independent nonprofit, with the goal of broadening the reach beyond denominational labels.

Brad Sugar, director of operations of Jewish Student Connection, comments:

> The students in the club take the responsibility for determining what they want to do. We suggest a variety of Jewish themes, but ultimately, the content is student-driven. We have two goals: (1) to engage the students with Jewish ideas and topics they are interested in exploring, and (2) to build relationships with them that enable the Jewish role model to advise them about other ways to engage in Jewish life, including synagogue youth groups, JCCs, Israel advocacy groups like AIPAC, and others.
>
> By establishing clubs in public and non-Jewish private schools, we are guaranteed a consistent meeting time with these students, who are coming of their own volition and are not forced by their parents or peers to do so. Our educators/advisors use this time not only to execute programming for the students, but also to get to know the students well enough to encourage them to take Jewish

*steps outside of the classroom (such as attending commu-
nity events, Shabbat hospitality at their educator/advisor's
home, or joining youth groups).*

*Our organization is unlike any other Jewish youth orga-
nization or group: (1) We are not a youth group. Therefore,
our end goal is not necessarily retained participation with
us; rather, we want the students to engage with another
Jewish activity. (2) We are not a membership/dues-based
organization. No student ever pays anything to participate.
(3) We operate directly on the high school grounds.*

The Campaign for Youth Engagement

Rabbi Jonah Pesner has brought the strategies of community organizing
to the Union for Reform Judaism in his role as senior vice president. First
up on the agenda is the Campaign for Youth Engagement (http://urj.org/
cye). In its first seven months alone, the initiative has hosted more than
a thousand one-on-one conversations with teenagers, youth leaders,
and laypeople dedicated to the cause of youth education. Pesner says:

*The number one learning was the importance of relation-
ships. Person after person told their stories about how they
were influenced by a youth director, a camp counselor, a
rabbi, other kids. So, now, we are shifting the emphasis
from programming to relationship building. We're developing training materials to teach teenagers how to have conversations with peers, how to hear and tell stories, and how
to build programming around what the peers say, not what
a few people think.*

The Reform movement knows this is a huge challenge; in the past,
some 80 percent of teenagers have left synagogue life after their Bar/
Bat Mitzvah.

Social Media

My daughter Havi and her husband Dave moved to a new community
shortly before their (beautiful, genius) daughter Ellie Brooklyn made
her grand entrance. Havi was eager to find other women with infants,

preferably Jewish moms with whom to share the experience of new parenthood. While there were many early childhood programs, synagogues, and JCCs in the area, not one Jewish institution offered any family education program targeted to parents with a child under the age of one. To be sure, the family received a warm welcome from individual rabbis and friends, and they signed up for the wonderful PJ Library—receiving a Jewish children's book in the mail each month from the Harold Grinspoon Foundation—but the only organized activity Havi could find was a business called My Gym. In her hunt for friends, she printed up what she called "Mommy Cards," a business card with her name, the name of her daughter, her e-mail address, and cell phone number, which she handed out to promising prospects she met in the checkout line at Target. "Thank God for Facebook," Havi sighed. "It became my community." Still, she admitted, "I am desperately seeking face-to-face friends, not just Facebook friends."

Will social networks really substitute for institutions? Will we ever need them again? If I can get community on Facebook, why invest in belonging to a Jewish organization? In *Relational Being*, Kenneth Gergen revises Descartes for the twenty-first century: "I link, therefore I am."[10] It is useless to deny the networking power of social media, e-mail, and the World Wide Web or to deny the reality that, for many, Facebook most definitely serves functions of community. The question is, how will we use it to enhance the building of relationships, whether virtual or face-to-face?

The Jewish community has only begun to marshal the power of social media to build relationships between individuals, between individuals and communities, and between individuals and Judaism itself. Pioneering users such as Lisa Colton of Darim Online/See3 Communications (a social media training and consulting firm), Rabbi Laura Baum of OurJewishCommunity.org (online virtual Jewish community), and Ed Case of InterfaithFamily.com (support for Jews and non-Jews raising Jewish children) have demonstrated the reach of the Internet as both a distribution system and a vehicle for networking.

Today, virtually every Jewish organization has a website, and many have Facebook pages, Twitter accounts, and even smartphone apps (Temple Sinai in Atlanta created one of the first, iSinai). These presences on the web are literally the face of the institution to the community, often the first stop for those seeking a Jewish connection. Unfortunately, the vast majority of these sites are disappointing—unwelcoming, unimaginative, uninspiring.

When I am invited to speak to an audience representing Jewish organizations in a community, I turn into a "mystery shopper," putting myself in the shoes of someone looking to connect. My first stop, well before making a phone call, is to visit the institution's website. In the past year, I visited thirty-five websites in a southeastern Jewish population center, seventy websites in a mountain community, and seventy-five websites in a major northeastern hub of Jewish life. I would characterize fewer than 10 percent as excellent.

Take synagogues, for example. Most of their home pages feature photos of buildings. Old buildings, new buildings—it doesn't matter. Or logos—lots of logos. Some have photos of sanctuaries—beautiful sanctuaries. With pictures of beautiful pews—empty pews. Stained glass—lots of stained glass.

That's what I want to join ... stained glass. That's where I can't wait to sit ... empty pews. One very large and famous congregation had a photo (I could not make this up) of one long staircase just going up ... and one (even longer?) going down.

The excellent websites featured photos of real people doing engaging things—celebrating, studying, dancing, repairing the world. The best of the best had slide shows, a rotating series of photos of people representing the diversity of the community, young and old, a vibrant panorama snapshot of the dynamism of a relational community.

Lisa Colton suggests two examples of note:

1. Temple Israel of Memphis, Tennessee, a large congregation with a full-time communications director—http://timemphis.org, with an introductory video from the rabbi; http://timemphis.org/worship/overview.htm, with a nice integration of people (photos and quotations).

2. Temple Israel, Dayton, Ohio—www.tidayton.org, simple, nothing fancy, but well organized, with people-centric photos that convey a sense of the community and its values.

Some organizations understand that even a Google search result can make a difference between a click and a pass. Google "The Kitchen San Francisco," a Next *Dor* site led by Rabbi Noa Kushner, and the search result reads:

> Home - *The Kitchen* | Slow Down, Jew Up
>
> *www.thekitchensf.org/*LOOKING. TO DO. JEWISH? US, TOO. *The Kitchen* is one part indie Shabbat community, one part *San Francisco* Experiment, and one part tool kit for DIY Jewish practice.
>
> 10 Brosnan Street San Francisco, CA 94103

Another approach to website home pages features engaging copy designed to attract those who approach Jewish institutions with hesitation or even skepticism. For example, on ikar-la.org, visitors see a slide show of statements of purpose:

> ikar is an ATTITUDE … a religious approach that fuses piety and hutzpah, obligation and inspiration, tradition and soul.
>
> ikar is a BIG IDEA … that Jewish life can by dynamic, compelling, creative and challenging.
>
> ikar is a CHALLENGE … that real spiritual practice must inspire a commitment to human dignity, justice and peace.
>
> ikar is a HOLY COMMUNITY … a sacred collection of people working to awaken the spirit and transform the world.
>
> ikar is a CATALYST … reanimating Jewish life and redefining what's possible in the 21st century.
>
> ikar is a WAY IN … for newbies and ringers, seekers and cynics, activists and ambivalents.

There's a tongue-in-cheek factor that's self-effacing and hip:

> You don't have to be a ringer to be touched by Shabbat davening at IKAR. You won't be the only one who doesn't read Hebrew, feels more comfortable in Shavasuna than Shabbes, or is wearing jeans and sneaks. This is truly an eclectic community—the shmoozers in the back are as likely rabbis and rab students as they are comedy writers, rocket scientists (yes,

we actually have one!) and baristas. The service is designed to welcome and stretch us all—wherever we come in, we ought to leave in a different place.

Rabbi Lizzi Heydemann established Mishkan, a new spiritual community in Chicago, in 2011. Here's the opening slide on Mishkan's home page:

Mishkan is inspired, down-to-earth Judaism.

We're about creativity and tradition, about building space for ecstatic prayer, music and meditation, for being intellectually stimulated and spiritually invigorated. We believe that Judaism is a vehicle for bringing more light, more goodness, more justice, and more joy to the world. We are from across the spectrum of denominations and backgrounds, LGBT and interfaith inclusive, open to everyone.

VOICES FROM THE COMMUNITY

Tips on using social media to build relationships from Lisa Colton:

1. Social Media Is about People

Social media is not about technology; it's about people, relationships, and communication. In the old "one-size-fits-all" communications paradigm, messages were broadcast in one direction to large numbers of people. In the new paradigm, individuals, families, and community are the center; the institution exists to support them and their shared goals; and the institution's messages are tailored to the community of individuals in order to earn each person's attention. From the user's perspective, when the institution is helping me clarify and achieve my goals, that's worth paying for with time, attention, and dollars. Sign me up.

Given that we are trying to strengthen relationships between synagogue/JCC members and the community as a whole, social media is much more than a soapbox; it is an opportunity to promote knowledge sharing, provide a platform for communal conversation, and add value, convenience, accessibility, and sometimes humor. Like the biblical Abraham welcoming the strangers as they approached his open tent, social media is a modern way of being open and welcoming.

2. To Get Heard, Start by Listening

Here's a little social media success secret: Don't worry about talking. Start by listening. Make listening a habit. Before social media, it was hard and costly to listen. Today, in just a few minutes of scanning Facebook posts or tweets, you can get the pulse of your community, learn important things about people in your network, and connect with a dozen individuals in meaningful, relevant, and personal ways.

3. Ask Questions

Once you're listening, start asking questions so you can listen some more! Rabbi Arnie Samlan asks a weekly Friday question on Facebook, "What did we learn this week?" which generates dozens of responses. Some congregations and schools make their Facebook pages a platform for communal knowledge sharing, asking such practical, relevant questions as "What's your best tip to keep young kids engaged at a Passover Seder?" or "How do you talk to your teenagers about forgiveness at Yom Kippur?"

4. Share Stories and Make Connections

Organizations seeking to strengthen community need to build more points of possible connection, and Facebook is an important, inexpensive, and efficient way to do so. A prospective member may get his or her first impression of your organization on your Facebook page. So, what does yours say? Does it look like a logo begging for attendance or like a vibrant community pursuing meaningful Jewish lives?

Facebook can become a conduit to in-person social connections. Inviting someone via Facebook to a relevant upcoming event not only welcomes the individual, but the exchange is also public, demonstrating a responsive, welcoming, and thoughtful culture to others who may be watching.

5. Open Communications Boundaries

In my experience, older people tend to default to private communications unless there is a reason to make the information public; conversely, younger people tend to make all communications public unless there is a reason to keep it private. While there is certainly a place for private exchanges, if we are in the business of building relationships and community, we need to be social. Open socializing is an accessible way of being welcoming to your current community members, as well as new ones. It builds trust and authenticity, the foundation of any relationship.

Each of us feels welcome when we connect with real people. Recently, an increasing number of posts from young adults, singles, families, and empty nesters are saying things like, "I'm going to Congregation ABC for services. They offer free tickets for High Holy Day services—anyone want to come?" How much more powerful it is to receive that invitation from a friend than from a newspaper ad!

So, be sure to identify active members who are trusted and have strong online networks. Encourage your members to share their experiences online and invite their friends into your community. Networks are powerful. Use them.

Undoubtedly, we will see new and different social media platforms emerge in the years ahead. Even now, Jewish college students have gravitated to Twitter as the primary vehicle for communication. Jewish communal leaders will need to keep pace with the rapidly evolving techniques of social interaction.

SPOTLIGHT ON BEST PRACTICES

Taking It to the Net

Inspired by Darim Online, Rabbi David Levy at Temple Shalom in Succasunna, New Jersey, invited congregants to contribute comments and ideas to his sermon. He posted texts about Judaism and the environment on the synagogue's Facebook page, incorporated responses from the community "like a primary text," and posted the sermon after delivering it during a service.

Rabbi Jonathan Blake, senior rabbi at Westchester Reform Temple in Scarsdale, New York, uses a social media platform called Formspring with which to communicate regularly with his community. Anyone can submit a question to him, and his responses are shared broadly with the congregation. Through this medium, Rabbi Blake has addressed questions as varied as "How do I ask for forgiveness?" and "What's your favorite restaurant?"

Passing the Baton

I write these words as the 4 x 100 meter women's relay race is under way at the 2012 London Summer Olympics. The team from the United States of America is hoping to erase years of doubt, sown by the failure of runners at the Beijing Olympics to successfully complete the event. Their failure was not due to lack of speed; it was caused by the inability to pass the baton from one runner to the next. Fortunately for Team USA, this year was different; all four runners successfully handed off the "stick" within the allotted twenty-meter "exchange zone," and the team won the gold medal in world record time. When asked for the key factor that propelled them to the top of the podium, Carmelita Jeter said, "We trusted each other. We believed in each other. We're a team."

In the Jewish community, we are terrible at passing the baton. We give almost no thought to how we "hand off" an individual or a family from one institution to another, from one life-cycle moment to another, from one school to another, from one group to another. Why? Is it that we don't trust each other, believe in each other? We certainly don't act as a team; each organization concentrates on its own agenda, often jealously guarding against "encroachment" from other groups. Certainly, some individual professionals in the community do see the big picture, always ready with a suggestion of how to take the next steps on a Jewish journey. But for the most part, our people fall through the cracks when our handoffs are sloppy and insecure. In a Relational Judaism, our community will figure out ways to transition people seamlessly from one space to another, from one experience to another, from one life stage to another. Just as in the relays, it will take coordination and teamwork.

Here are three hopeful signs that we can do better, all using social networking and media as the initial engagement strategy.

1. MazelTot

MazelTot, an initiative of the Rose Community Foundation launched in 2009, is a network of thirty-five Jewish organizations working together to engage expectant parents and families of children under age five in Jewish life. MazelTot provides parents with easy access to information about Jewish life in Greater Denver and Boulder, Colorado, and with big discounts that make trying new Jewish experiences more affordable. At mazeltot.org, thirty-five local partner organizations post the programs and activities they offer to help families celebrate Jewish life, learn together, make new friends, and create community.

Mazeltot not only connects families to Jewish institutions, but it also helps young families connect with one another. Families can reach out to the MazelTot Family Networker for help navigating the community or to be introduced to other Jewish families in their neighborhood for playgroups. The MazelTot Family Networker has created twenty neighborhood-based MazelTot playgroups, facilitating parent and child friendships.

A collective marketing campaign promotes mazeltot.org, a central web platform where parents can explore hundreds of Jewish classes, events, retreats, preschools, camps, and celebrations offered by MazelTot partner organizations. After taking a few minutes to sign up (for free), parents can redeem up to three big discounts, allowing their family to participate in Jewish programs and events at very low or no cost. Parents also receive a weekly e-mail blast from MazelTot highlighting upcoming events and programs.

Lisa Farber Miller, senior program officer at the Rose Community Foundation, explains why they created MazelTot:

> New and expectant parents are searching for Jewish friends, resources, information, services, and connections. The want and need Jewish friends and community to share their parenting journey. They need help to create their own Jewish family traditions. This searching creates a teachable moment, an opportunity for parents to explore their Jewish choices and to begin or deepen their engagement in Jewish life. MazelTot is there to help them in a nonthreatening way. Seventy-two percent of surveyed parents agreed that mazeltot.org played a significant role in connecting them to Jewish life. New parents are most interested in forming new friendships with other Jewish families. The feature that most appealed to parents after the discounts is the opportunity to meet other Jewish families with young children. All of our participating synagogues and agencies have learned that it is not enough to offer programs; parents are seeking authentic relationships and sometimes need help to connect with one another. Our agencies are now asking themselves how to modify programs to create opportunities for participants to make friends and to relate to staff.

2. Community Concierge

The Builders of Jewish Education in Los Angeles (www.bjela.org) has deployed two professionals who provide "concierge services" to assist families making choices for the Jewish education of their young children. Debra Markovic, LA city concierge, and Rachel Kaplan, San Fernando Valley concierge, are contacted by parents searching for parent and me groups, preschools, day schools, religious schools, summer camps, and other points of connection to Jewish LA. They also monitor a number of "mommy" sites/forums for questions posted about finding an appropriate educational opportunity and offer their services. Together, they have connected with more than one thousand families. They maintain a website, http://jkidla.com, send out bi-monthly e-mail blasts, and are active participants in social media to get the word out about the JKidLA/Concierge Services program. Debra Markovic comments:

> *Ultimately, we're really a portal for people looking to connect with Jewish schools, camps, and parent and me programs. Our first task is to listen carefully; there is always a story. "We're an interfaith family. I'm comfortable with this; my husband would be comfortable with that. My child has certain needs. I'm a working parent and need extended child care." We are open to whatever information they are willing to share with us. We help them find a comfort level in the Jewish community. Some people do stay in touch for a number of years, and we are able to guide them in their transitions from one institution to another.*
>
> *Being a concierge means we need to have good working relationships with all the schools, all the programs. We make site visits; we know them well. Then, we are able to do the matchmaking between the family and the institution.*

In St. Louis, the Jewish Federation hired twenty-six-year-old Joel Frankel to be an "Israel engagement professional." His concierge-style service is devoted to finding, connecting with, and bringing together young Jews returning from Israel, two thousand of whom have been on a Birthright Israel trip. "Young adults feel a powerful bond when they return from Israel. I'm here to help them find their niche in St. Louis," he says. His process begins with a phone call or an e-mail to young adults who have recently been to Israel, followed up with coffee or lunch. He learns about each individual on a personal level, giving him a deeper understanding of where they might fit into St. Louis's booming young Jewish community. "After connecting with people individually, I leverage the structures already in place to connect people to each other."

In Birmingham, Alabama, the task of recruiting and retaining people to the city of fifty-two hundred Jews is not easy. So the Federation hired Caren Seligman as both a recruiter and a concierge. Tracking down college students who have moved away; fielding phone calls from newcomers; and extending a warm welcome, complete with a kit of Shabbat candles, kosher wine, and free one-year memberships to the JCC, occupy her days. Leaders in Columbus, Ohio, begin this recruitment effort even earlier. The community has launched Growing Jewish Columbus, a collaboration of the Columbus Jewish Federation, Jewish Family Services, and Ohio State University Hillel that brings together college juniors and seniors and connects them with each other, their Judaism, Columbus and its Jewish community, and local employers and career opportunities.

3. GrapeVine: The Jewish Journey Connector

If you have ever purchased an item on Amazon, you know that the next time you visit their website an array of suggestions for additional things you might be interested in will pop up. How do they know what you like? They know a lot about you. They track your purchases and your searches. The same is true of Netflix, Pandora, Google, and Facebook; these savvy web-based services are designed to connect you to the things, information, and people that will likely interest you.

Imagine if we could do the same thing for individuals looking for personalized suggestions to take the next step on their Jewish journey. The idea would be to provide an Internet-based platform enabling a fundamental shift in the Jewish community from a program-centric to a relational orientation. While it is estimated that up to 80 percent of Jews are engaged in some institution in the community at one point or another, fewer than a quarter are "affiliated" at any one time. In short, we get people, but we don't retain them. As most businesses know, it is far cheaper to retain a customer than it is to recruit one.

In an effort to "link the silos" in the Jewish community, Sacha Litman and his colleagues have launched GrapeVine, initially funded by a grant from the Jewish New Media Innovation Fund, a pilot collaboration of the Jim Joseph Foundation, the Righteous Persons Foundation, and the Schusterman Family Foundation. GrapeVine is an intriguing project that uses social media to encourage the next generation of Jews to engage in Jewish living and community.

How does it work? GrapeVine sends Jewish opportunities (events, articles, blogs, and informal gatherings) that are individually targeted for every Jew in the community according to his or her unique needs, interests, life stage, and geography. Using multiple communication channels—e-mail, Facebook, web, iPhone and Android apps, texts—to reach Jews where they are paying attention, a sophisticated learning algorithm keeps track of every person's prior involvement and current interests and improves over time to provide the opportunities that are a better fit, even as needs change. Individuals are able to navigate their own Jewish journey by getting connected with the right opportunities, programs, and people that meet their interests and life stage at the right point in time. Organizations are able to place their offerings in front of a wider audience of potential target participants than can be accomplished on their own, and perhaps most importantly, each program can track the impact it has had on their alumni's long-term Jewish identity and activity. The whole community benefits from a reliable method of creating an ongoing relationship with individual Jews, even as their needs, interests, location, and life stage change.

This potentially groundbreaking initiative puts people first by acting as a virtual concierge for continuous engagement, as well as supplementing and supporting the professionals in the community. GrapeVine has launched in New York City, Toronto, Columbus, and Rhode Island and secured national partnerships with the Jewish Telegraphic Agency, MASA, Hillel, Moishe House, and others. As other communities come online, it will be very interesting to see whether the promise of GrapeVine is realized.

Fundraisers' Wisdom

Nonprofit organizations are just that—nonprofit. They do not exist to earn a profit, but they must bring in revenues. Most Jewish nonprofit organizations bring in the vast majority of their revenue as tax-free contributions from their constituents and donors. Although some nonprofits operate revenue-generating activities (programs, services), their financial success depends on the ability of their boards and staff to raise money. What is the single most important activity impacting their effectiveness in raising money? Building relationships.

Of all the qualifications for senior executives, excellence in fundraising is usually at the top of the list. I spoke with some of the best. Here are their thoughts on how each builds relationships.

Abraham H. Foxman, National Director of the Anti-Defamation League

How do you build relationships? You have to like people and take the time and energy to know what interests them and what their concerns are. If you don't like people, you don't do it. That's the beginning and the end of it. You yourself need a sense of worth, value, and self-respect. You can't be insecure; if you're not sure about your own self-confidence, then you have a problem.

If you like people and you care about people, you take the time to remember them. I read the newspaper with Post-It notes in hand so I can follow up. If I read something I think someone will be interested in, I send it to them, with a note in my own handwriting. They know I'm thinking of them. I'll give a book from my personal library or one I have written to someone who visits me in my office. It's more important to call somebody when they're down than when they're up. Most people are more inclined to call to congratulate people rather than commiserate because it is much harder to do. That reverberates. Before holidays, I spend a day or two calling people. It's a time-consuming effort, but it goes a long, long way to let people know you care.

People give to people; they don't give to institutions. They do give to institutions, but only if they care about the people who run them and in whom they have confidence. At the end of the day it's, who asks them? Who is involved? What company do you want to be with? There are exceptions. God forbid, your child suffers from a certain disease, you'll support efforts for the cure, regardless of who's involved. In order to get people's attention, they have to have respect for you, your integrity, your credibility, and then you have a better chance that they will support your cause.

Dr. David Ellenson, President of Hebrew Union College–Jewish Institute of Religion

When I took this position, I went to visit the best fundraiser I knew in the Jewish community—Rabbi Isaiah Zeldin. He built the magnificent Stephen S. Wise Temple and the Milken Community Jewish High School. He gave me a tutorial on fundraising. I'll never forget this. First, he said, there are causes for which one raises funds: cancer, Israel, education. How much people give depends on how they feel about the cause. However, the second and more important fundraising comes from relationships. He said, "I am with people at the most intimate high and low moments of their lives. I marry people, I bury them. I give their children a Bar Mitzvah, a Bat Mitzvah. I am with them at baby namings and I am with them in the hospital. The closeness of the relationships I enjoy gives them confidence and trust in me and the causes I promote."

How do you build relationships? You talk with people, you hear their stories. I remember Stanley Gold, one of our HUC board members, said to me when I applied for the job of president, "If you want to be president of HUC, you have to be prepared for at least twenty meals a week with donors. No one will blame you for not wanting to do that. But, if you want to do this job, that's what you're required to do."

Dr. Arnold M. Eisen, Chancellor of The Jewish Theological Seminary of America

When I took this job, everybody told me that fundraising is all about relationships ... and that is true. In the case of a rabbi, there is a natural relationship with people when you do their life-cycle events, when you comfort them. There was a question about whether I, as a person who is not a rabbi, could do this job. My friend David Ellenson is a rabbi; he officiates at his people's weddings and funerals. It's a level of connection I can't have. But people want to talk to me about their Jewish lives. As a scholar of American Judaism, I find that they want to connect. And the fact that I'm not a rabbi means I'm sitting in the congregation, and we share that experience of being a congregant. I feel privileged to have people come into my office and want to talk about their Jewish lives. That is the basis out of which the giving comes.

Jerry Silverman, President and CEO of Jewish Federations of North America

There must be trust to build relationships. Donors invest in both mission and organization because they have a passion for it, but they'll also invest because they trust that the people who lead the organization will steward their money directly into areas that create meaning and purpose. How do you build trust with donors? One lesson I learned from Patrick Lencioni's Five Temptations of a CEO is don't let yourself fall into the trap that the organization will not let people get to know the real you. You are not infallible as a leader; you should be able to say, "I made a mistake, I messed up," so your staff knows it's okay to mess up. He calls this "vulnerability," when your people get to know you more intimately, when you're approachable. It is critical for you to let people in so they really know you, and you show your interest in getting to know them, understand their passions, their interests, what's meaningful to them.

The key to fundraising is knowing and understanding the expectations of the donor. I ask this question to the donor: "If you invest in this project, what does success look like?" I really want to know what they see as success, what success looks like through their eyes, not through our eyes.

And they must touch the product. The greatest way to sustainability of investment is emotional. When I led the Foundation for Jewish Camp, we took investors to camp and let them see for themselves what their dollars achieved. How do you establish an emotional tie? You have the donor touch the product ... on a mission to Israel, or to the former Soviet Union, or visiting local agencies, or visiting a project or the people for whom you are making a difference in their lives. That's the best way to connect them—to see the dollars in action.

Bottom line: know your people individually, know their expectations, know their touch points, and build your relationship on the basis of that knowledge.

John Ruskay, Executive Vice President and CEO of UJA-Federation of New York

It's not about "fundraising." For me, fundraising is enabling people to do mitzvot, to evoke in people a sense of gratitude for the extraordinary privilege that most of us enjoy— the gift of life and living with remarkable opportunities. The core skill—difficult to teach—is "hanging out." When I meet with someone I'd like to engage in the act of hesed or tzedakah—to provide means to help us do our mission— the first thing I try to do is hang out with the person, be with the person ... and have the person be with me. Over time, I explore interests—what does the person really care about, where is the opportunity to think together, dream together, imagine together, work together? Only when I've built a relationship can I find the appropriate way to use their expertise, where they would like to be involved in the Jewish enterprise.

I stay connected periodically with a wide range of people. I will ask people to have a breakfast, a meal, and catch up. We catch up on personal things, communal issues, on what's happening in the world. Naomi Levine once said the most important thing for fundraisers is to be au courant, so people will want to be with you, so they feel expanded and grow with the interaction. This is new. Federation fundraisers used to be facilitators, a model that emerged from social work. We're in a whole different place today. Every interaction with a donor is a serious discussion about the Jewish present and the Jewish future; it's much more substantive.

You need to arrive at key moments in people's lives—especially when there's an illness, a hospital visit, a shiva. By "arrive," I mean to be able to say, "How can we help?" If there's bad news about a person in the newspaper, a phone call says, "We're with you; we're not walking away." It means so much.

Community is at the core of our enterprise—inspiring, caring community motivates people to say, "I want to be part of it"—not because they have to, they don't; not because of guilt, they have little; but because community provides meaning, purpose, connection. There's no one formula for what provides powerful community. For some, it's about leadership or music or prayer; for some, it's about study; for others, it's about service. For all of these things, relationships are the spokes in the wheel, the thread through which people are linked into the enterprise. If someone just drops in for a program and then leaves, you will not feel connected. You feel entirely different when a fellow classmate or leader inquires about how you're doing with your sick parent or what happened in that job interview. Connecting a person over time requires both meaningful substance and relationships with others.

Esther Netter, CEO of Zimmer Children's Museum

It's a privilege to ask people to give to something that will forever link their loved ones in memory. Once you know someone, their story, and their interests, you propose your cause as a link to them. Once the gift has been made, the relationship really begins. You can't just drop them. You

*have to cultivate the relationship, pay attention, be there
for them. Fundraising is sacred work. Im ein kemach, ein
Torah—"Without sustenance, there is no Torah" [Pirke Avot
3:21]. Asking for money is an invitation to be in relationship
with Torah, with Jewish learning.*

If we had to summarize the suggestions and advice of these master
fundraisers, we might say that there are six steps of relational
fundraising:

1. Build personal relationships.
2. Know someone's story, passions, and concerns.
3. Understand the capacity to give.
4. Make the "ask" to support a cause meaningful to the
    individual; have the donor "touch" the "product."
5. Express appreciation.
6. Follow up; stay in touch.

5

The Twelve Principles of Relational Engagement

Sizz gutt tzu zein tzusamen—"It's good to be together."

YIDDISH PROVERB

Slowly, there is a developing recognition and understanding among many synagogue leaders that the primary means for the establishment and continuity of community is not an emphasis on programming, but a renewed dedication to creating sacred relationships within that community.

RABBI RICHARD ADDRESS, *SEEKERS OF MEANING: BABY BOOMERS, JUDAISM, AND THE PURSUIT OF HEALTHY AGING*[1]

HOW, THEN, DO LEADERS of Jewish institutions build relationships between individuals and each of the Nine Levels of Jewish experience? What are some of the strategies, best practices, and best principles for going beyond welcoming? And will it make a difference? Can a relational engagement strategy make a difference in how people feel about their Jewish institutional affiliation? Will it change the "revolving door" phenomenon and improve retention rates?

The answer is: "Yes, it can."

Let's begin with an exciting relational success story, the transformation of the Bar/Bat Mitzvah experience for families at Central Synagogue, a large Reform congregation in midtown Manhattan. The result: a near-total reversal of the typical 80 percent drop-out rate among teenagers. Here is the story in the words of one of the key professionals, Cantor Angela Buchdahl:

> One day, we picked up the New York Times to read about a Jewish family whose celebration of their daughter's Bat Mitzvah was held at a Fifth Avenue boutique and featured an appearance by a famous movie star. We were surprised to learn it was a family from our congregation.
>
> We had tried to tackle the challenge of the ostentatious Bar/Bat Mitzvah celebration from the top down: we gave sermons from the pulpit. People shook their heads in agreement ... and nothing changed. One of the great things about relational work and community organizing is the starting premise: most people actually want to do the right thing most of the time. You appeal to people's best selves. And, you engage them in the conversation that allows them to express where they really are.
>
> When we invited people to start sharing their stories about the Bar/Bat Mitzvah culture, we realized they were not happy with what the expectations were, but they felt helpless to do anything about it themselves. They didn't want their child to be the only one not having the dancers, the games, the theme parties, even though they said, "This is not who my kid is." But, when they sat together, peer to peer, and shared their stories and honestly asked the deeper, bigger questions about values, then suddenly, they were in relation with each other. They were no longer changing the culture just because someone told them to do so.

We had house meetings with parents of sixth graders, but it was too late. So, we began doing the house meetings with parents of fourth graders, who found a safe place to share their stories. Once you've heard that story from someone who had been out of a job for more than a year ... and had no idea how they could afford even a modest celebration, you begin to realize that what you do affects other people in a very real way. So a kind of shift started to happen. We started to see real changes within the first year in the way people celebrated their kids' Bar and Bat Mitzvahs. But we got much deeper than that. In the next year, the conversation turned to the larger values, beyond the celebration. "Why are we doing this in the first place? What kind of children do we want to raise ... period? Why are we in this enterprise called 'Jewish life'? And why does it matter?"

We thought we would see changes in the types of Bar/Bat Mitzvah celebrations ... and we have. What we didn't expect was that the opportunity to build a different, deeper relationship among the group of parents ... and with the clergy ... has led to a huge improvement in retention. We used to have ten, twelve kids in the confirmation class, three years after the Bar/Bat Mitzvah; we have tripled that number within four years of this initiative. We had twenty-three students in our eighth and ninth grade program seven years ago; now we have more than ninety kids. And, we are not losing the parents. I don't think one family has dropped their membership after the Bar/Bat Mitzvah year, even if their kid does not continue in the religious school program. The adults have found new friends and meaning in belonging to the congregation.

Why this success? We've changed the conversation and changed the culture. There's more. These mutual conversations have led the clergy to rethink our Shabbat morning service ... what we wanted to teach and what we want them to walk away with. We have a whole new core of leaders, people who would never have been involved in synagogue leadership. Instead of just being on some committee, which is not often the most rewarding experience, the fifty people we've trained to lead house meetings, to engage their peers, to organize the groups of families from fourth grade on through high school—they feel like they are doing something meaningful. They feel very connected to Central Synagogue and to their Judaism in a much deeper way.

We have now adopted the relational strategies for engaging the entire congregation. Last year, Peter Rubinstein, the senior rabbi, and I attended fifty house meetings; he took twenty-five, I took twenty-five. Every member of the congregation was invited to one in someone's living room. Being in people's homes made people feel like they were part of a much smaller community. It was very powerful. They absolutely loved it.

Let's look at the Twelve Principles of Relational Engagement that inform Relational Judaism.

1) Personal Encounters

"All real living is meeting."[2] This famous saying from Martin Buber encapsulates his theology of relationships centered on the personal encounter of an "I" with a "Thou." As Rabbi Dennis Ross explains it:

> Just as a suspension bridge spans an expanse between two shores, the *I–Thou* relationship is a bridge of words spanning the space between people. And, most important, at the same time we build that interpersonal bridge, we build a bridge to the *Eternal Thou*, God. As Buber describes it, "With every *Thou* we are stirred with a breath of the *Thou*, that is, eternal life."[3] When we speak to people we also speak to God.[4]

Where do we personally encounter our people? If it is only in our institutional buildings, we are prisoners of our edifice complexes. Yes, there is a palpable power for clergy and professionals to meet people in their studies and offices for certain conversations. But, there is an even greater power when a Jewish professional invites people into his or her home.

I met Rabbi David-Seth Kirshner of Temple Emanu-El in Closter, New Jersey, in the first year of his tenure there. Rabbi Kirshner had served as chief development officer for The Jewish Theological Seminary of America and was taking his first major pulpit assignment, a large Conservative synagogue. I asked him, "Rabbi, did you do anything special to meet your people during your first year?" "Yes, I did," he said. "Before I accepted the position, I insisted the board create a budget line for catered and waitered Shabbat meals in my home once a month. I did not want to burden my wife with this, but I knew how important it was to offer hospitality to the membership. In the first eight months, we hosted more than two hundred people." Rabbi Kirshner has continued the practice every year; by his fourth year in the pulpit, he and his wife have hosted more than five hundred people in his home—five hundred people who now have a different relationship with the rabbi. Rabbi Kirshner told me that one of his guests reported to another, "The rabbi—he's a normal guy! He likes sports. He can talk politics." The rabbi has borrowed another practice from the world of fundraising and business. He usually has three breakfasts a day, each with a different member of the synagogue. In addition to his teaching two mornings a week at the synagogue, he has these breakfasts outside the building. "Ron, it's been a game changer!" he confided.

This is what presidents of universities do; their homes are an extension of their offices. When I reported this best practice at a recent convention of the Rabbinical Assembly, some of the rabbis were rolling their eyes in disbelief: "Ron, my home is my sanctuary ... it's my only relief from a 24/7 job." "Ron, I have two young kids who are *vilde hayehs* [wild animals]; I could never have anyone in my home." To these rabbis, I asked if any of them had been on a cruise ship. What's the coolest thing that can happen to you on a cruise? You get invited to the captain's table. During many of my visits to synagogues as a scholar-in-residence, I notice a prime table at the Shabbat *Kiddush* luncheon with a sign "Reserved for Clergy." Why not transform the table into a "rebbe's *tish*," and invite new members or members you haven't seen in a while to join you for lunch?

When Rabbi Philip Ohriner moved to Saratoga, California, to serve Congregation Beth David, he and his wife Rabbi Shoshana Ohriner demonstrated relational leadership based on their deep commitment to the Jewish value of *hakhnasat orchim*, "hospitality." They invited groups of people to their home for Shabbat dinners and luncheons, hosting more than 450 individuals within the first two years in the community. Rabbi Ohriner explains:

> We host groups of twelve to fourteen for Shabbat and holidays. We want to welcome them into our home, but we have an agenda. We want them to experience what it means to sit down for a Shabbat meal with friends and family, what it feels like to participate in the rituals. We hear each other's stories. We learn about the Torah portion. We also have a four-year-old and a fifteen-month-old, so part of the experience for our guests is seeing a real family interacting! We also give out cards with step-by-step instructions for the basic rituals so families can go home and make Shabbat for themselves. I know the experience has made an impression on some of my congregants who report that the experience helped them cultivate their own Shabbat observance. Others begin showing up for services or classes as a result of getting to know my family and me a little bit better outside of synagogue life.
>
> We see these acts of *hakhnasat orchim, hospitality,* as an integral component of our rabbinates. My congregants appreciate the invitation; they appreciate that we've opened ourselves up to them, and we appreciate the opportunity to build a relationship with them on a more personal level. I have had conversations with four hundred and fifty members of my congregation. So, when they need me, we have a relationship.

Rabbi Ohriner feels confident he has connected with most of the membership of his congregation, but it has not resulted in an uptick in membership numbers. He wondered aloud to me, "How can I reach beyond the people we already have to engage the unaffiliated?" I suggested that he ask the people with whom he now has a relationship to tap into their social networks. "Ask for referrals from them. Suggest they say to their friends who might be receptive, 'You know, I had dinner with this terrific young rabbi; I think you would enjoy meeting him. May I give him your contact info?' Or, how about saying to the members you invite to your home who ask, 'What can I bring?' 'Bring me the name of a colleague of yours at Google or Facebook whom I can invite on your recommendation to come to my house for Shabbat dinner or for lunch or to meet for coffee.' Build on their social networks and extend your hospitality to an audience of un-engaged, under-engaged, once-engaged-and-not-now-engaged people. Build a relationship with them; they already know someone in the congregation; this could result in an increase in membership."

VOICES FROM THE COMMUNITY

David Suissa, president of the Jewish Journal in Los Angeles, is a passionate advocate for the Jewish people and a perceptive observer of all branches of Judaism. He reflects on the importance of personal encounters:

> I'll tell you what can transform Judaism. It's the Friday night Shabbat table. For me, it's the secret sauce of Jewish survival. It's our weekly Thanksgiving holiday. I sometimes have guests at my table who want nothing to do with Judaism, but when they experience the warm dance of the Shabbat table, when they see me bless my kids and ask everyone what they learned that week, when we all enjoy good food and meaningful and lively conversation, they can't wait to do it again. You build relationships around that table. It is that table and those relationships that have kept our people going for two thousand years.

For clergy and communal professionals, willingness to host people in your home is not about giving up status; it's about *enhancing* your status in the eyes of the community. Once you've broken bread with someone, especially in your home, you have a different kind of relationship with him or her. Once you have taken people on a retreat or to Israel or to a convention, you have a different kind of relationship with them. Once you know their names, their stories, their passions, their concerns, their families, you can be a rabbi or Jewish role model to them in the best sense of that word.

Most clergy are very good at making personal visits to those who are hospitalized. Is there any time in life when you feel as vulnerable as when you are confined to a hospital bed? Showing up to comfort the person who is ill and support the family camped in the waiting room is a *mitzvah*, a much-appreciated act of kindness that deepens relationship. The same is true for those meetings with family members to prepare a eulogy, for those moments just before and after a funeral, for arranging and officiating at a shiva minyan in the home. These are moments of encounter when clergy, as well as other communal professionals, transcend the boundaries of public space to enter the inner sanctum of family.

People love to see the rabbi outside the walls of the synagogue. Rabbi Ed Feinstein tells the story of meeting a preschool mother and her three-year-old walking down an aisle of the local supermarket on a Friday afternoon. "Mommy, look!" the little girl screamed. "It's God!" He laughed and warmly engaged them with banter, checking in on how they were enjoying the preschool program, and wishing them a "Shabbat shalom."

The emphasis on building relationships is as important in JCC settings as it is in synagogues. Allan Finkelstein, president and CEO of the Jewish Community Centers Association (JCCA), reports on efforts in the JCC movement toward "engagement" rather than "affiliation":

> *We're developing metrics to assess the level of informal conversations with staff members. We see much more engagement in our programs when relationships are at the heart of what we do. And, we're working hard to change the ambience of the JCC. The Baltimore JCC launched a campaign to train staff members to interact with members and guests as they walk down the halls. Even though they*

*may be busy with their work and in a hurry to get to the
next meeting or the next task, there is nothing more important than greeting our people, creating the kind of warm
ambience that should characterize our institutions.*

At the Jewish Community Center of San Francisco, Rachel Brodie
serves as the CJO—"chief Jewish officer"—charged with helping the
entire institution to think how to best serve its mission to enrich Jewish life and peoplehood. Brodie relates:

> *We are looking to move from a transactional relation-
> ship with our members to something deeper. It's a work
> in progress. We're improving our "customer service,"
> using people's names and such. There is a time and place
> for large-scale events, but there is also value in putting
> resources in individuals. For the kind of transformative
> experiences of relationships, everybody knows that has to
> be done on a smaller scale.*

There are certainly groups in the JCC where relationships are para-
mount. Parents whose children are involved in the early childhood
center often become a close-knit microcommunity. The patrons of a
JCC health and fitness facility also form deep relationships. My own
father-in-law, Abe Kukawka (may he rest in peace), joined the health
club at the Omaha JCC upon retiring at age sixty-five and participated
in exercise classes and enjoyed the facilities nearly every day of his life
until, literally, the day he died (in the *shvitz*, no kidding) at the age of
one hundred. His best friends were a bunch of guys who were "regulars" at the health club who shared coffee and conversation at a "round
table." The "J" was his community.

Andy Paller directs an impressive "benchmarking" effort by the
JCCA to apply rigorous research to identify impact on outcomes from
the variety of activities at JCCs. Through surveying members, users,
and staff, and the collection and analysis of detailed JCC participation
and financial data, the benchmarking initiative is designed to "raise
the bar" for JCCs, with close to eighty (out of one hundred and fifty)
JCCs opting into the program and through the sharing of continental

findings with the field. Here is Paller's summary of the applicable results from 2011:

> At JCCs where users report higher levels of staff-participant interaction and of encouraging transitions, we see people more deeply involved in different departments in the JCC. In turn, membership retention, donor contributions, and reported Jewish growth levels improve. When JCC management decides this is important and staff is trained, the impact goes up. We've seen a big improvement since beginning our benchmarking in 2006. In 2011, 53 percent of all JCC users said they had an informal conversation with a staff person on at least 50 percent of their visits to the JCC, and 69 percent said at least 25 percent of visits. Similarly, we are doing better in "cross-selling": 47 percent, 61 percent, and 73 percent of users in the largest JCC departments (Fitness, Camp, Early Childhood) reported that staff sometimes or frequently encouraged participation in another area.
>
> Engaging people in a welcoming way can be challenging in a large building, with people coming and going. As one staff person put it, "People race into the building running to their class, iPod plugged into their ears, with a 'get out of my way, I don't have time for a conversation' attitude. It's hard to do this." A lot of energy and training was put into warming up the welcome when these findings were first identified, to help staff get better at doing this, with measurable results. This is an important challenge since that measure is correlated with increased retention, likelihood of a financial gift, improved Net Promoter Score (willingness to recommend to another), and number of program areas used.
>
> We're convinced that when JCCs do a better job of engaging in personal relationships, it positively impacts our work. However, this is an operational area that requires ongoing attention to maintain and increase results. This

may include ongoing training as well as continuing to reinforce the importance of informal conversations and encouraging transition, and being aware of need to retrain new staff and staff moving into new roles. Some staff just don't know how to do this. We need to train them in how to engage in conversation and build relationships. Informal conversations are easier in smaller JCCs; it's a reflection of relationships in community, longevity of staff, the culture of "friendliness." We're identifying tools to assist in this process, from better name tags that identify someone as staff and allows a member to address them by name, to systems in many Js where swiping a membership card brings up their photo and their name pops up on the screen, allowing the staff at the desk to call the member by name and begin a short conversation to check in with them.

The next best thing to personal face-to-face encounter is a phone call. Unfortunately, most Jewish institutions make phone calls to constituents only when they are seeking donations or rustling up attendance at a program. If that is the only time the institution bothers to pick up the phone, what is the message being sent? Since the publication of *The Spirituality of Welcoming*, many synagogues have taken up the call to phone every member of the congregation at least once a year, often before the High Holy Days, Passover, or Hanukkah, just to send wishes for a happy holiday. The uniqueness of the experience is reflected in the reactions the institutional callers often receive from the other end: befuddled silence. "You're calling just to say, 'Happy New Year?'" the incredulous member will say. "You sure I'm not late with my dues?"

There are moments I wished I received a phone call rather than an e-mail or a letter. When my mother of blessed memory died, my rabbi was there for me in person. However, on the first *yahrzait*, the anniversary of her death, the communication I received from the synagogue was a short notice reminding me of the *yahrzait* date and informing me that my mother's name would be read in the synagogue. The notice was printed on the outside of an envelope, a request for a donation. There was no explanation of why there was an expectation of a contribution, no discussion of the tradition of giving *tzedakah* on such occasions. The message was "send money." I can only imagine the reaction of members who don't know about this tradition, who may think to themselves, "I already gave you thousands of dollars in dues; now you want more?"

Once again, great relationship-builders find the time to make regular phone contact with their people. Some leaders maintain a regular call list to VIPs in their organizations; what about everyone else? But, beware robocalls. I received one from a congregation, and frankly, it felt disingenuous. I understand the allure of automatic messaging systems, but there is nothing more powerful than a personal encounter, whether by phone or, preferably, face-to-face.

2) Telling Stories

Narratives of the self are not fundamentally possessions of the individual, but possessions of relationships—products of social interchange. In effect, to be a self with a past and potential future is not to be an independent agent, unique and autonomous, but to be immersed in interdependency.
KENNETH J. GERGEN, *REALITIES AND RELATIONSHIPS: SOUNDINGS IN SOCIAL CONSTRUCTION*[5]

Telling someone your story is sharing the experience of your life. Sharing experiences with others in turn becomes the story of your life.

A story is shared by means of conversations. As my colleague and Synagogue 3000 partner Lawrence A. Hoffman teaches, it is our conversations that define our very identity:

> With the demise of ethnicity, issues of identity become prominent. No longer are we simply what we were "born to be." We are "what we decide we want to be." The result is a frantic competition for identity markers. We are, among other things, nationals (American, Canadian, British, French, or Spanish); religious (Jew, Muslim, Christian); denominational (Reform, not Conservative; Shiite, not Sunni; Lutheran,

not Catholic); and gendered (women, not men; gay, not straight). Increasingly, as well, we are called upon to stake out claims on a political-social divide (liberal, moderate, or conservative). We may also be thought of as soccer moms, Native Americans, suburban professionals, millennials, or boomers. Of all these identity markers, the religious and denominational sides become optional; they end up competing for their share of our discretionary time and attention alongside lifestyle choices (vegetarian), cultural proclivities (art-movie buff), and even hobbies and the things we say we are "into" (stamp collecting, yoga, running).

How do we keep track of these multiple identities? How do we express their relative importance to others?

The answer, increasingly, is through conversation. How else do people regularly know that we are, say, professing evangelicals, passionate feminists, ardent Catholics, active Democrats, or Jews for whom Zionism matters deeply? The most evident marker is the extent and the intensity of the conversations we have on these subjects. Imagine the totality of our conversations for any given week collected in a pie chart. Mark off the wedge devoted to talking about Judaism, multiply that wedge by the intensity with which we have the conversations, and you get the degree to which Judaism is our identity.

Dale Carnegie famously quipped that the person someone most likes to talk about is herself or himself. When do people in Jewish institutions, especially new members, get to talk about themselves? Most of our organizations begin their relationship with new people by handing them a demographic form to fill out. And then no one looks at it. We can do better. We can develop ways to hear the stories of others.

When you meet someone new for the first time, what do you talk about? You talk about who you are, where you're from, your family, your work—you tell your story. This is what we should be doing with our people, certainly with new members … and even with members we have had on the books for years.

The second step in building a relationship with another, then, is to have face-to-face conversations, to share our stories. By "stories," I mean the general outline of our life's journey. I'll often ask a new acquaintance, "What's your story?" In the South, people ask "Where y'at?" And, I'm often asked to tell mine. These quick life reviews are generally no more than a few minutes in length, revealing the highlights of home of origin, places of education, career, major moves, family status. They sometimes lead to a game of "Jewish geography," a mutual point of connection for social networking.

VOICES FROM THE COMMUNITY

Gary Wexler, president of Passion Marketing, is a go-to consultant for branding, marketing, and advertising in the Jewish nonprofit sector:

> I have switched my entire marketing approach from the emphasis on branding and social marketing to conversation. I've realized in the nonprofit sector, who owns the conversation, wins. The job of the nonprofit marketer is to explore which conversations in the community the nonprofit can own. How do you frame those conversations? How do you host them? Who should be in the conversation? Who is the influencer? Who is in their network? What are the big ideas to move the conversations? Then, you create the branding and social marketing to follow the framing and big ideas that will become the engine of the conversation. This is not a mass-marketing approach; it has to be done in targeted segments, where it can actually create results and be affordable. That's why I'm facilitating Conversational Dinners with small groups of donors in the cities where I consult. Those dinners by far are the most powerful big idea for nonprofit marketing.

The importance of sharing one's story is poignantly portrayed in the classic film *The Bellboy* (1960). Jerry Lewis plays Stanley, a sweet, clueless bellboy working in the glamorous Fountainbleau Hotel in Miami Beach. The movie has no plot; it consists of a series of vignettes featuring Stanley messing up in one way or another: delivering suitcases to the wrong room, walking twenty-five rambunctious dogs, pretending to conduct an invisible hotel orchestra, reshaping a wet sculpture in hilarious fashion—all setups to showcase Lewis's extraordinary rubbery face and slapstick physical comedy. Throughout the entire film, Stanley never utters a word; he is completely silent, obeying instructions and commands from his superiors and hotel guests.

At the very end of the film, Stanley and a group of bellboys gather to plan a protest action against the management of the hotel. They bicker among themselves so loudly that Stanley, until then quite the passive observer, slams his hand on the table and stands up in a gesture to demand quiet. Shocked, the bellboys stop their squabbling. Just then, Mr. Novack, the general manager of the hotel, walks in, sees Stanley in what appears to be a position of leadership, and berates him, "Aha, so you are the ringleader, eh, Stanley? And I thought you were a nice, quiet young man ... I've given you a home away from home here, haven't I, Stanley? And this is the way you repay me! You're nothing but a troublemaker!"

Stanley vigorously shakes his head in disagreement. "Stop shaking your head!" Novack yells, exasperated. "What's the matter with you? Can't you talk?" Stanley thinks for a moment ... and then to the surprise of all, he answers in a perfectly normal, serious tone of voice, "Certainly, I can talk. I suspect I can talk as well as any other man, Mr. Novack." Novack replies, "In that case, how is it we never heard you talk before?" Stanley answers brightly, "Because no one ever asked me!" He then whistles a tune and walks out of the room, leaving Novack and his fellow bellboys dumbfounded.

Lewis, who wrote, starred in, and directed the film, then offers the message of the movie. He has the narrator break the fourth wall separating the players and the audience by addressing the viewer directly: "So, you see, there was no story ... but there is a moral ... and a simple one: You'll never know the next guy's story ... unless you ask!"

You will never know the next guy's story unless you ask.

How many people seeking to enter Jewish life are never asked to share their story? Instead, they are given brochures touting the organization and what it does ... or asked to fill out a form ... or begged to volunteer for a committee ... or solicited for money. The message is, "We put our programs first. Let us tell you *our* story ... and then, maybe, maybe ... we'll have the time to listen to yours."

It should be the other way around.

When Rabbi Zoë Klein became senior rabbi of Temple Isaiah in Los Angeles, she was advised by the board to "tell her story" to the congregation. She felt differently:

> *The way people really feel connected to you is not if they know your story, but if they feel you know their story. If the rabbi knows your story, then you feel like you are seen, you matter, you are in relationship. So, I set up small groups in my study—six to eight people—to share a "Sacred Stories Haggadah" experience; we had a little Kiddush, karpas appetizer, we told the story of the congregation, and then I would invite people to add their own stories by answering the question "What was your journey that brought you to this place?" We concluded with a blessing. Some 250 people shared their stories with me and with each other. It was powerful.*

Rabbi Will Berkovitz, an early leader of Jconnect, puts it this way:

> *There are two kinds of conversation we have with young Jews. At a big event, when we meet someone new, we ask them a few questions to get to know them ... and then immediately link them with others who might share something in common—Jewish geography, affinity, profession, or interest. This happens in the space of just a few minutes of conversation. Our goal is to link them into a microcommunity, a smaller subset of our larger network.*
>
> *The second type of conversation often happens over coffee. We know that in the emerging adult world, young people ages twenty-one to forty are trying to answer the*

> questions "Who am I? What do I want to do with my life?
> What is my career path? Where do I want to live?" So, we
> ask: "What's life-giving in your life? What's challenging in
> your life? What are you trying to do; what's your purpose?
> And, what would it look like if what you're trying to do actu-
> ally came true?" If we create a structure for them to find
> answers to those questions, they will engage.
>
> A mentor of mine once gave me great advice: "When
> you meet another person, listen so hard, it will give you
> a headache." I "listen hard," and then I act on what I've
> heard to guide my new friend to a community where it's
> okay to ask these deeper questions. People are looking for
> a unique place to ask and explore these questions.

The key characteristic of someone who "listens hard" is empathy. Putting yourself in the other's shoes, identifying with the feelings being
expressed, focusing on what the other is saying instead of thinking
about what you will say next—these are the key components of an
empathetic personality.

When applying for a job as a flight attendant at Southwest Air-
lines, several candidates are led into a room filled with customers and
human resource staff. One of the candidates is invited to take a seat
at the head of the table and asked a surprising question: "What was
the most embarrassing thing to ever happen to you?" As the candidate
begins to speak, the people doing the hiring are not focused on the
person telling the story. They are looking at the other candidates for
the job to watch *their* reactions. If they are exhibiting schadenfreude
(deriving pleasure from another's misfortune), there is no chance of
them being hired. It turns out that empathy is the most important
characteristic for a flight attendant stuck in a crowded silver tube trav-
eling at five hundred miles per hour at thirty thousand feet.

Some of our organizations are beginning to create safe spaces and
times for participants to tell their stories. The Federation of Jewish
Men's Clubs, the Conservative movement's men's organization, created
an initiative called Hearing Men's Voices. Local chapters are taught
how to have a "talking circle" where guys can tell "the story of their

journeys as Jewish men." The goal is to surface deep relationships among the guys as they become increasingly more comfortable in sharing the issues that shape their lives as men.

In New York City, the Jewish Education Project (formerly the Board of Jewish Education) invited me to speak about Relational Judaism to a large convening of teams from synagogues and schools engaged in LOMED, an initiative to rethink Jewish education (lomed.wikispaces.com). During the year that followed, Cyd Weissman and her colleagues conducted dozens of opportunities for "sharing sacred stories of our lives" by teaching strategies for engaging in deeper conversations than the usual surface chitchat.

Sharing stories is at the heart of an initiative at Valley Beth Shalom, a Conservative synagogue in Encino, California. Rabbi Feinstein and his colleagues Rabbi Joshua Hoffman and Rabbi Noah Farkas are experimenting with a new approach to inducting new members into the life of the community. It begins with a "new member covenanting ceremony"— a wonderful experience on a Sunday morning in August and then again at select times during the year. A small group of new and prospective members gathers for bagels and coffee in the lobby of the synagogue, where they meet a rabbi, the executive director, and a lay leader.

On the morning I observed, there were four couples, all in their late thirties and early forties, with young kids, and a few single people, also middle-aged. After ten minutes of schmoozing, the group was invited into the sanctuary, onto the bimah, where they sat in a circle in front of the *aron ha-kodesh*, the holy ark. Everyone was asked to introduce herself or himself to the group and answer the question "What brought you to Valley Beth Shalom?" The kids had the run of the sanctuary while the adults shared their stories. The synagogue leaders shared their stories, too. The rabbi, Joshua Hoffman, talked about his little kids and their involvement with the preschool and the day school. There was no hard sell about the synagogue and ways to get involved; rather, the rabbi simply said that this was the beginning of a process to enter into a "covenant between you and the congregation." They were all invited to join the next step in the process—a four-session small-group experience called Our Jewish Home, "home" meaning the spiritual home of the congregation (see below).

The rabbi then did something quite extraordinary. He said that belonging to a synagogue was a sacred act and invited the entire group to gather inside the ark. Yes, Valley Beth Shalom has a walk-in *aron ha-kodesh*, with two very tall doors that when opened reveal a space in which a small group can stand. Rabbi Hoffman opened the ark and everyone smushed into the space. The kids were oohing and aahing at the Torah scrolls, while the adults realized they probably had not been that close to an ark since their own Bar or Bat Mitzvah, if they had one. The rabbi transformed the moment into something quite special. He offered a brief *kavanah* (meditation) about the sacredness of relationships and then offered a blessing of *Shehecheyanu*. The people were moved, some to tears, by this powerful, uplifting, spiritual experience.

SPOTLIGHT ON BEST PRACTICES

A fascinating innovation at IKAR has been the transformation of the *Yizkor* memorial services from a private to a public affair. Members are invited to submit short essays about the loved ones remembered. The stories are compiled in a *Yizkor* "memory book" distributed during the Yom Kippur *Yizkor* service. The resulting document is filled with touching, poignant, funny, and moving stories that reveal as much about the writer as about those whose memories are being honored. People not only read the stories, but they also comment on them to the mourners, deepening the relationships in the community.

Providing invitations and opportunities for conversation can be an important and appreciated aspect of the value proposition offered by Jewish institutions. In a recent *New York Times* op-ed book *Alone Together: Why We Expect More from Technology and Less from Each Other*, psychologist and professor at Massachusetts Institute of Technology Sherry Turkle warns that we are sacrificing conversation for more connection. "The little devices most of us carry around are so powerful that they change not only what we do, but also who we are … we've become accustomed to a new way of being—'alone together.'" Turkle describes offices where employees sit glued to their computers, iPads, and smartphones, texting each other rather than talking together. A sixteen-year-old boy who uses texts to communicate almost everything says wistfully, "Someday, someday, but certainly not now, I'd like to learn how to have a conversation."

As Turkle laments, the move from conversation to connection has reduced "messy and demanding" human relationships to edited postings of who we want to be, not who we really are. "It's a process in which we shortchange ourselves. Worse, it seems that over time we stop caring, forgetting there is a difference." The technologies provide the "illusion of companionship" without the demands of relationship. Turkle argues there is no substitute for face-to-face conversation that unfolds slowly, requires patience, and allows self-reflection. "We think constant connection will make us feel less lonely. The opposite is true." She writes movingly of walking the sand dunes on Cape Cod, where "not too long ago, people walked with their heads up, looking at the water, the sky, the sand and at one another, talking. Now they often walk with their heads down, typing. Even when they are with their friends, partners, children, everyone is on their own devices. So, I say, look up at one another, and let's start the conversation."[6]

Let's create institutions of Relational Judaism that welcome the conversation.

SPOTLIGHT ON BEST PRACTICES

As exciting as a listening campaign or house meeting can be, it can be challenging to create a culture of empathetic listening. Sometimes someone dominates the discussion, hopes to have individual problems solved, or keeps the story they tell at a surface level. Community organizers suggest the following ten steps to maximize the effectiveness of storytelling:

1. Be clear in the PR/invitation about what will happen.
2. Build in snacks and schmooze time early in the evening to get that level of conversation out of the way.

3. Choose the first storyteller in advance. Work with that person to share a model story.
4. Teach the value of *derekh eretz*—respect.
5. Have a timekeeper, and be willing to cut people off in a gentle way. Be consistent about time.
6. Grant permission not to speak, but encourage people to trust the process.
7. Bring God into sacred time—keep the story rooted in Jewish experience.
8. Create a safe place for sharing real stories about real struggles.
9. Check in with the group to assess agreement to the ground rules of the meeting before proceeding. "Is it okay with everyone that we'll cut you off after five minutes?"
10. Thank people for sharing their stories.

I observed Rabbi Stephanie Kolin train the leadership team at Stephen S. Wise Temple, Los Angeles, in the art of holding a one-on-one conversation. She distinguished what a one-on-one is … and is not:

> A one-on-one is not: an interview, chitchat, a monologue, a date, therapy, pastoral counseling, selling, preaching, giving opinions, prying. A one-on-one is: beginning of a relationship, a facilitated conversation, sharing public stories about who we are and what we care about, listening carefully, building trust, enriching for both, finding commonalities, being truly curious about the other, a sacred exchange, asking "why" questions, listening for "self-interest," hearing concerns and worries.

A good one-on-one lasts between thirty minutes and an hour and, if the person is someone you would like to engage more deeply, concludes with an offer to meet again or join in organizing.

Community organizers are justifiably hesitant to put in writing their approach to engaging people in one-on-one conversations and listening campaigns. It is difficult to put into words what is essentially a process that can truly only be experienced. Thus, the best way to learn these skills is to participate in trainings and seminars sponsored by the expert practitioners of the art. In the Jewish community, the go-to organizations of organizers are Just Congregations at the Union for Reform Judaism and JOIN for Justice: Jewish Organizing Institute and Network. A good description of the process may be found in *Where Justice Dwells: A Hands-On Guide to Doing Social Justice in Your Jewish Community* (Jewish Lights Publishing) by Rabbi Jill Jacobs.

There are a number of additional creative strategies for organizations to engage people in conversation: Open Space technology—any participant can list a topic of interest and gather others wishing to discuss the issue; the World Café—small groups meeting around a question; StoryLooms—knitting together tactiles to tell stories; Digital StoryWeavers—on-the-spot video of conversations; Word Cloud of Commitments—a visual depiction of word frequency used in stories; and live texting of responses during conversations, dialogue, and lectures. At a unique Rosh Hashanah "experience" sponsored by The Tribe, Miami's Next *Dor* site, young Jewish adults texted emotions and responses to the event, which were projected onto large screens set behind the pulpit.[7]

3) Learning Together / Doing Together

Margaret Thatcher once famously said to a volunteer group: "True companionship comes not from *being* together, but from *doing* together."

One of the most effective Jewish ways of "doing together" is to invite people to learn together. For centuries, Jews have been gathering in the *beit midrash*—the house of study—to sit in pairs around tables in face-to-face encounter with a text between them, reading the words of a text out loud and working together to decipher its meaning. The very word that describes this pedagogic process—*hevruta*—reveals the core of the relational experience. *Hevruta* comes from the Hebrew root *haver*, "friend." The Talmud famously states, *O hevruta o metuta*, "Either one has friendship, or else one has death" (*Ta'anit* 23a).

Why is the classical model of Jewish study relational? Chancellor Arnold M. Eisen offers his perspective:

Text study is good precisely because it puts you around the table. It's very important to be around a table at which you all share, where everybody has equal access and the right of insight into it.

And because you're not sitting there talking to one another about yourselves but you're talking to another about the text, it gives you the distance that you need in order to talk about yourself. It gives you the distance to be personal and build relationship. There's another advantage to study: it doesn't make demands of conviction or commitment of you at the first instance. People like to learn. Once they've learned they can contribute to the conversation, you usually can't stop them ... which is good!

Most North American Jews have never experienced serious Jewish learning. Baby boomers quit the mostly boring afternoon Hebrew schools of their youth as soon as the Bar/Bat Mitzvah party was over. Yet, with the guidance of a skilled teacher, adults who are introduced to *hevruta* learning—who meet with a rabbi on Saturday morning or Wednesday evening for an hour of learning, who enroll in the local branch of the Florence Melton Mini-School, who are lucky enough to be invited into a cohort of the Wexner Heritage Fellowship, who travel to Jerusalem to study at the Hartman Institute, who take courses at the American Jewish University's Whizin Center for Continuing Education, who take in a lecture broadcast from the 92nd Street Y, or who attend a Limmud Conference—all embrace the opportunity to delve into classic Jewish texts and hear the thoughts of visionary Jewish teachers.

Almost three decades ago, Leslie Wexner (later joined by his wife, Abigail), recognizing the need to identify and inspire the next generation of Jewish leaders, established The Wexner Foundation. The three major initiatives of The Wexner Foundation are the Wexner Heritage Program, with cohorts of twenty carefully selected young volunteer leaders in cities across North America (currently there are more than 1,700 alumni); the Wexner Graduate Fellowship, with cohorts of twenty nominated professionals-in-training studying in graduate schools renowned for preparing Jewish community leaders (currently there are 354 alumni); and the Wexner Israel Fellows, cohorts of ten young Israeli leaders who receive intensive graduate-level work at the Kennedy School of Government at Harvard University (currently there are 216 alumni). Larry Moses, president emeritus of The Wexner Foundation, reflects on more than twenty-five years of intensive work in leadership development:

> When we first began the Wexner Heritage initiative, the theory was that serious Jewish learning would be foundational in developing future leaders. Thus, our courses and intensive institutes focused heavily on providing the Wexner Heritage members the highest level of adult Jewish learning taught by the finest Jewish scholars and teachers in the world. While the individual learning was truly effective, we were surprised to find that the interpersonal bonding of the participants was as important as the study itself, and, in fact, one was intrinsic to the other. Many Wexner Heritage cohorts continue to meet—at their own expense—years after their initial two-year commitment. The Israeli Fellows have spun off affinity groups interested in specific areas of work. Families gather together for holiday celebrations. Jewish community rabbis, educators, and communal professionals share best practices and deepening relationships across ideological, geographical, and organizational boundaries, making use of web-based social networking platforms. Perhaps the greatest success of the Wexner leadership programs is building individual leaders into cohorts, and then cohorts into a larger leadership community, all fueled by learning and the values of the Jewish people. In a word, it is truly about "relationships."

A second best principle of building relationships among people is to do something together. This is the idea behind "committees" in institutions bringing people together who share the same passion to "get something done," whether that is working to repair the world, supporting key constituencies within the community, or ensuring the long-term financial stability of the organization.

"Doing a *mitzvah*" is another Jewish value, one that can be done individually or collectively. There are all sorts of examples of strategies to encourage people to "do *mitzvot*," ranging from one-shot "*mitzvah* days" to sustainable campaigns. I much prefer the latter. One such campaign was launched by Chancellor Arnold M. Eisen to reinvigorate the base of the Conservative movement—the *Mitzvah* Initiative. Emanating from The Jewish Theological Seminary of America, the approach seeks to encourage the adoption of a personal "signature *mitzvah*" through small-group discussion, reflection, text study, and consideration of the key questions of relationship, such as the following:

- What are the relationships and responsibilities that give my life meaning and purpose?
- How can I express this in an authentically Jewish way?
- What can I learn about my own relationship to Judaism and Jewish life?

The goal is to create a personal relationship with the concept of *mitzvah* as a path to enriching spiritual growth and meaning.[8]

Sharing a Shabbat or holiday meal is another way to "do something together." At Beth Am, a Conservative synagogue in Baltimore, the year 5772 introduced an initiative to connect members to one another around the Shabbat table for good food and conversation. The Year of 613+ Shabbat Dinners saw dozens of families inviting other families to each other's homes. Hosts posted reports on the experience on a dedicated website, inspiring others to participate as well.

4) Connecting

The key to connecting is caring. Listen to Rabbi Steven Carr Reuben, a Reconstructionist rabbi who has served Kehillat Israel in Pacific Palisades, California, for twenty-seven years:

> One of our HUC rabbinic interns once asked me, "Why does everyone in this congregation seem so happy?" I thought about it. The truth is we're a full-service synagogue like every other place, but one of the key elements in our success is that, regardless of their background—Jewish, non-Jewish, or

whatever—our people feel that we care about them. We take people seriously; we validate who they are. The proudest feeling I have about this Reconstructionist place is that we are as self-consciously nonjudgmental as any synagogue could be. Relationships grow out of that kind of attitude. It boils down to one thing: everybody wants a little attention. Care about them, care for them, and they will connect with you forever.

Connecting to Friends

Richard Address is another rabbi who recently took on a pulpit position after serving in a national organization for more than thirty years. He met some two hundred people in "meet and greets" over the first summer in the job.

I asked every single one of them why they belong to M'kor Shalom. Not one said, "Because I am committed to the interpretations of liberal, progressive Judaism as embodied in the Reform movement." They all said, "I enrolled my kid in a preschool, I met some other parents, we became friends, we share our lives together."

Tzivia Getzug Schwartz conducted focus groups for the Los Angeles Jewish Federation as the leadership considered new initiatives to engage young Jewish adults. "In all the focus groups, it became very clear that everyone is looking for social connection." Consequently, the LA Federation is creating NuRoots, an ambitious citywide effort to engage young Jews.

Some institutions connect people by affinity, people who share something in common. Federations organize their fundraising groups by affinity: women's groups, real estate guys, lawyers, young Jewish adults. Some synagogues have had success with men's groups (Guys Night Out, Brews with Jews), elder adult learners, the usual "sisterhoods" and "men's clubs." Other communities have found affinity groups didn't work. IKAR discovered that the lawyers in the community did not want to be with other lawyers on their "downtime."

Neighborhood groups often work well. As a result of a year-long CBCO listening campaign, Congregation Emanu-El in San Francisco, one of the largest Reform synagogues in the country, learned that the members felt disconnected and lonely. Community engagement manager Sandy Rechtschaffen recruited forty lay leaders to implement Emanu-El in the Neighborhood, a strategy to divide the city into seventeen neighborhoods, each one led by a minimum of two members. After discovering that many members had no place to go for Yom Kippur break-fast, these neighborhood groups confirmed hosts for fourteen potluck break-fasts in which four hundred people attended. Following this enormous success, the neighborhoods now sponsor other communal celebrations such as Hanukkah candle lighting, Shabbat meals, *Havdalah*, and Passover Seder matching.

A second effort to build relationships at Congregation Emanu-El has been to decentralize the "caring community" outreach into the neighborhood groups. The congregation alerts the neighborhood "*liaisonim*" of an illness, death, or *simcha* of a member, and they make contact with an appropriate phone call or e-mail. Instead of one committee responsible for a shiva meal, each neighborhood uses the Meal-Train software platform (www.mealtrain.com) to organize meals. "We had one member fighting pancreatic cancer who received meals from her neighbors for fourteen months," reports Sandy Rechtschaffen. Neighbors are also encouraged to attend services and other events at the temple as a group. Rechtschaffen has written a comprehensive manual to guide the lay leaders and offers support throughout the year. Notice, this relational effort is not managed or staffed by the five rabbis in the congregation, although they are available as Judaic resources. The goal is to create "horizontal" connections among the members in addition to "vertical" relationships with the clergy. Rabbi Carla Fenves comments:

> *People are eager to be* known. *The solution is to break down our big numbers into smaller, local communities. Being known is not just about the rabbi knowing your name; it's about congregant-to-congregant connection. Bring Judaism to the neighborhood. The rabbi doesn't have to be there for it to feel like a synagogue event or feel like people can meet each other. Our kids go to fifty*

*different schools; how else will we meet each other if not in
the neighborhood? People are desperate for community,
face-to-face community.*

At IKAR, an annual large-scale fundraiser called Wandering Jews
features potluck Shabbat dinners in people's homes situated in neighborhoods. Some synagogues run *Havdalah*-by-Zip-Code in members'
homes.

SPOTLIGHT ON BEST PRACTICES

Beth El's Our Shabbat Tables

Beth El Synagogue in Omaha, Nebraska, is a medium-size Conservative congregation with a mix of fourth-generation families
and newcomers attracted to town by a relatively healthy economy
and a lovely quality of life. Synagogue leaders realized that many
members did not know each other. In a bold initiative to build
relationships, Beth El launched Our Shabbat Tables, bringing
together members of all ages for Friday night dinners at fellow
congregants' homes. In the first year, 130 people participated, far
exceeding expectations. In August, interested hosts and guests
gather at the synagogue for a fondue dinner, during which they
are matched and meet each other. This ameliorates the hesitancy
of guests to walk into a host home "cold." The matches are made
based on shared demographics and interests, with the groups
meeting for three dinners during a three-month period. Most
groups consist of three or four couples or families and six to eight
individuals. Interestingly, the synagogue itself provides the kosher
meals—mains and sides—while the participants bring wine/juice,
challah, salad, fruit, and dessert, all coordinated by the host family. Funding comes from an optional one-time small donation
from participants and a grant from a funder. Sophie Ambrose
comments, "The Shabbat get-togethers have been special for me
because I've been able to connect with members of our community I might not have had a chance to interact with otherwise."

Then, there is the belief that some people will self-organize. In many schools, new friendships are forged in Mommy and Me programs, in Mothers Circles, and in PJ Library groups, and the parents whose children share day school carpools end up celebrating birthday parties together. When there are good ingredients and when the "chemistry" is right, sometimes the groups form naturally. Institutions can help facilitate the creation of groups by providing bonding experiences and ensuring that every "program" has a social component in which participants interact and get to know each other on some level.

SPOTLIGHT ON BEST PRACTICES

The *Ruakh* Rally and One People / One Lunch

One of the interesting innovations at Congregation Shirat Hayam in Swampscott, Massachusetts, is the weekly "synaplex" model of multiple minyanim and activities running parallel to each other on Shabbat morning. Although many synagogues offer such options, there is often concern that the separation of small groups to worship diminishes the sense of community and the opportunity to connect people to one another. Shirat Hayam has developed a unique and quite exciting answer to this challenge. At precisely 11:45 a.m. each Shabbat morning, all the alternative minyanim in the building are required to end, and hundreds of people, young and old, gather together in the main sanctuary for what is called the *Ruakh* Rally. Think rousing song session at summer camp or youth group convention. There are songs of peace, Israeli melodies, and a unison singing of "Hatikvah." Immediately following the conclusion of the "rally," everyone enters the Shabbat Café for a full-on, sit-down lunch. According to Rabbi Baruch HaLevi, the charismatic leader of the community, "Regardless of the money involved, it is worth its weight in gold. It is the unifying force of the day. An hour or two into it, people are still schmoozing the day away." In fact, this is one of the key indicators of a relational community—if people hang around talking with one another after a program, service, or meal is over, relationships are in place.

Working the Sanctuary

Rabbis have introduced "relational moments" into worship services in a number of ways. At Valley Beth Shalom in Encino, California, congregants are encouraged to stand with arms around a neighbor during the *Kiddush* on Friday night and at the conclusion of the Shabbat morning davening. Recently, the rabbis asked congregants to move over next to anyone reciting the Mourner's *Kaddish* if the mourner was standing alone. Just before the *Kol Nidre* prayers begin, Rabbi Ed Feinstein encourages family members to turn to each other to "ask forgiveness" from each other before asking forgiveness from God.

Any number of congregations suspend the worship for a few minutes of what churches call "passing the peace." Congregants are invited to "turn to someone around you" to extend greetings. Rabbi Karyn Kedar stops the worship services on Friday night at Congregation B'nai Jehoshua Beth Elohim in Deerfield, Illinois, and instructs congregants to "'stand up, go across the sanctuary, and meet someone you don't know.' It takes time ... you have to be crazy to do it ... but is there anything more important? No, there is not." Rabbi Peter Berg at The Temple in Atlanta invites congregants to turn to each other and answer this question: "What crossroads are you at this week?"

One day, I received a phone call from Rabbi Wes Gardenswartz at Temple Emanuel in Newton, Massachusetts, a suburb of Boston. He was in his office, meeting with the current president of the synagogue at the time, Mike Benjamin. They told me that Emanuel was a large Conservative congregation, successful by every standard, with a modern building, a big staff, and terrific lay leadership. This was the kind of synagogue I loved to work with—a great place that wanted to get better, go deeper. There were some challenges: many families disappeared once their youngest child left for college. They gained and lost roughly the same number of household members each year—a revolving door synagogue. The key issue was the transactional nature of the relationship with many of the congregants; once their needs had been met, they retreated or dropped their membership entirely. So I was invited to be the scholar-in-residence during a weekend at the congregation based on *The Spirituality of Welcoming*. The key session was a board/staff retreat on the art of welcoming, copies of my book were distributed, and this determined group of clergy, staff, and lay leaders went to work.

Much to my surprise and delight, two years later Rabbi Gardenswartz along with the new president Amy Klein called me again. "We want you to return to Emanuel, both to see what has happened here and, more importantly, to push forward with Welcoming 2.0." When I returned, indeed the place was different. On Shabbat morning, greeters met congregants and visitors at the front door of the building and again at the entrance to the sanctuary. The signage was much improved; you could actually find the sanctuary and the rabbi's study. On Sunday morning, the lobby was transformed into the Java Gate Café, a playful allusion to the "gates" of entry into the life of the sacred community: prayer, study, justice, and so on. And, significant progress had been made in deepening the relationship with families early on in their membership experience, denting the transactional culture. But, amazingly, on Friday night I was advised that the biggest change by far was the senior rabbi himself. "Wait, Ron," Amy marveled. "You won't believe what has happened. It has changed the culture of our community."

I could hardly wait for Shabbat morning services to begin. Typically in a Conservative synagogue, there are twelve to fifteen "regulars" who show up at the very beginning of the prayer service, along with the family of the Bar/Bat Mitzvah and their guests who take the invitation literally. At Temple Emanuel that morning, a layperson led the first section of the davening. When Rabbi Gardenswartz arrived, he entered the bimah from the side, greeted the people sitting there, and then, while the worship continued, proceeded to walk down into the sanctuary. He warmly greeted the Bar Mitzvah family and their guests. He walked up and down the aisles, wishing those in attendance "Shabbat shalom." Then, remarkably, he made his way to the back of the sanctuary, stationed himself right next to the greeters, and joined them in welcoming everyone who entered that room. For nearly an hour, until just before the Torah reading, Rabbi Gardenswartz stood there, offering a handshake, introducing himself to newcomers, kibitzing with the regulars, and acting as a model for his congregation to embrace the *mitzvah* of *hakhnasat orchim*, hospitality, as people trickled into the service. When I commented approvingly, the president of the shul said to me, "Ron, you liberated Wes from the bimah."

Rabbi Gardenswartz never learned how to do this in rabbinical school. Nor do Jewish communal professionals, teachers, and educators learn it. But, this is a skill everyone who works within the Jewish community needs to have in a Relational Judaism, both to offer a sincere welcome—the first step in building a relationship—and to model welcoming behavior for the other professionals and lay leaders on our institutional teams.

SPOTLIGHT ON BEST PRACTICES

Rabbi Alan Silverstein is known as the social networker of his Conservative congregation, Agudath Israel in Caldwell, New Jersey. I asked him how he builds relationships with his congregants and guests ... in the sanctuary itself:

> My view of the world is this: when somebody comes into my house, I must, to the best of my ability, properly welcome them, make them feel comfortable, and network them to others. This is the mitzvah of hakhnasat orchim. The congregation is my house. If somebody comes into a shul, they partake of the davening, listen to the sermon, but they don't connect with people, it's a diminished experience for them. So, first and foremost, this is a calling, a mission.
>
> I use my vantage point on the bimah to locate people I don't know who have come into the sanctuary and don't seem to be connected to some cluster of guests. Once I spot that person, I motion to my surrogates—the cantor, education director, executive director, membership committee people, and outgoing lay leaders—to come up to the bimah, and I'll say to them, "See those folks in the fourth row from the back on the left? Can you do the mitzvah and greet them and find out if this is their first time here? Are they visiting, or are they members of the

shul who haven't been here in a long time? How can we best meet their needs?" You wouldn't expect someone you don't know to come into the living room of your home and not make an effort to find out who they are. That's the second thing: identify the people who need to be networked.

Third thing: once we identify folks, I have to figure out how to make them feel networked, even while they're in the sanctuary. If I see it's a young couple with little kids, I'll have someone from the same demographic group go over to them, welcome them, and invite any or all of that group who wants to come to Torah Tots, Mini-minyan, or any of the other parallel activities about to happen to come with them so they don't go alone. If they send the kids to junior congregation and they come back into the sanctuary, I'll have people in their demographic come over and say something like, "You know, it's not real comfortable sitting by yourself, why don't you come over and sit with a bunch of us ... and then we'll all go to sit-down Kiddush together." Some people will say, "No thanks, I prefer to remain here." But most of the time, people say, "Oh, that's really nice." So there's some bonding going on even during the service.

To the extent we can, we offer a low-anxiety honor—read in English, open the ark—and most people are delighted. We don't give them an aliyah in Hebrew unless the person walks in comfortably wearing a big tallit, davening up a storm. Bottom line: make people feel comfortable. Even so, some will say, "I came to be left alone and meditate, and all these people are bothering me ..." But I would rather err on the side of our value of hakhnasat orchim than on the side of indifference.

Fourth thing: when the service ends, we have a Shabbat virtual community format every week. We don't allow the Bar Mitzvah to upend our communal gathering. Even if you want to have a catered Kiddush luncheon following the service, you have to first participate in the congregational Kiddush with your guests for about forty-five minutes, and then we'll set up your private luncheon in another room. We get some pushback about this, but it's a statement of what we're about. At the community Kiddush every week, we set up small nursery-school-sized tables for kids with kid food (peanut butter and jelly), and then we invite young couples with kids to join the other young couples with kids over in that section of the room. If we have new empty-nester guests, we make sure that, in addition to the key staff greeting them, we have outgoing people in the same demographic greeting them. I have a whole group of people who don't feel put upon to engage people in conversation. I want ambassadors. I realize we're not going to be perfect at this. People will slip through the cracks, but we don't beat ourselves up about it. We try the best we can. It's an art, not a science.

How do I teach my people to do the mitzvah? Modeling. People have a pretty clear sense about my own personal Judaism. So, if I take time out to do this mitzvah, they get the message that it's important for them to do it, too. By now, it's ingrained in the culture of our place.

My primary emphasis in terms of welcoming is on new people who have joined the shul, particularly if they are new in the area and they don't have a network yet in town. They need relationships. If I can help them define their relationship in a setting where the people they are relating to are engaged in Jewish stuff as well as Little League, that will help define their Jewish journeys because they'll be doing it with peers.

We offer a million different opportunities for engagement. We have a couple hundred people in adult learning, we have all sorts of tikkun olam options, we have *tefillah options, Israel options, world Jewry options, Torah study options ... but it will all fall by the wayside for most people if they're not engaged in relationships.*

Food is a remarkably effective vehicle for encouraging connection. Many synagogues begin and end their Shabbat worship experiences with an opportunity for people to gather around food. A "pre-service proneg" or "snack and yak" cheese and wine/juice hour on a Friday night and a full-on Shabbat dinner or luncheon following services both build community. At Chicken Soup Shabbat at Congregation Or Hadash in Atlanta, volunteers ladle out chicken-stock or vegan broth into oversized logo mugs while individuals personalize their "dinner" with rice, noodles, or matzah balls; add challah and brownies for an inexpensive sit-down Shabbat dinner experience. Federations rarely have a meeting without snacks, and many JCCs have installed cafés in their lobbies serving Starbucks-quality coffee and light meals. Situated on the JCC campus, the Rose Blumkin Home for the Aging in Omaha, Nebraska, goes a step further; during the lunch hour on Fridays, the Star Deli offers deli-starved Jews in Omaha a full array of hard-to-get kosher delicacies. The prayer experience in many synagogues has become much more welcoming and engaging; of that, there is no doubt. The relationship between congregant and clergy has been fundamentally transformed from observer to fully involved participant. Just as "relational art," defined by Nicolas Bourriaud as "a set of artistic practices which take as their theoretical and practical point of departure the whole of human relations and their social context," has thrust museum and gallery patrons into "festive, collective and participatory space,"[9] so too have clergy fashioned a relational worship that, at its best, immerses everyone into relationship with each other and with God.

Gabby Kozak, membership director at Temple Sinai, a Reform congregation in Oakland, California, masterfully used Facebook as a platform to engage members of the community. GabbyTempleSinai was her Facebook page, and over four hundred members "friended" her. She says:

> I learned so much about what was happening in our members' lives by reading their Facebook posts. Most people are not calling into synagogues to report on the car accident that gave them whiplash or the thrill of witnessing a child's recital. But I would know about it instantly, report some things to the clergy, and always respond with a word of comfort or encouragement. When I saw them in the synagogue, I didn't have to ask, "What's happening in your life?" I knew. I could refer to things happening in their lives I already knew about. It helped me keep up with them.

Connecting to Families

The hottest show on Broadway at the moment is *The Book of Mormon*. It pokes fun at Mormon missionary work. But, the Mormons do two remarkable things to connect with their families. The first is a program called Family Home Evening. This is a dedicated time each week (Monday night for many) when the family does something together. No TV, no computers, no cell phones; just time together. The Mormon Church produces outstanding curricular material for use in the family—text studies, activities, games—all designed for intergenerational family education.

The second thing the Mormons do is home visits. Every active Mormon gets a monthly visit from two volunteers from the local church. They come equipped with resources, network people to needed services, and act as a sounding board for the church.

In a similar vein, with the support of the Dorothy and Myer S. Kripke Institute for Jewish Family Literacy, the Covenant Foundation, and the Gladys Crown Foundation, Shevet: The Jewish Family Education Exchange continues the important work of professional development for those working directly with Jewish families. In addition to an online community of practice (shevet-jfee.org) and workshops at regional convenings and national conventions, the faculty gathers each year to consider trends in family life and strategies for Jewish family engagement. Among the most recent topics: trying to better serve families with newborn through two-year-olds, welcoming interfaith and LGBT families, guiding families to co-create and co-view digital media (with consultation from Sesame Workshop), maximizing impact of PJ Library, encouraging non-Jewish members of Jewish families to connect with Judaism (with the cooperation of the Jewish Outreach Institute), creating Jewish grandparenting circles, serving Jewish families living in small Jewish communities in the South (in partnership with the Institute of Southern Jewish Life), supporting families with special-needs children, fostering pride in multiracial and multiethnic Jewish families, and "accompanying" all families as they proceed on their Jewish journeys.

SPOTLIGHT ON BEST PRACTICES

Rabbi Ari Moffic directs an innovative outreach effort to build relationships with young interfaith couples to encourage them to create Jewish families. Based in Chicago, Rabbi Moffic averages ten contacts per week through InterfaithFamily.com, the sponsoring agency of the project. She meets each of the couples for coffee to hear their stories and then invites them into workshops on marriage and family life. The couples often create relationships with others in these small group settings and through online support networks. Ari acts as a concierge, encouraging them to connect to synagogues and other avenues of Jewish learning and experiences in Chicago and beyond.

Joshua Mason-Barkin, director of congregational learning at Temple Isaiah in Los Angeles, describes an innovative family education model called *Tiyul: Shabbat B'yachad*. Forty-one families meet on Saturday morning or afternoon three times per month.

After a one-hour family service, kids adjourn to classrooms organized by grade, while parents gather for an adult learning experience. Many of the parents did not know each other when they joined
the program. One of the parents suggested a camping weekend,
which has become a much-anticipated annual experience.

> It turns out that eating communal meals together during
> the weekend or for potluck lunch or dinner Saturday night
> is critical. The conversations begun in the adult learning
> continue. And, now, the families see each other socially.
> Plus, the kids want their Bar/Bat Mitzvah ceremonies to be
> in the family worship, not during the usual private service.
> This has become their community, their relationships.

Valley Beth Shalom in Encino, California, has created a two-year
"new member engagement" process to follow up their creative
covenanting ceremony. In the first year, Our Jewish Home offers
small groups of new families four sessions:

1. An initial meeting in a lay leader's home. Personal stories
   are shared and linked to the "master Jewish story" through
   a Torah learning experience. Families are given a copy of
   the *Tanakh* (the entire Hebrew Bible) as a welcome gift.
2. Meeting at the synagogue, families are taken on a physical
   and programmatic tour of the congregation. The message
   is "you are needed here" and "we can help you find your
   place."
3. One of the new member families hosts session three, during which individuals complete a "learning plan" for next
   steps of involvement in the four pillars of the congregation: *Torah* (wisdom), *Avodah* (spirituality), *Chesed* (care for
   others), and *Chevre* (social encounters).
4. Session four is a Shabbat morning family service. New
   families are welcomed into the congregation with a group
   aliyah; the synagogue hosts a luncheon after services.

Year two of the induction process is titled Living a Jewish Life. A small group of families meets with a rabbi monthly over the course of the year in each other's homes, culminating in a family retreat over a Shabbat weekend. The curriculum consists of "big Jewish ideas," how to celebrate holidays in the home, and how to talk to your kids about God. Individuals are encouraged to join an affinity group or volunteer on a committee in order to engage in the life of the broader synagogue community.

During the two years, clergy are on the lookout for potential future leaders of the congregation. Some become mentors/ambassadors to subsequent new members; others eventually become members of the board. The goal is to create strong relationships with the clergy, with each other, with Jewish practice, and with the synagogue community.

Connecting to Young Professionals

When the American Jewish Committee approached its one-hundredth anniversary in 2005, the leadership asked a tough question: what did the organization need to do to reinvent itself, to attract smart young leaders interested in policies affecting the Jewish community? The answer: AJC created ACCESS, a new structure to build relationships with young Jews. In the words of Daniel Inlender, a young ACCESS leader in Los Angeles, ACCESS

> *gives my generation a voice at the table, and, yes, access to the highest levels of debate and policy formation. Participating in these conversations, taking intensive trips to Washington, D.C., and abroad, all help build relationships between members and with the organization.*

By focusing on the needs and interests of young Jews that may, in fact, be quite different from the senior leadership and empowering them to act, ACCESS has "unlocked the magic of creating a structure for young Jews within a traditional organization," according to the review in *Slingshot*, a prestigious annual listing of fifty innovative initiatives in the Jewish community.

Connecting to Teenagers

At Temple Beth Elohim in Wellesley, Massachusetts, there are, count 'em, five full-time Jewish educators who work in some way with a teenage engagement program called *Havayah* (Hebrew for "experience"; www.tbeyouth.org). Laura Hyman, director of *Havayah*, explains:

> We have a lot of staff who spend time building relationships with kids—take them for coffee, see them at temple, encourage them to go to camp. They come all week long, at different times, and when they are there, someone on staff can connect with them. For example, we have a group called JAWs: Jewish Actors Workshop— twenty-five kids who work with an educator, a graduate of the program, and they love him. We do a lot of building community in small groups. We have kids who like to cook, who do art, a choir, a leadership course, several *Rosh Hodesh: It's A Girl Thing* groups, several boys' groups *(Jew Man Group)* ... teenagers are interested in gender-based programming; they want a safe space to talk about their own issues with an adult. We run several *Shabbatonim* each year, regular youth group events, a teen-to-teen mentoring program, and social action projects. Our senior rabbi, Joel Sisenwine, says, "If the kids know the aleph-bet, but they don't know each other's names, we have failed." Our culture is all about relationships. The key is having full-time staff around all the time; they keep tabs on a lot of the kids.

5) Experiences

Personal encounters, telling our stories, and connecting people to each other create the foundation for engaging in a Relational Judaism. But, then what? How can institutions move the newly engaged into "action"?

Graham Hoffman makes the startling observation that the "program paradigm" is so strong that it has taken seven years to "change the vocabulary" in the Hillel system:

Programming is the only thing young leadership has been trained to do. Beginning in youth group, at summer camps, in synagogues and JCCs, it's all about creating cute titles, setting up seats, ordering enough food, getting the PR out, and hoping people show up. When are these young leaders taught how to do relational work? Almost never.

The assumption has been that if people come to a program, they will meet others and build friendships. Yet, many participants will say they come to programs and barely meet anybody. Rabbi Rick Jacobs, president of the Union for Reform Judaism, comments:

Programs don't sustain anything. You can have fancy brochures, all sorts of adult learning, Torah study on Shabbat morning. But, then you walk in and wonder: Did anyone know that I was there? Did anyone care that I was there? Buber is the underpinning. If synagogue is based on fancyshmancy Judaically closed I–It relationships where it's all instrumentalities—we want to get people in the building to do this or that—it doesn't work. We are deconstructing the programmatic synagogue; I don't know one that has been sustaining, that is not a lot of smoke and mirrors. The synagogues where it's happening are all built on relationships, webs of deep personal relationships. That's the Jewish tradition.

Rabbi Steven Wernick, CEO of United Synagogue of Conservative Judaism, understands the importance of a relational community; he has literally changed the language of Conservative congregations from "synagogue" to *kehillah*—community. Rabbi Wernick comments:

It's all about relationships today. If "identity" and "affiliation" were the bywords of the past, "engagement" is all about relationships. It's essential for clergy to get out of their offices ... and for kehillah leadership to be part of that relationship building. You can't expect professionals to be the only ones to do that. Relationships are all about the trust that people will make the right decisions based on

> *shared values. Successful synagogues are doing this. We have to move from membership to meaning and from programs to purpose.*

Transforming "programs" into "experiences" is the first "action" task of Relational Judaism. In the field of education, teachers are trained to think of two major goals for every lesson plan to shape the experience in the classroom: *cognitive goals*—what we want students to know as a result of the experience—and *affective goals*—what we want them to feel. We need to add a *relational goal*—how we want our people to deepen relationships, between themselves and others and between themselves and the Nine Levels of Relationship: self, family, friends, Jewish living, community, peoplehood, Israel, the world, and God.

Experiential education has emerged in recent years as one of the most effective efforts to engage people with Judaism. "Immersive experiences," such as summer camp, retreats, conferences, trips to Israel, social justice missions, intensive study opportunities, and organic farming, take the Sovereign-Self Jews out of their daily lives and insert them into real, natural, authentic Jewish environments. These experiences share certain characteristics:

1. Content—something is learned
2. Emotion—something is felt
3. Food—something is eaten
4. Role models—someone leads
5. Action—something is accomplished
6. Celebration—some recognition of achievement

Another important aspect of transformative experiential education is the understanding that the participants are full partners with the leaders in shaping the flow and outcome of the experience. "Programs" often feature an educator, a communal worker, or clergy doing something *to* or *for* the participants. In "experiences," the leaders do something *with* the participants. Barry Chazan, philosopher of Jewish education, calls this "person-centered" Jewish education, a curriculum of Jewish experiences and values, taught through an interactive process within a group experience that truly engages the learner.[10] Joseph Reimer adds that experience is most impactful when it is accompanied by narration and interpretation, something Jews are especially good at, because we have been doing exactly that with the experience of receiving the Torah at Sinai since the event itself.[11] Daniel Libenson has called for a new "education of discovery" in which Jewish leaders and engaged citizens alike embrace the paradigm shifts that will shape the Jewish future.[12]

Relational educators would do well to look at the evolving new model of elementary education championed by Shimon Waronker at The New American Academy in Brooklyn. Eschewing the Prussian model of education adopted by Horace Mann for the public schools of America, a factory model designed to create docile workers for the coming Industrial Revolution (see *The Cult of Efficiency* by Raymond Callahan), Waronker is pioneering a new model that reflects the collaborative and networked reality of the twenty-first century. The guiding vision is a "relationship driven" school where a four-person teaching team moves with their students from grade to grade from kindergarten through fifth grade. As at Ivy League colleges, students are grouped in "houses." Big tables replace individual seats (think the communal table at Le Pain Quotidien), encouraging group conversations and collaborations. The approach offers "unprecedented levels of targeted support, instruction and mentorship for both teachers and students." In the words of *New York Times* columnist David Brooks, The New American Academy

> does a tremendous job nurturing relationships. Since people learn from people they love, education is fundamentally about the relationship between a teacher and student. By insisting on constant informal contact and by preserving that contact year after year, [the school] has the potential to create richer, mentorlike or even familylike relationships for students who are not rich in those things.[13]

It did not surprise me to learn that Headmaster Waronker is an observant Jew, a Chabadnik.

Imagine a new model of Relational Jewish Education that puts relationships between students and teachers, teachers and families, and kids and the Nine Levels of Relationship at the heart of the enterprise. If relationships can transform an American public school serving mostly minority students, it can certainly transform our Jewish schools, which are in urgent need of a new approach to engaging our youth.

Arnold M. Eisen and others have concluded that among all the efforts to engage young Jews with Judaism, three stand out as the most effective: Jewish summer camps, Israel trips, and Jewish day schools. All three share a common approach: they are experiences that thrust participants into intensive, authentic Jewish living situations. All three immersive experiences feature similar characteristics: (1) substantial time, (2) community, and (3) experiential participation. Summer camps and Israel trips are 24/7 experiences, while Jewish day school students spend the majority of their waking hours engaged in the activities of the school. Excellent camps, trips, and schools pay careful attention to creating an actual community that influences behavior, teaches values and content, and enhances the sense of "membership" in the group. All three provide participants with the best way to learn the norms of a culture—experiential engagement with Jewish living. It is one thing to be told how Jews live or even to watch others live Jewishly; it is quite another thing to be immersed within an authentic total Jewish living situation in which learning comes from doing, identity is built from living, and community emerges from relationships.

Why can't we do this in Hebrew schools? The answer is, "Of course, we can."

In my Practicum in Experiential Education at American Jewish University, I take my graduate students in Jewish education on site visits to coffee shops, stores, museums, and educational organizations that have learned how to shape engaging "experiences." It is the world their students and families live in. The Starbucks "experience" includes learning a foreign language (because when is "tall" the smallest serving of coffee?), personalization by writing your name on the cup, and access to a guide for ordering ("I'll have a venti decaf mocha latte with two shots"). At a time when virtually everything can be done on the Internet, shopping malls have necessarily sought to offer "experiences" that cannot be had online. Build-a-Bear Workshops and Color Me Mine studios offer opportunities for creating personalized crafts. Barnes and Noble bookstores have cafés and train sets in the kids' departments. At The Grove in Los Angeles, the outdoor mall itself has become a destination, featuring a concierge and the taping of a popular television program, *Extra*. Westfield Shopping Towns sport activities for kids, including a dedicated indoor playground space, carousels, and even a "Ladybug Express" electric train that circles the hallways. An outlet mall in New Jersey brought in a Lego store that not only sells Legos but also offers classes in Lego construction. American Girl Place entices kids and their parents with museum-like displays of historical dolls (including "Rebecca," a Jewish immigrant girl from the Lower East Side), a beauty shop (for the dolls), a doll hospital, and a tearoom.

SPOTLIGHT ON BEST PRACTICES

The Apple Store Experience

Have you ever visited an Apple Store? The Apple Store is one of the most popular and profitable retail outlets in America, generating an average of $5,600 per square foot and attracting more than twenty thousand visitors a week. Why? Especially when most Apple products can be bought in a box store or online for less money, why would people pay full price in the Apple Store? Here is the answer according to Carmine Gallo, in his book *The Apple Experience: Secrets to Building Insanely Great Customer Loyalty*:

1. Steve Jobs famously stated the purpose of Apple products was "to enrich people's lives" by enabling them to be creative, to share themselves with others, to conduct their businesses more efficiently, and on and on.

2. Apple Store employees are thus a noncommissioned sales force trained to spend as much time as necessary to "build lasting relationships" with customers.

3. "Specialists" offer a warm welcome to those entering the Apple Store within ten seconds or ten feet of the front door.

4. Long tables with fully loaded and wired computers, phones, iPods, and iPads are available for people to use and explore.

5. Each store features a Genius Bar for in-depth consultations with trained experts, who work to "rebuild relationships" with those having difficulties.
6. Purchasers of Mac computers can sign up for One to One private counseling sessions, a $99 one-year membership program. Apple understands that the more you understand, use, and enjoy their products, the more likely you are to have a long relationship with the company.
7. The Apple Store teaches its employees to follow five steps in each and every interaction: Approach with a customized, warm greeting; Probe politely to understand the customer's needs; Present a solution the customer can take home today; Listen for and address unresolved questions; End with a fond farewell and an invitation to return. Yes, the acronym is: APPLE.[14]

Imagine a Jewish institution applying these principles in fashioning a model of "quality service experience" for engaging people. It would begin with a clear vision that the goal is to enrich lives with meaning and purpose, belonging and blessing. Every staff member, every lay leader would practice radical hospitality. They would spend time with each and every individual one-on-one, probing politely for their story to understand their needs. The institution would present a wide variety of Jewish experiences that don't stay in the building, but empower people to "take it home." It would begin by focusing on what many Jews already do—Passover Seder, Hanukkah candle lighting, Bar/Bat Mitzvah celebrations, *brit* and *simchat bat*, weddings, funerals, Yom Kippur break-fasts—and equip them to offer and engage in the experiences with joy, creativity, and meaning. The relationships created would lower barriers to participation and enable people to share their innermost questions and challenges. Everyone would feel inspired and grateful, eager to recommend engagement and affiliation to others. If Apple can do it, why can't we?

SPOTLIGHT ON BEST PRACTICES

The Playground Minyan Experience

Rabbi Noah Farkas has created an engaging Shabbat morning worship experience for families with young children at Valley Beth Shalom in Encino, California. In a preschool classroom immediately adjacent to the early childhood center playground, a portable ark and chairs are set up for a fairly traditional Conservative davening. Lay leaders share in the organizing, prayers, Torah reading, and sermons. But the proximity of the playground allows kids free access to and fro, while parents can pray and watch their children through the classroom windows or join them.

In addition, Rabbi Farkas created a safe space for moms and dads to be with the littlest children in davening space. "My vision is a mom holding a baby and reading Torah for her community. Our children learn to be Jewish by watching us be Jewish. The minyan is a sacred space in which a baby's cry is an accepting amen to any prayer."

Bottom line: think "relational experiences," not "one-off programs."

6) Volunteerism

Volunteerism in the Jewish community is in trouble. I hear the complaints from institutional leaders all the time: "People are too busy." "Dual-career households have decimated a key source of volunteer help." "It's easier to get people to write a check than to donate time."

I think there are other issues at play. There are often so few people volunteering to join "committees" that those who do are made the chairperson immediately. And, once on the committee, it becomes a life sentence—you never get off! Neither pleas nor "please" is working.

The institutional approach to recruiting volunteers is in need of transformation. In the old model, people were given a list of committees to join, and the organization's leaders hoped for the best. Even when individuals checked off something on the intake form, many institutions rarely followed up. The approach is backward. This list of committees emphasizes the priorities and programs of the institution. In a Relational Judaism, the approach to engagement puts people first, not a predetermined list of generalized issues such as "youth committee" or "social justice committee." Rather, individuals are asked to identify their talents, abilities, and passions. Then, and only then, can the institutional leaders link the person with a team or a project-based group to join. This is a far more labor-intensive process than giving people a check-off list, but it has the potential to be much more effective in engaging volunteers.

Time is another problem when it comes to recruiting volunteers. People really are very busy, juggling work, family, and social obligations, especially with the constant pressure of our social networks demanding instantaneous response. One answer is to appeal for volunteers on a time-limited basis. "Are you able to give us three weeks of your help? We have a specific task to do, there will be no long meetings, and when the event is over, we're done." Most people will find the time to respond to this "ask."

Another consideration to improve volunteerism as a path to engagement is to think about how you yourself were recruited to be a volunteer. When I ask people to reflect on this question, the answer I hear most often is, "I was tapped on the shoulder. Someone asked me." The power of personal invitation rests on the foundation of relationship. Asking someone to help out is asking the person to enter into a social contract. If someone you know or respect asks you to participate, the chances of a "yes" are exponentially increased. This is as true in recruiting volunteers as it is in fundraising; personal relationships, knowing someone's passions and concerns, understanding capacity, making the ask, expressing appreciation, following up—these are the critical steps in a relationship-based organization.

Volunteers can be recruited after people share experiences together. Take a mission to Israel, build a Habitat for Humanity house, work a soup kitchen, put on a play, create a quilt, have an adult Bar/Bat Mitzvah … and you are likely to be able to call on people you were with to help out. Find people who share the same passions and interests, who believe in the same cause, and you can gather support. Look to those in the same life stage—singles, parents of young children, parents of teenagers, empty nesters—and recruit them with engagement opportunities shaped to their interests and needs.

The language of volunteerism needs transformation, as well. Changing the business language of "committees" into the relational language of "teams" and "partners" will go a long way toward creating a different ambience among the volunteer corps.

The experience of volunteering itself will be different in an institution informed by Relational Judaism. Working with others on a project can bind people together, but only if attention is paid to relationship building. We learned this lesson in Synagogue 2000 when we insisted that the leadership team begin every session with "check-in," a brief opportunity for every person in the room to share something about her or his personal life. I am reminded of the power of the quilting bee, when groups of women would join together to craft beautiful quilts, but through sharing the stories of their lives as they worked, they crafted deeper relationships among themselves.

The truth is that people eagerly volunteer to help with those organizations in which they have a vested interest. Rabbi Dara Frimmer of Temple Isaiah in Los Angeles observes:

> *The moms in our preschool will do just about anything we ask them to do if they believe it will benefit their children. And they volunteer for other organizations around town whose causes speak to them. Our task is to make the experience of volunteering so compelling and so meaningful and so rich in relationships that they will want to continue to give of their most precious commodity: time.*

For me, volunteering in the Jewish community is a sacred act. We can apply the lesson of the megachurch, which has successfully convinced their volunteers that, whatever they do, they are doing sacred work. The guys who direct traffic, the women who give up their worship experience to greet people, the teams who operate the food pantry, the teenagers who help out in the Sunday school—they have been told over and over again by their pastor that they are doing God's work and that they are partners in the continual process of creation. I am not just speaking of synagogue volunteering; Jewish Federations, support organizations, and Jewish Community Centers all would benefit from reminding their constituents that giving of their time and talent to build community is a *mitzvah*, a sacred responsibility and opportunity. Elevating volunteerism to this level can only enhance the experience for all.

SPOTLIGHT ON BEST PRACTICES

Rabbi Charles Simon relates the following example of elevating volunteerism in his book, *Building a Volunteer Culture* (Jewish Lights Publishing):

> *I remember a senior rabbi in a New England congregation who asked a congregant to accept a volunteer position as an usher for a forthcoming holiday. The volunteer tentatively accepted. The rabbi then personally escorted her to the office, introduced her to each member of the support staff, and explained how each of these people would be available to assist her. The volunteer left the synagogue feeling that she had sufficient support to do her job well.*
>
> *That volunteer rose to a position of prominence in the synagogue after just three years. After each volunteer activity, she was thanked both privately and publicly. Within a few weeks after each time she volunteered she was asked anew to assume another responsibility Once she was asked to train a new volunteer to take her place. On another occasion she was asked to work on a small committee with a specific, well-defined goal. Step by step, she became more enamored of the synagogue and its community. Step by step, she was integrated into the synagogue committee and leadership structure.*[15]

7) Follow-Up

All the engagement efforts in the world will be for naught if there is little or no follow-up. This is a chronic problem in Jewish institutional life. Demographic forms are filled out and collected, even entered into a database, and then no one calls. With the exception of some fundraisers, we do a generally poor job at cultivating and sustaining relationships with our people.

Lisa Colton comments on how most synagogues track their members:

> In most cases, the databases we are using (and the ways in which we use them) are designed to track contact information, attendance at events, and perhaps donations history. Rarely are we using such tools to track, manage, and deepen relationships. As organizations seek to align their work for success in this connected age, we need to focus on strategy, tactics, and culture. Once you have a strategic direction, don't neglect the next two very important steps. Which database do you need, how will your staff use it, and what values and behavior do you need to model to pivot to a relational, connected culture?

A key component of a relational approach to building community is tracking relationships. In an earlier time, organized professionals kept files on each person with whom they had built a relationship. "He has a great Rolodex [a physical card system]" was a common accolade for someone with many contacts. The best of the best at maintaining relationships would use these files and Rolodex cards to keep in touch with the people they met. Today, we have lists of "contacts" on our smartphones, "friends" on Facebook, and "circles" on Google+. Not so long ago, if I wanted to remember someone's birthday, I needed to look for a notation on the person's Rolodex card on my office desk; today, I get an automatic e-mail sent to me a week in advance reminding me that so-and-so's birthday is on such-and-such date. And yet, I yearn for a more personalized response. For Jewish professionals and lay leaders, personal phone calls, handwritten notes, and anything but a form letter or generic e-mail blast can make a huge impression.

SPOTLIGHT ON BEST PRACTICES

Jill Seigerman warns about the weakness of Internet-based communications:

> When we started the community organizing initiative at Central Synagogue a few years ago, we thought an Evite would be the best way to invite congregants to small gatherings to meet with the clergy. We invited congregants to a cocktail party, an intimate gathering, in a member's home with the clergy, to talk about the synagogue and the larger Jewish community. Most people never opened the e-mail invitation; they thought it was regular synagogue correspondence or spam. So, we created a beautiful, personalized invitation that we mailed to the congregants. That worked. We had a 30 percent response rate, the highest we had ever had. People appreciated getting an invitation in the mail.

Rabbi Zoë Klein of Temple Isaiah in Los Angeles, relates:

> When I meet someone, I always ask if I can take a photo: of their dog, their house, their kids. I attach the photo to my follow-up e-mail thanking them for the meeting. We have developed a large adult learning program. I wondered, "How do I employ relational power in this setting?" So, after each class, I let people know that I saw them. I spend a couple of hours sending personal e-mails, saying something that lets them know that I recognized they were there.

We are in the era of "big data." Virtually every company and organization is marshaling the power of computing and the access to personal data in order to learn more about their customers and clients.

The technology to track all this data is called customer relationship marketing (CRM). The basic idea of CRM has crept into nonprofit organizations, as well. Hillel invested hundreds of thousands of dollars to create REACH, the custom-tailored tracking system for Senior Jewish Educators and Campus Entrepreneur Interns to document and follow up every interaction with students on campus. Synagogue 3000's Next *Dor* Network pilot sites are required to submit data using an off-the-shelf CRM software called Karma. The community concierges in Los Angeles use SalesForce. Jconnect and other initiatives simply use data-rich Excel spreadsheets to catalog information about the people who are met.

Here is a screen shot of REACH:

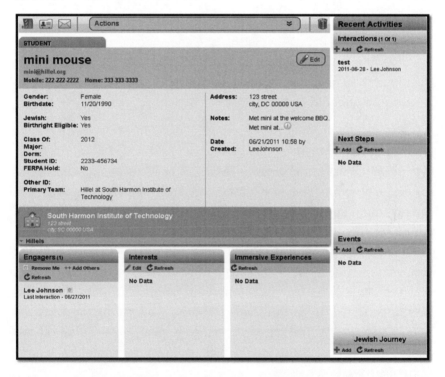

The key to effective data tracking, of course, is the accuracy of the information entered into the database. Frankly, there is often pushback from staff, who feel the effort takes away time from other duties. Remind objectors that doctors are required to take notes on every interaction with patients in a personalized medical record and that therapists keep detailed accounts of each session with clients. The pay-off is a better understanding of your people and a more effective way to follow up with the relationships you are creating, which is, of course, the reason for the data collection in the first place. The bottom line: the leaders embracing Relational Judaism have a wide array of technologies to assist in tracking, maintaining, and building relationships. It takes discipline to enter the data after an encounter, and it takes commitment to follow up to maximize the capability that the era of big data promises.

SPOTLIGHT ON BEST PRACTICES

Some organizations do a good job following up with alumni. At Camp Ramah, Rabbi Ami Hersh is spearheading the development of a smartphone app, Ramah365, designed to keep the thousands of former and current campers connected to each other and to the institution.

8) Transition Points

We do well in our comfort zones. Many of us focus on one area of our institutional work. The early childhood professionals are engaged in the preschool at the JCC and have little connection to the teen youth educators. The synagogue-sponsored day school educators have ten-uous relationships with the program director. The leadership in the various departments of Federation hardly know what their colleagues down the hall do … or, more important, whom they know. It is very easy to be siloed, to work in our own areas, to lose the forest for the trees. As mentioned earlier, we don't do a great job handing off our people from one institution to the next, from one program to the next, from one stage to the next.

There are six transition points on a family's Jewish journey through Jewish institutional life:

1. From institution shopper to member/affiliate
2. From preschool to religious school or day school

3. From Bar/Bat Mitzvah to high school
4. From high school to college
5. From postcollege to young Jewish adulthood
6. From child rearing to empty nesting

Among the questions our people ask:

- We were blessed with our first child. Where can I find other parents with the same age children to talk about parenting? Mommy and Me / Daddy and Me programs?
- Where do I look for preschool?
- What next after preschool? Day school? Religious school?
- How do I go shul shopping?
- Where do I connect with the Jewish community: Federation, Jewish fraternal groups, Zionist organizations, defense agencies?
- Which Jewish summer camp is best for my kids?
- How do I connect with Jewish role models: rabbis, cantors, educators, communal professionals, teachers?
- How do I connect my teenager to a youth educator?
- What about a trip to Israel with the family?
- Once the kids have flown the coop, how do I sustain connection and community?

I understand that it is challenging enough to organize and implement programs, and most leaders cannot imagine how they would find the time to ensure that their people are well coached to make decisions about their next steps when transitioning between these life stages. Yet, the "tap on the shoulder," the gentle encouragement that animates the question "Have you thought about …?," the offer to refer and recommend the next "address" for engagement or the next opportunity for a meaningful experience with other Jews and Jewish living—these are fundamental characteristics of a professional and lay leadership working in a relational culture and our best chance at retaining the affiliation of those in our communities.

Transition Guides

As we saw above, the idea of a "concierge" to assist those with young children to find appropriate points of connection has been quite successful. In MetroWest New Jersey, an early childhood consultancy has taught preschools that forging relationships with families begins with their first inquiry. Building social connections and a web of friendships among the families themselves meets their need for community. If the preschool is in a JCC or synagogue, building bridges to the professionals and lay leadership of the institution can increase the chances of keeping the family engaged with the community after the child moves on to kindergarten or elementary school. Preschool directors ought to ask parents about their plans and help them make decisions. Incentives in the form of reduced tuition, free or discounted membership in a synagogue or JCC, free tickets to family High Holy Day services—all can help to increase the chances of continuing a family's affiliation with an institution.

But, the need for such guidance doesn't end at preschool.

We need the linker of silos, the concierge at the resort who knows all the activities, tourist sites, restaurants, and experiences not to be missed. Imagine a real live Yelp / Zagat / Angie's List referral service. Like a high school college guidance counselor who knows both the individual student and the colleges well and can thus suggest potential successful matchups, we ought to invest in transition guides who are available at these key decision-making moments when Jewish engagement can be sustained or end.

Institutions embracing Relational Judaism will have staff or laypeople who have built relationships with their members and stand ready to help them make decisions about next Jewish steps. In a synagogue, this could be the executive director, a community relationship manager, or a relationship director, certainly as valuable a position as a program director. At Shirat Hayam in Swampscott, Massachusetts, there are "synaguides" who help members and guests navigate the options offered by the congregation. In a JCC, it could be a "cross-seller," a benchmark person, or someone like Rachel Brodie, who after seven years directing Jewish Milestones—an outreach effort to guide unaffiliated Jews into Jewish engagement—now works as the CJO, the "chief Jewish officer," of the JCC of San Francisco. The person could be age related, like a SCORE mentor (a retired business executive), who has a bank of experience on which to draw. At Denver's Judaism Your Way, the staff handles walk-in, call-in, and e-mail requests for connections to all things Jewish, and a trans-denominational rabbi serves the large percentage of unaffiliated people in the area. Each needs training in listening skills, resource accumulation, counseling skills, and follow-up/tracking to feed back into the database of recommendations.

9) Reengagement

In a transactional, program-centric, fee-for-service institution, it is no surprise that once the "service" is completed, the connection between the individual and the organization is easily severed. This is particularly true in synagogues. When the youngest child becomes a Bar/Bat Mitzvah or leaves for college, it is not just the kids who disappear; the parents often drop out, too.

If the institutions wait until these critical transition points to build relationships, it's too late ... way too late. People will simply walk away. But, if their best friends are in the organization, if they are deeply connected to the mission, if they derive meaning and a sense of purpose from their experiences, they will want to go deeper and continue their engagement.

Is there any chance of reengaging those who have dropped out of membership or affiliation? Perhaps.

Certainly, it is worth some effort to reengage those who were once involved in the organization. In the business world, companies work hard at reconnecting with customers and subscribers who have stopped their newspaper deliveries, switched mobile communication providers, or not returned to a particular hotel brand. My inbox was filled with pleas from a weekly magazine when I failed to extend my subscription and from Netflix after I, and millions of others, quit when they radically changed their cost structure. They know that it costs far more to recruit a new customer than to reengage a previous one.

David M. Elcott and Stuart Himmelfarb are tackling the challenge of sustained connection with their B3: The Jewish Boomer Platform initiative to engage—and reengage—Jewish baby boomers to leverage their talent, experience, and resources for the benefit of the Jewish community. In his report *Baby Boomers, Public Service, and Minority Communities: A Case Study of the Jewish Community in the United States*, Elcott rejects the notion that affluent, talented, and time-rich baby boomers will automatically volunteer in the Jewish community.[16] He quotes one focus group participant, a highly influential woman in New York City:

> I am the person you are worried about. I am highly edu-
> cated and pretty demanding. I feel less connected at this
> point in my life. Being involved in the Jewish community
> is not at the top of my list. I am no longer a member of
> a synagogue or of the JCC. I am not really interested in
> volunteering in a Jewish organization. My experiences in
> the Jewish community have not been fabulous. I will look
> elsewhere.[17]

Elcott concludes that Jewish organizations will need to create new approaches to engage baby boomers—using their professional and avocational talents, for example—to secure their involvement in volunteering and those looking for "encore" careers:

> Jews will choose to use a Jewish agency … as long as it is
> equal to or better than a comparable non-Jewish agency. But
> there is little to support the assumption, or even the hope,
> that Baby Boomers will provide the same fidelity to the Jew-
> ish community that was assumed with the prior generation
> and upon which this minority community grew to depend.
> Their allegiance is up for grabs, and as Baby Boomers move
> into this new life passage, the competition for their attention
> and involvement will certainly increase.[18]

The best practice for reengaging the disengaged is a personal invitation from a leader to become involved again, to relearn the person's passions and talents, to put them to use in meaningful service to the community, and to rebuild connections to the Nine Levels of Relationship.

10) Relational Space

Doug Pagitt is the pastor of Solomon's Porch, a "holistic missional Christian community" in Minneapolis, Minnesota. It is not "your father's church" ... not by a long shot. Pagitt's father, a big megapastor, took his young son on a tour of his megachurch complex and said, "Someday, son, this will all be yours." Pagitt answered, "I don't want it." Instead, he helped found the Emergent Church, a backlash to the megachurch movement. Along with colleagues Brian McLaren and Tony Jones, Pagitt reinvented "church" by focusing on traditional ritual, serious Bible text study, commitment to social justice, and building relationships. To physically reflect this shift, Pagitt and his congregation renovated an old church by tearing out the pews and installing big comfy couches, small sitting areas, and coffee tables—all designed to look like a private living room. As Pagitt puts it, "Do something with sacred space that aligns with your theology." This is a "relational space," conducive to conversations, face-to-face interaction, and relationship building. An entire wall features a collage of pictures of the diverse faces of people in the congregation.

Rabbi Karyn Kedar understands the power of relational space. She and her lay partners at B'nai Jehoshua Beth Elohim in Deerfield, Illinois, have created a spectacularly welcoming environment for building community. At the entrance of the synagogue building, an expansive lobby that looks like a reading room in a modern public library invites members and visitors to interact with each other. There are small sitting areas for conversation, a play area for children, a café, and tall tables for stand-up chats. Key values of the congregation— "Faith," "Courage," "Wisdom"—are inscribed in both English and Hebrew on columns framing the space. One wall features enclosed bins for collecting food, shoes, clothing, and other items for distribution to the needy. There is no library room stuck in the back of the building; the collection of books is sprinkled throughout the lobby on shelves, offering easy access for reading. An oblong alcove in the rear of the lobby contains the memorial plaques, a quiet meditative area for reflection. In the entryway to the building, an unfinished segment of the wall sports a simple Lucite sign: "The world is not completed. We are completing it."

Find ways to build relational space in lobbies, office waiting areas, lounges, and in synagogues—even in the sanctuary itself.

Beyond the Walls

One of the principle strategies of a Relational Judaism is to loosen the fetters of buildings. In the paroxysm of growth that fueled the Jewish community in the 1950s and 1960s as a result of the post–World War II baby boom and the move to the suburbs, hundreds of synagogues, schools, JCCs, Hillel Houses, Jewish country clubs, and other places of Jewish communal gathering were built. These edifices served—and continue to serve—the important function of providing a safe Jewish space within which to congregate, learn, worship, act, and celebrate.

Yet, there are those who find the thought of stepping inside these places intimidating, even anathema. For some, it is fear—fear that someone will ask you to do something that you are clearly uncomfortable or unwilling to do. For others, there is simply no need for Jewish health clubs or golf courses now that we have been almost totally accepted in the mainstream American society. For young Jewish adults, the attraction of these places is limited.

For organizations that understand this hesitancy and still want to reach these populations, the emergence of Judaism in the public space seeks to bring Jewish experience out of the buildings and into the homes, workplaces, shopping malls, and restaurants where most Jews live and spend time. To cite just a few examples:

- "When Three Stars Appear"—a Jewish family education experience of *Havdalah*, the ceremony separating Shabbat from the rest of the week, held at the local planetarium/observatory, where one looks for stars
- Hillel sponsoring Jewish celebrations in dorms and Israel advocacy at tables in the campus quadrangle
- Chabad rabbis taking shoppers on a kosher-for-Passover tour of local supermarkets
- Rabbi Dan Moskovitz of Temple Judea in Tarzana, California, teaching Torah and building a sukkah at a local Whole Foods market

- Wexner Heritage Foundation teaching Jewish studies courses in law offices
- Jewish Outreach Institute's "Mothers Circles," a small-group experience for interfaith moms raising Jewish children, meeting in each other's homes
- American Jewish University's public lecture series at the Gibson Amphitheatre in Universal City, California

An interesting wrinkle in public-space Judaism is the popularity of "pop-up" stores and events. These are one-off or short-term experiences designed to attract crowds that otherwise might not come to the normal bricks-and-mortar building. For example, a well-known gourmet French chef, Ludo Lefebvre, gave up his successful restaurant in Los Angeles to go on the road to cities across America where, in a week's time, he and his wife create a pop-up restaurant called LudoBites, which serves one meal only before moving on to the next community. My son Michael's best friend, Andrew Kessler, created a pop-up bookstore in Manhattan with three thousand copies of exactly one book, *Martian Summer: Robot Arms, Cowboy Spacemen, and My 90 Days with the Phoenix Mars Mission* by, you guessed it, Andrew Kessler. In December 2011, a pop-up 1950s-style record store in the popular Mission District of San Francisco called Tikva Records attracted hundreds of people to listen to and buy Jewish music during the run-up to Hanukkah.

Taking Judaism and Jewish experiences out of institutional buildings to where the Jews are is a powerful strategy to reach the unengaged and under-affiliated.

11) Relational Membership Models

How does a Relational Judaism membership model look different from a fee-for-service model? In the fee-for-service model, I pay dues up front and you—JCC—give me access to the gym, the pool, the library, the classes, the preschool for my kids, the summer camp, and the cultural arts programs. Likewise, I pay dues up front and you—synagogue—give me High Holy Day seats, a religious school for my kids, and a rabbi on call. But in the Relational Judaism model, I am welcomed into a relationship with others in the community—professionals and lay—who care deeply about me, learn about me, network me, teach me, and are there for me in good times and bad. And once in relationship, I will give back to the community my time and my treasure out of gratitude. The truth is that those who have this level of relationship with a community often give larger donations beyond the normal "dues."

Rabbi Stephanie Kolin relates a horror story:

> I have a neighbor whose mother died recently. She called a rabbi at a large synagogue in town to ask if he would officiate at the funeral. The rabbi says he's sorry, but the synagogue policy prevents him from doing the funeral: "We can't officiate at funerals and weddings of nonmembers." My neighbor doesn't understand this; she is completely turned off, rejected, bereft. She doesn't know where to turn. Do you think she'll be joining a synagogue anytime soon? And yet, these life-cycle moments are exactly when you can make Jews. Aren't we shooting ourselves in the foot by adhering to policies like this instead of opening our doors when people reach out?

This relational model of membership must begin at the very beginning of the relationship between institution and individual. The megachurches understand this fully: from the minute you express interest in belonging (not "joining"), you are inducted into a culture of relationships with the people of the spiritual community and with God. In a four-session seminar, you are taught not simply about the benefits of belonging to the church; you are also taught about the obligations and responsibilities of being a member of the church.

Some Jewish spiritual communities are not shying away from this approach; they are openly embracing it.

IKAR

According to Melissa Balaban, executive director of IKAR (http://ikar-la.org), the leadership has steadfastly held to several core values: lower the bar for entrance, raise the bar for participation, offer a warm welcome, and create high expectations among the community that everything will be done with excellence. She explains:

> At IKAR, someone can come to services as much as you like and enjoy the sit-down Shabbat lunch, for no cost whatsoever. However, once you decide to join IKAR as a member, you agree to do four things:
>
> 1. Community building. *We have a bare-bones staff, so we need your help. You can host a house party. You can build our website. You can coordinate High Holy Days. We'll find something for you to do. The first expectation is that you will give of your talents.*
> 2. Learning. *The second expectation is that we expect you to be learning. Everyone is on a learning journey, even if you're a rabbi or rabbinical student. That's the ikar ("essence") of Judaism.*
> 3. Social justice. *The third expectation is that you will find a way to engage in the sacred work of social justice. We expect you to engage in our* Minyan Tzedek *work—food justice, immigration issues, direct service to those in need. You will receive a "spiritual pledge card" on the High Holy Days to make your commitment.*
> 4. Financial contribution. *Everyone at IKAR gives something. Some give $18, a lot give $180, some give $1,800 or much more. We make recommendations to you for your fair share. We expect that you will value your experience at IKAR so highly, you will be motivated to give generously to support your community.*

Kavana

Kavana (http://kavana.org) is an independent Jewish community in Seattle, Washington, led by Rabbi Rachel Nussbaum. It does not identify with any specific denominational label. Its mission:

> To create a supportive communal environment in which individuals and families can use *"kavana"*—intention—to create a Jewish life that is spiritually fulfilling, intellectually satisfying, fun, and meaningful.

Kavana is the first Jewish spiritual community organized as a "co-op," a cooperative model in which "partners" share in the task of creating Jewish life for themselves and for the group. As a pluralistic and nondenominational community, Kavana attracts participants from very diverse backgrounds and provides multiple entry points for Jewish involvement. Although one of its offers is "personalized Judaism in a community context," Kavana acknowledges and embraces the dynamic tension between the needs and interests of individuals and the obligations of community. As might be expected in a co-op in the Pacific Northwest, Kavana believes that Jewish communal life "will best thrive in settings which are local, organic, and intimate."

The most unusual aspect of the co-op model is how individuals and families become "partners." As at IKAR—and most other synagogues and JCCs—everyone is welcome to participate in virtually every aspect of the community. However, Kavana expects that regular participants will choose to become partners, to better support both themselves and the community in the process. Partners get special benefits that non-partners do not, including access to the rabbi, staff, and other partners to create their own "personalized Judaism in a community context." They receive discounts on event fees, have the opportunity to participate in governance, and help set policies of the community. Partners also accept certain obligations, including meeting with the rabbi to define what partnership will look like for each person, participating in various activities regularly, and making contributions of time and money. There is no minimum contribution required to become a partner of Kavana. The organization cites the Talmud teaching that the longer someone has been part of a community, the greater the responsibility to maintain it: "After one month of living in a city, you were expected to contribute to a fund for the poor. After one year, you were also expected to contribute to a fund that maintained the walls of the city." The goal is for partners to become producers of their own Jewish lives, with the support of an engaging rabbi and a vibrant community.

A Community Passport

In London, the Liberal Jewish community offers an innovative Passport to Liberal Judaism program targeting young Jewish adults ages twenty to thirty-five. For a monthly fee, individuals receive a "passport" good for access to all Liberal Judaism synagogues, complimentary tickets to High Holy Day services, and discounts at a variety of events. Membership fees for those under the age of twenty-two (or in full-time education) are £7 per month, £84 (about $135) annually. Fees start for those aged twenty-two at £8 per month, £96 (about $154) annually, and rise with every birthday by £1 per month or £12 per year. The maximum fee is £20 per month or £240 (about $384) per year at age thirty-five.[19]

Might a major Jewish community in North America adopt a similar strategy?

Chabad ... Again

Whenever the subject of money comes up, leaders of most membership-based Jewish institutions will say, "We could never go to voluntary dues or depend on contributions. People won't pay. We would be out of business."

Perhaps, just perhaps, someday the community will begin to present the notion of "membership in the Jewish people."

Of course, Chabad has already mastered this approach; *shluchim* do not distinguish between "members" and "nonmembers." Every Jew is seen as "belonging" to the Jewish people, and "every Jew" is the target of Chabad. How do they raise a billion dollars annually? From people (as noted below, mostly non-Orthodox Jews) grateful for the relationship with a Chabad rabbi and from deep-pocket donors who appreciate their approach to engaging Jews with Judaism. Chabad turns the membership model upside down. Instead of "first pay your dues and then we'll serve you," Chabad believes "first we'll serve you and then you'll pay your contribution."

SPOTLIGHT ON BEST PRACTICES

In a widely read piece in *eJewish Philanthropy*, "Scrapping Synagogue Dues," Rabbi Dan Judson, a doctoral candidate at Brandeis University studying synagogues and money, presents the intriguing story of one large Conservative synagogue in suburban Boston, Temple Israel of Sharon, Massachusetts. In 2008, the congregation was facing a significant problem of declining revenue from dues. The price point had become so high that families were leaving. Even though members could apply for "dues abatement," it was clear that the process was embarrassing, so families just left. When the recession hit, things reached the point where a complete rethinking of the dues structure was urgent.

The first thought was to move to "fair share" dues, common in many synagogues, requiring 1 to 1.5 percent of the adjusted gross income of the family. According to Rabbi Judson, this was a nonstarter. What they came up with was even more radical; they abandoned dues altogether in favor of voluntary contributions. Members were told a "sustaining amount" each family would need to pay to meet the budget. They were encouraged to give more if feasible, but the message was, "You tell us how much you're going to pay."

Initially, revenue did decline, but at a lower rate (4 percent) than the decline in the previous year under the old system. However, within three years, revenues were actually up, despite the lingering recession. Moreover, the synagogue gained a net of twenty new families, reversing the previous steady decline of numbers. Some disaffiliated families returned to membership. Most important, the voluntary system fundamentally changed the nature of the relationship between members and the congregation. The whole culture of money was transformed from the formerly mandatory system, which often required synagogue leaders to chase down late payers and subject others to the humiliating abatement process, into a more pleasant voluntary ambience. Rob Carver, president of Temple Israel, concludes:

> *I hear complaints all the time from synagogue leaders that people treat synagogues like a fee for service business. But in fact synagogues don't do anything to counteract this mentality other than complain. We have done something proactive here; we have said that we care about you, that we want you to have a true stake in what we do here.*[20]

See www.tisharon.org/a_unique_dues_alternatives for how the idea is presented.

For twenty-five years in bucolic Vermont, members of the Woodstock Area Jewish Community, Congregation Shir Shalom, have embraced an entirely voluntary financial support policy. According to Stuart and Antoinette Matlins, cofounders of the synagogue, "Participants value the community and its style and want to see it thrive. This approach, combined with a welcoming congregational style, particularly to interfaith families, has allowed many people who no longer participated in synagogue life, and many among them who had the usual complaints about dues/pay to pray, to get over their hurt and hostility and join in our congregation."

Rabbi Jessica Zimmerman, director of congregational engagement for Synagogue 3000, alerted me to the interesting approach of Northern Virginia Hebrew Congregation. The synagogue requires dues to join, but it lists two options for religious school costs: subsidized tuition and regular tuition. After presenting the families with a transparent accounting of the real expenses in operating the religious school, often the most expensive line in a synagogue budget, parents can decide to pay "full freight" or a reduced, subsidized amount. In the end, the congregation raised an extra $20,000 by giving members the choice.

VOICES FROM THE COMMUNITY

At Shirat Hayam in Swampscott, Massachusetts, the congregation is experimenting with a "revenue revolution." Two aspects of their effort are intriguing. First, they have transformed the generic annual High Holy Day appeal into the *Lev* Initiative, the name derived from the instruction "And Adonai spoke to Moses, saying: Speak to the people of Israel, that they bring me an offering; from every man that gives it willingly with his heart, you shall take my offering" (Exodus 25:1–2); the Hebrew word for "heart" is *lev*. Rabbi Baruch HaLevi and Ellen Frankel explain:

> The Lev Initiative is designated or directed giving.... We make phone calls and sit down with people face-to-face. We discuss investing in areas within synagogue life that they are connected to, utilize, and that they want to see flourish.... With the Lev Initiative, we have far surpassed previous fundraising efforts. We have done so in a way that makes it personal, that connects people with what they use and with what they love.[21]

Even with their success in adopting the strategy of donor-directed giving, a common practice in Jewish Federations and other organizations, Shirat Hayam has gone a step further in raising revenues. They make transparent what other synagogues know, but rarely admit publicly: the "nonprofit" organization needs to have "profit" centers. At Shirat Hayam, these include a preschool, the Bezalel Academy offering private or group lessons in the arts, a University of Judaism of courses for adult learning, shulcasting funerals, virtual *Yizkor*, and legacy video testimonials. But, perhaps the most radical of ideas is the Zuzzim think tank, an independent group of entrepreneurs and business owners who are committed to creating and implementing business-to-business and business-to-consumer networking to facilitate Jews doing business with one another. When they do, a percentage of profits is donated to the synagogue or another Zuzzim member institution. This is taking the "buy scrip to shop at your local supermarket and we get a 5 percent kickback from the store" model a huge step further. Whether any or all of these creative ideas for raising money will work remains to be seen, but give Rabbi HaLevi and his colleagues props for thinking out of the box and developing new revenue streams to support Jewish institutions in an era when the dues model is under fire.

The Church Model

Josh Nathan-Kazis, a reporter for the *Forward*, investigated the question, do churches and synagogues of comparable sizes raise the same amount of money? Churches raise most of their money through voluntary weekly contributions, while synagogues depend on dues. It turns out that both raise about the same amount of money.[22] According to Dan Judson, the success of churches in raising voluntary contributions is not simply the passion of the people for the community:

> Protestant America has spent the past 100+ years developing a concept that they call "stewardship," which provides a theological understanding for people to give to their church. We don't have that. My sense is that if the voluntaristic approach to giving becomes an important paradigm for synagogues, it will have to develop its own comparable Jewish language.

In a Relational Judaism, we will need to create that language, language rooted in the fact that meaningful relationship leads to commitment, financial and otherwise. Part of the language has to create a transparency about what it costs to operate our Jewish institutions. To those who question, "Why do we have to pay to pray?" Rabbi Ed Feinstein answers, "You don't pay to pray. Praying is free. But, you want a prayer book? Lights? Air conditioning when it's ninety-eight degrees on Yom Kippur day? A rabbi to respond when your mother is in the hospital? Those things cost."

A good beginning would be for our communal institutions to be much more transparent about the real costs of doing business. I don't know one synagogue that makes its audited financial statement available to the public on its website; some churches do this … and so does every 501c3 nonprofit organization in America. We also need to teach that what exists now was built by earlier generations who knew we would need it; our responsibility is to sustain it … and keep building for our descendants. It doesn't help to make the financial challenges a whispered conversation. Another idea: invite committed donors to give testimonials about why they support the organization, the value the institution offers, and the good feelings that come from their investment in the Jewish future.

When we create institutions that put people first, that elevate "membership" to "belonging," that offer experiences of individual Jewish growth and deep relationships with the Nine Levels of Relationship, we will see *relational giving* as an imperative that is joyfully and gratefully accepted as part of our new institutional culture.

12) Relational Leadership

What is the role of the leader in a Relational Judaism?

In my conversations with a number of professionals who "get" relational work, two models of leadership emerge: personal relationships and community relationships. Some leaders focus their energies and time on building relationships with as many individuals as they can, while others believe it is more important to empower peer-to-peer microcommunities of relationships. The two approaches are not mutually exclusive; in fact, the best relationship builders I know manage to do both.

Many clergy and Jewish communal professionals claim they are so tied up in committee meetings and other programmatic responsibilities that they barely have any time for building relationships. Yet, Rabbi Rick Jacobs, who served a large Reform synagogue for eighteen years, observes, "If people say they don't have time to do one-on-one meetings, they're just pretending to be too busy."

Listen to Arnold M. Eisen, chancellor of The Jewish Theological Seminary of America:

> I would say that for the average rabbi, the most fulfilling thing that he or she does involves relationships. It is why they find life-cycle moments so meaningful—because of

the relationships that are involved. They get a chance to relate as a human being to other human beings on a deep level; they all find this to be a great privilege. I hear people complain that the Chabad rabbis have all the time in the world on their hands. They can afford to sit in the hospital for hours because they don't have to go to ten committee meetings … and they're right. But you're right that it's more important to go to the hospital than to those ten committee meetings. We all know this: you can lose a congregant forever if you're not there for them at the moment when they need you. People will forgive the rabbi for bad sermons but will not forgive the rabbi for bad pastoral care.

VOICES FROM THE COMMUNITY

I am sitting in the audience at a major conference of Jewish communal professionals. Just before my friend is to give the keynote speech, I ask him how things are going in his world. He shakes his head disapprovingly, knowing of my interest in synagogue life:

> You won't believe this, Ron. Four generations of my family have been members of our synagogue. My mother-in-law was hospitalized this summer, and the senior rabbi never showed up to visit. She was devastated. They've decided to leave the congregation. Their friends are there, their community is there, but the rabbi didn't have time to visit? They're outta there.

Relationships, even long-term relationships, can be severed in an instant; there is something quite emotional about the relationship between people and Jewish institutions. I understand this may be a rare occurrence, but the exception proves the rule: it's all about relationships.

The middle name of JCC is "community." Joy Levitt, executive director of the JCC in Manhattan, tells staff:

> *Your job is building relationships, not programming. I get this question all the time: "How much time should I be spending on programs?" and "How much time should I be spending on building relationships, listening to what people need?" They think: "I'm a programmer. I've got a schedule. I've got to fill my page. I've got to meet my budget. So, I'm going to come up with a whole bunch of programs, and I'll hope and pray that people will come." Some programs will be good; some not so good. It's a little bit of a hamster wheel. That's different than being available, meeting people when they walk into the building and hearing what they need and want. Almost everything good that we've developed here has come from a relationship with one of our people who has suggested things for us to do, from conversations with people who feel like you know them, you're listening to them, you care about them. Staff need to figure out how to balance their organizational responsibilities and their time on building relationships. If you're so busy that you don't know the people you're working for, you're not doing the right work. At the end of the day, that's actually the job—to put the notion that everyone is made in the image of God in the center of your work.*

Scheduling Time for Relationships

There is no doubt that the lives of Jewish communal professionals and clergy are extraordinarily demanding. For some, it feels like a 24/7 job, 365 days a year. The balancing of personal and professional responsibilities is challenging, often on a daily basis. A healthy community requires healthy professionals; I will be the first to insist on downtime, days off, vacations, and respites for our communal servants.

However, if building relationships is the key to building communities of meaning and purpose, belonging and blessing, then a reallocation of time on task is an urgent requirement in our Jewish institutions.

Measuring Success has gathered data on how clergy and professionals spend their time. Data from a survey of twelve New York–area synagogues reveals rabbis spend 9 percent of their time performing pastoral counseling—one-on-one or small-group interactions with members of the community. This is time well spent, as individuals who met with a rabbi at least once a year for pastoral counseling had both higher Net Promoter Scores and Jewish Growth Scores. When the analysis is broadened to include interactions such as shiva and hospital visits, social gatherings with congregants outside the synagogue, and maintaining donor relationships, rabbis spent 21 percent of their time on average personally interacting with approximately 17 percent of their constituency.

What would it mean for a synagogue if a rabbi doubled down and spent 40 percent of his or her time in Jewish conversations with individual congregants? The data suggest it is the personal relationship that affects the likelihood to recommend the congregation to a friend and moves individual Jewish growth. After sharing this data with the leadership of the twelve synagogues, Measuring Success reports rabbis have been changing how they use their time.

Measuring Success also conducted time-on-task analysis for senior management in Jewish Federations across North America. On average, time spent in internal meetings, office work, and day-to-day operations (43 percent) was more than double the amount of time senior management spent cultivating donor relationships through one-on-one meetings (20 percent). Time cultivating donors is linked with top donor gift increases, higher agency health scores, higher board attendance scores, and higher average campaign gifts. It also turned out to be good for the senior managers themselves—the more time spent with donors correlated to a higher promotion rate.

But, what if I work in a large institution? How many "relationships" can I realistically create and maintain? Robin Dunbar, a British anthropologist, asserts that there is a finite limit to how many relationships the average human being can have at one time. He arrived at this conclusion by developing an equation based on the size of the neocortex relative to the brain to determine the size of any primate's social grouping. He explains the "Dunbar number" for humans:

> The figure of 150 seems to represent the maximum number of individuals with whom we can have a genuinely social relationship, the kind of relationship that goes with knowing who they are and how they relate to us. Putting it another way, it's the number of people you would not feel embarrassed about joining uninvited for a drink if you happened to bump into them in a bar.[23]

For a Relational Judaism professional, recruiting other colleagues and lay leaders to build relationships and create peer-to-peer microcommunities is absolutely essential. In an institution committed to creating a relational culture, everyone will find time to connect with others, including the microcommunity of the professional staff within the organization. Allowing time for building good working relationships among colleagues is fundamental in creating a "culture of honor" and avoiding a "culture of blame."

For both professionals and lay leaders, I suggest a simple exercise: create a time chart over the course of two weeks to track how hours are actually allocated. Ask a simple question: Is this time I am spending building relationships, strengthening our community? Is it absolutely necessary for me to be there? Might someone else be empowered to do certain tasks that can free me to do the work I uniquely must do to engage people with the Jewish experience?

Then, invest in a course, a book, a strategy for improving your time management. If building relationships is a goal, then schedule time in your weekly calendar for one-on-one meetings. Find a way to meet people in public space; get out of the building. Open your home and engage people on a different level of relationship over a Shabbat dinner table, a holiday celebration, a "house party." Set a goal of connecting with a specific number of people each week. Work with others to create ways to engage people in peer-to-peer relationships in small groups, in neighborhood *havurot*. Become a relational leader.

SPOTLIGHT ON BEST PRACTICES

Rabbi David Paskin of Temple Beth Abraham in Canton, Massachusetts, has a button on the synagogue web page, Meet with Rabbi Paskin, that enables anyone to schedule a meeting with him during available time slots.

Rabbi Greg Litcofsky, now senior rabbi at Temple Emanu-El in Livingston, New Jersey, got hooked on community organizing while in rabbinical school at Hebrew Union College–Jewish Institute of Religion in New York. In his previous position as an associate rabbi of Temple Shir Tikva in Wayland, Massachusetts, Rabbi Litcofsky used his passion for organizing to lead his community. Here's his story:

> *Organizing is a skill set to be a leader, to build community, starting with people, not programs. When I got the job at Temple Shir Tikva, I immediately set about to meet the congregants. I asked my senior, Neal Gold, and the president, Trudy Sonis, "Whom should I meet?" Within the first few months, I had done thirty to forty one-on-one meetings. These were not justice meetings; they were just relational meetings. The meetings were never held in my office, always at the bagel shop, at Starbucks, some open space. People would joke about Greg and his coffees, but for me it was my legacy. I did good programs, but I am most proud of my relational work.*
>
> *During these one-on-ones, I would ask questions to get to know them: "What are you most proud of? Why did you join Shir Tikva? Why did you move here? What are your hopes for the synagogue?" Then, I shared my story with them. At the end of the conversation, I would ask their advice: "I'm thinking about developing*

experiences for young families. What do you think? Am I missing something ... or on to something?"

You know what I realized? My young family leadership team came from these meetings. I wasn't just having nice conversations. I was building relationships with some who evolved into Jewish leaders. I wanted the people to feel they could own it, be part of it, work with me to bring vision to fruition. You can't do that without relationship.

Rabbi Charles Simon, executive director of the Federation of Jewish Men's Clubs, has instilled a culture of caring relationship in the Conservative movement's men's organization. He comments:

Building relationships is about trust and taking risks. When I took over the Men's Clubs, the leadership meetings were full of tension and disagreements. The guys didn't really know each other. The culture had to change. So I taught them how to hug. Literally, I would hug each and every one of them. In the first three minutes of engaging them, I would ask them about their lives, their families, their health. It was a personal check-in. Slowly, I taught them by modeling a culture of engagement. My language was being mirrored in action.

Amy Dorsch of United Synagogue Youth says:

I think we assume that the nature of a teenage Jewish youth group is social—that friendships will just form automatically through our programs. That may be true, but what's going to make them come to us? Technology is great, but it is disconnecting us from reaching out to our kids personally. I think we're really feeling the effects of the lack of personal contact. I see the difference between the chapters with full-time youth directors who really know their constituents or make the effort to be present over the phone and in the community and the part-time advisor who posts programs on Facebook and expects forty kids to show up.

Rabbi Daniel G. Zemel of Temple Micah in Washington, D.C., comments:

Here's how I work. I have no committees ... at least, no committees that I'm on. But I have lots of ideas. So for me to spread my message of what I think Temple Micah is all about, I have to talk to people or the ideas stay with me. I read a lot. When I read books that I think can make the people of Micah a better Jew, I'll ask six to eight people to read the book, and then I'll meet with them over the course of a few months to discuss what it means for Temple Micah. These aren't "committees"; I have a lot of "thinking groups" at Temple Micah. So, I build relationships with them around these ideas.

The most important part of my job is to know my people. I have lunch with members at least two times a week. I call them up; "I want to get to know you, why you wanted to join Micah." I target new members especially. I want to know why they joined. The rabbi has to know the community. That's what the Talmud says: "Go out and see what the people are doing." I follow up ... and I network people ... after my conversation with them. Once I get to know them and they get to know me, then I can put them on the map of Temple Micah—this person can do this, this person can do that. Then, I connect the people to a purpose.

Rabbi Zoë Klein of Temple Isaiah in Los Angeles comments:

> For a long time, we clergy would go into the preschool classrooms to tell stories to the kids. We'd go to three classes in a row on one morning; it was exhausting. But, we were still getting complaints from the parents: "We don't know the rabbi." What? What other rabbis are on the floor with your kids? Eventually, the preschool director said, "You know what I think they want? They want you in the lobby to say 'hello.' More than the three hours you tell stories each week, they actually want the fifteen minutes in the morning to say, 'Hi, how are you?'" So, we started greeting people in the lobby ... which freed up our schedules ... and people felt connected and good. It didn't seem logical at first, but it makes sense.

Rabbi Noah Farkas of Valley Beth Shalom in Encino, California, offers a succinct summary of a relationship-based vision of leadership:

> Leadership is not something you do to people. Leadership is gathering people to do something together. The ability to act comes from organizing people, hearing their stories and concerns, and then agitating them to use their power to change the world. Rabbis can give a good sermon, executives can cast a vision, but that's nowhere near as powerful as building relationships that lead to action.

Cantor Howard Stahl of Temple B'nai Jeshurun in Short Hills, New Jersey, comments on the role of the *hazzan*:

> The best part of my job has nothing to do with music. I never really consider myself a musician or a singer. I don't have the personality for it. To me, it's all about relationships. I could be sitting with a congregant, helping

> *them through a difficult time, or sitting with a kid—a two-year-old, a four-year-old, even a twenty-year-old—and watching them absorb everything like a sponge. It's communicating with the congregation on a multitude of levels: laughing, crying, sitting over a cup of coffee schmoozing, or really learning.*[24]

The truth is that no one leader—rabbi, cantor, educator, JCC director, Federation executive—has the time to build relationships all day. Moreover, leaders of large institutions can never be in relationship with everyone. Peer-to-peer relationships are as important in building community. Thus, the task for the communal professionals is twofold: build personal relationships *vertically*—between staff and many, many individuals—and build relational microcommunities among individuals *horizontally.* "This is the only way to reach scale," according to Rabbi Jonah Pesner. "It took Rabbi Jeremy Morrison two years working full-time at the Riverway Project at Temple Israel of Boston to reach one thousand people, but once he recruited young leaders to build their own relational subcommunities, the initiative really took off." This is the power of relational leadership—it takes the collaboration of professionals and lay leaders to fashion a relational community.

Listen to Rabbi Dan Smokler of the Bronfman Center for Jewish Life at New York University:

> *My job requires me to engage 180 Jewish students on campus each year. I build relationships with individuals, but I also try to grow microcommunities. If I can get eight couples to celebrate a potluck Shabbat dinner once a month, if I can get ten students to learn together on a regular basis, they will be sharing significant Jewish experiences together that don't rely on a single staff member. My goal is to link an individual to a social and self-sustaining community. Eventually, I'll age out. I don't want to be spending every night meeting one-on-one in coffee shops and bars. I want to be with my own family. More importantly, it is community that has staying power.*

When it comes to leadership, relationships matter. No excuses. Find the time to build an institution of relationships, beginning with you. The famous saying in *Pirke Avot* 1:6, *Aseh l'kha rav, uk'nei l'kha haver,* "Make for yourself a rabbi/teacher/mentor/leader and acquire a friend," is a fundamental principle of Jewish education. In Relational Judaism, additionally, we will reverse the dictum: *Aseh l'kha haver, uk'nei l'kha rav,* "Make yourself a friend to your people, and they will make you their rabbi/teacher/mentor/leader."

The Costs of Relational Leadership

Inevitably, the question will be asked, "What are the costs of our professionals spending time building relationships and microcommunities?" No doubt, the single greatest expense in the Relational Judaism transformation is time. This will be labor-intensive work; there is no way around it. Large organizations will need to hire new relational positions. Smaller institutions will need to reallocate time. This is not about bigger and fancier buildings; we've already been through an "edifice complex" in North American Jewish history. Expensive programs may bring people out of their homes for an event, but the effect is transitory. Spend the money on time, on six-dollar coffee receipts, on Shabbat luncheons for all. Build a staff that understands our most important task in Jewish organizational life is to connect with our people and to connect them with each other and with the Nine Levels of Relationship with the Jewish experience. We can afford no less.

VOICES FROM THE COMMUNITY

At the JOIN Conference, I asked a group of rabbis who had already trained in community organizing how they could rearrange their schedules to allow for more relational work. Here were their top answers:

1. Lock the office for certain hours of the week to ensure staff will be out of the building, building relationships.

2. Just as there is a fixed time for learning on the calendar to study with two *hevruta* partners, schedule one-on-one relational meetings the same way.
3. Protect time away from the building to meet people.
4. Carve out time for the leadership team.
5. Empower laypeople to write and deliver *divrei Torah*.
6. Reduce time reading blogs and article research.
7. Turn Shabbat once a month into a relational meeting.
8. Turn and talk during services.
9. Invest in money for more staff.
10. Invite people to members' homes for Shabbat and holiday meals.

I will add one more suggestion for loosening up time for professionals: excuse them from unnecessary attendance at meetings of lay leaders. A rabbi does not have to be present at every single committee meeting of the congregation. Federation staff members do not have to clutter their calendars with endless meetings. Empower your dedicated professionals to spend their precious time building relationships.

A Word of Caution

I know you, my friends. I know that when you, my lay leader friends, read about this "best practice" or that "strategy," your first inclination is to underline it, Post-It note it, and run to your rabbi or executive director or president and say, "See, if you only did this, or we only did that, we would solve our problems." I know that you, my professional friends, read these "spotlights" by colleagues and think, "Hmm, that's interesting, but my community is so different, it'll never work."

If you are serious about transforming your communities from program-centric to relational, remember two crucial guidelines as you seek to implement change:

1. Think "application," not "replication." Every organization, every community is unique, with its own set of

challenges and opportunities. As you review these many examples of relational best practices and discuss them with your leadership team, consider how to adapt them, not necessarily adopt them. Focus not on the best practice but on the underlying best principle that informs what the organization and their leaders are doing.

2. There are no quick fixes. Please reread the opening chapter of the book. Transforming our institutions into relational communities will not happen by devising and implementing another new program. The whole point of the book is that this moment in Jewish history requires a total rethinking of our goal, our strategies for engagement, and what will count for our success. Success is not more butts in seats at programs; it is more relationships between our people and between our people and the Nine Levels of Relationship with the Jewish experience. We cannot continue to count on programs to engage our people. The fundamental principle of every "best practice" cited here is this: to shift the shape of Jewish engagement, we must put people first—learn their stories, learn their passions and their talents, lead them to a meaningful engagement with Judaism, sustain their engagement throughout their lives, particularly at key transition points, and build relationships with others in a relational community. Do this and you will discover and create your own path toward a Relational Judaism.

6

The Challenges Ahead

Options for a Shrinking Community

I am invited to give two lectures—one in the fall, one in the spring—for an adult education series at a synagogue in Southern California. I drive into the potholed parking lot, gather my notes, and head into the building. Across the entryway in large letters is the name of the congregation: "Temple Beth Disney." (Not really. I have changed the name for reasons that will become clear in a moment.) As I walk through the covered walkway, I notice traffic cones and yellow tape surrounding several of the columns, obviously in desperate need of repair. When I enter the building itself, a faint mist of mold greets me. Clearly, the nearly fifty-year-old facility has seen better days. The social hall is set up with long tables and chairs—a bingo parlor. The small sanctuary with its fixed pews and boiler plate bimah is uninspiring.

The president and interim rabbi ask me to stick around after my talk to discuss the challenges facing the congregation with a small subset of the board. "We've lost so many members; they've moved away, they've quit, they've died, we're getting older. Our school is down to thirty kids. We have a nice loyal crowd that comes on Shabbat and holidays, but it is shrinking. The only thing keeping us alive financially is the revenue from the bingo games and rental fees from a church that meets here on Sundays." We spend an hour exploring strategies for recruitment, engagement, and retention.

Six months later, I return to the congregation for the second lecture. As I pull into the parking lot, I think I have made a wrong turn. A fresh coat of asphalt has smoothed the surface of the lot. The crumbling columns in the entryway have been totally resurfaced with sparkling stone facades and new lighting. My eyes drift to the sign above the entry. It reads: "Romanian Church of God." I blink twice, checking my GPS to see if I have gone to the correct address. I have. I walk into the refurbished lobby and meet the president of the synagogue. "We decided to sell the property to the church. Now, instead of their renting from us, we're renting from them. It will buy us some time." I feel like someone has punched me in the stomach.

The economic downturn in the past five years has impacted the Jewish community and its institutions. Already reeling from the high cost of Jewish living, many individuals and families struggling with job loss and reduced discretionary income simply cannot afford escalating costs of synagogue and JCC memberships, Jewish day school tuitions, donations to Federation and other organizations, trips to Israel, and other engagement activities that are funded from voluntary contributions. Consequently, some institutions have been selling buildings, merging, and downsizing in every possible way ... rather than reinventing our structures and models and assumptions.

Rabbi Aaron Bisno of Pittsburgh has called for "courageous conversations" on this issue.[1] But, the answers he floats—new business models, mergers, collaborative religious schools—still ignore the fundamental challenge we face: transforming the institutions of Jewish life into a relational model. To my mind, virtually everything a person could possibly want or need Jewishly is readily available at much less cost and trouble via Internet and rent-a-professional ... except deep and lasting relationships, face-to-face relationships with people, both lay and professional, who care about you and care about connecting you to others, and work to help you build relationships with the Jewish experience on the Nine Levels.

Was the explosion of synagogues, JCCs, Federations, summer camps, and Jewish organizations after World War II a demographic blip? Was the move to suburbs, the influence of Kaplan disciples wanting to build synagogues and centers, and the relative affluence of the community a perfect confluence of events and place and ideology? Will only synagogues and centers that are well situated demographically continue to thrive on the twentieth-century model?

With the exception of the growing Orthodox population, it seems likely that smaller numbers of people will lead to smaller organizations, fewer professional positions, and less revenue. Just as changes in health care have transformed the positions and compensation packages for doctors, Jewish clergy and communal workers are not likely to make the same salaries, with increased competition for fewer available jobs. Smaller institutions may actually accelerate the transformation to more relational communities if … and only if … the leadership embraces the opportunity for change rather than shriveling in despair.

The Challenge Facing National Organizations and Movements

Steven Windmueller, emeritus professor of Jewish communal service at Hebrew Union College–Jewish Institute of Religion in Los Angeles, has predicted a "third American Jewish revolution" that will see the decline in denominations and umbrella national organizations reflecting the corresponding decline in demographic numbers and financial resources. There are a number of factors contributing to this prediction:

- Individuals and families have fewer discretionary dollars or flexible hours.
- There is a marked decline in ideologically-based social movements.
- Life-long loyalty to traditional institutional relationships has given way to a growing investment in single-issue causes and more short-term commitments to specific social causes.
- In today's marketplace there are multiple options with regard to affiliation and participation.

- [There is] a general loss of trust and confidence in national institutions and movements.

- Social networks have replaced traditional membership and affiliation patterns.

- Younger folks have far less interest in and loyalty to the institutions of their parents' generation.

- Consumerism (namely: "how can I benefit?") is driving institutional affiliation patterns and the corresponding notion of "membership" is seen as an anathema.[2]

In 2008, Synagogue 3000 sponsored the first-ever gathering of leaders of "emergent" Jewish spiritual communities. We found a dozen "independent minyanim" that had sprung up since the turn of the millennium, places like Mechon Hadar and Romemu in New York, Brooklyn Jews in you-know-where, Kavana Cooperative in Seattle, and IKAR in Los Angeles. Each of them was founded by rabbis and lay partners who had been trained and raised in the Conservative or Reform movements. None of them wanted to be shackled with a denominational label. Today, Mechon Hadar deploys consultants to more than one hundred independent minyanim in cities across North America. Although together they represent a small sliver of Jewish affiliation, they, together with the rising ranks of the "Just Jewish," could nevertheless be harbingers of a post-denominational Judaism.

The same phenomenon occurred when the evangelical megachurches emerged on the national scene in the 1980s. Pastors like Rick Warren and Bill Hybels discarded denominational designations, preferring to call their congregations simply "Saddleback Church" and "Willowcreek Community Church." They realized the labels were off-putting rather than welcoming.

Another factor eroding the pull of denominations is the porous nature of formerly rigid boundaries among and between religions. A survey conducted by the Pew Forum in 2007 found that 44 percent of Americans change their religious affiliation at some point in their lives. According to Putnam and Campbell in *American Grace*:

> Many Americans—at least one third and rising—nowadays choose their religion rather than simply inheriting it....

Religion in America is increasingly a domain of choice, churn and surprising low brand loyalty. That is the demand side of the religious marketplace. On the supply side, we would expect successful "firms" (denominations and congregations) in such a fickle market to be especially entrepreneurial in "marketing" their product.[3]

But, (dis)loyalty is not the most dangerous threat to the national movements and organizations. It's "playlist Judaism," according to Rabbi Kerry Olitzky, executive director of the Jewish Outreach Institute, citing a key factor in the rise in the numbers of "Just Jewish" Jews:

I no longer have to buy the entire package in order to have the service I want…. You don't need to restrict yourself to Jewish institutions to engage Jewishly. There have been 300 startups in the Jewish community in the last ten years. That doesn't reflect less engagement. What it says is the institutions that exist are not meeting our needs.[4]

I believe in the importance of the synagogue denominational movement. Both the Conservative and the Reform movements have faced the reality of downsizing, but they are also working assiduously to transform themselves into organizations responsive to the needs of local synagogue communities. Likewise, Jewish Federations of North America, Hadassah, Anti-Defamation League, American Jewish Committee, International Hillel, Jewish Community Centers Association, and all other "national" headquarter organizations serve the important function of equipping local affiliates with the proper personnel, training, and institutional support. But in the coming years, they will all need to demonstrate their own "value-added" if the communities that they serve continue to shrink.

Jewish Professionals: Fewer Jobs, Great Opportunity

The Great Recession has had another huge impact; it has significantly reduced the number of jobs available in the Jewish community. Synagogues have fewer positions for rabbis, cantors, and educators; JCCs have cut back staff; Jewish communal organizations have downsized; and Federations have scaled back their rosters. Meanwhile, the Jewish professional schools and seminaries continue to produce student-loan-laden graduates seeking employment in a shrinking job market, made all the worse by long-serving communal workers who cannot afford to retire.

Listen to Rabbi Joel Nickerson of Temple Isaiah in Los Angeles, California:

> *There was an awful economy when I was ordained. I was one of five—out of fifteen students—who had a job right after ordination in 2009. I only landed a job because I went outside of the synagogue world to Hillel. Two other people had internships that became jobs, and two others were international students who returned home. No one else had jobs. It was really terrible; some of them are still struggling. It may be a little better now, but there are more rabbis than jobs, that's for sure.*

Where some see crisis, I see opportunity. My proposal: Let us transform our program-centric institutions into relational communities. Let us do so by creating new jobs and transforming old programming positions into a series of relationship-building slots in existing organizations, with professionals spending their time building relationships with individuals and creating relational microcommunities among individuals, to deepen the relationships with those already affiliated with us, to engage those who can be attracted to Judaism, and to retain people long term, whether in our existing institutions or in new start-up groups. For example:

> *Relationship director*: a full-time position responsible for recruiting, inducting, and advising members of JCCs and synagogues
>
> *Community concierge*: a full-time position working out of Federations to engage unaffiliated Jews in Jewish experiences
>
> *Roving rabbis*: a full-time position for outreach rabbis dedicating their energies to building relationships with unaffiliated Jews and guiding them into communal connections
>
> *Engagement rabbis*: a full-time position for rabbis in synagogues devoted to engaging specific target populations—young Jewish adults, families, empty nesters

We have done this before. When the leadership of the American Jewish community realized that the vast majority of Jewish young people were attending college, we invented Hillel. When most young people were married shortly after graduation, there was almost no gap between the time they left campus and ended up affiliated with a Jewish organization. Now, of course, with various factors pushing marriage off well into their thirties, we have a whole generation of young Jewish adults with nothing but a smattering of local efforts. There is no "Hillel" for Jews ages twenty-five to forty. And, the numbers are significant. While Hillel estimates there are 380,000 Jewish collegians at any one time, sociologist Steven M. Cohen estimates there are at least 800,000 non-Orthodox Jews ages twenty-five to thirty-nine. The community currently invests $77 million annually in Hillel with the hopes of reaching, at best, 10 to 20 percent of the 380,000 college students. What does the community spend to engage young Jewish adults postcollege, post-Birthright? *Bupkes* (another technical term, meaning "hardly anything").

Just as Chabad began its remarkable growth on college campuses, let us begin a "non-Orthodox Chabad" targeting these eight hundred thousand young Jewish adults. The key is to create a cadre of passionate young rabbis and community organizers trained in the vision and engagement strategies of Relational Judaism. Lawrence A. Hoffman and I were asked by Jay Kaiman, executive director of the Marcus Foundation, to conduct research among our current rabbinical students at Hebrew Union College–Jewish Institute of Religion, New York, and the Ziegler School of Rabbinic Studies at the American Jewish University in Los Angeles to assess their interest in such positions if we had them. Our students were overwhelmingly positive; the best of the best of our future rabbis would jump at the opportunity to do this engagement work. To be sure, the rabbinical seminaries will need to find room for courses in relational engagement strategies, interpersonal skills, and entrepreneurship; they can and they must.

Imagine an "army" of passionate advocates for Judaism, spending their time creating relationships, networks, and experiences for young Jews and others living with Jews and/or raising a Jewish family. Imagine every Jewish population center in North America employing a "roving rabbi" or "community concierge" who devotes her or his full time engaging the unengaged and deepening relationships with Judaism and Jewish institutional life. Imagine synagogues hiring "engagement rabbis" and transforming their program directors into relationship directors. Imagine every JCC hiring a "chief Jewish officer." Imagine Jewish schools and camps sharing a relational rabbi to help bridge the gap between summers and the rest of the year. We won't need buildings for this; Synagogue 3000 has demonstrated through our Next *Dor* initiative that these engagement professionals can work out of existing supportive mainstream synagogues or other institutions in the community. They can work collaboratively with local Moishe Houses, Birthright Israel alumni, Federation young leadership, ACCESS, and synagogues with young adult efforts.

What we need is a *bold continental engagement effort* that uses social media, database technologies, and excellent relationship-building strategies to identify, network, track, and support young Jewish adults as they navigate "emerging adulthood" from singles to settlers to CHIPS, a family with young children. The goal is to reach individual Jews and build a relationship with a Jewish role model who can guide each person to deepen his or her relationships with the Nine Levels: self, family, friends, Jewish living, community, peoplehood, Israel, the world, and God. If the community can raise hundreds of millions of dollars to send hundreds of thousands of first-timers on a free trip to Israel, surely a coalition of national foundations and funders and local Federations and Jewish Community Foundations can pool their dollars for a $100 million initial campaign to begin this work.

If we moved the needle of engagement even 10 to 20 percent, it would significantly impact both the quantity and the quality of the Jewish future. We have the talent, our young professionals need the jobs, and there is clearly enough money in the coffers of our foundations and funders to build a Relational Judaism, beginning with our young adults. The payoff will be more young Jews in significant relationships with the Jewish experience and a much better chance that they will join, sustain, and create the best of our Jewish institutions and organizations in the twenty-first century.

What are we waiting for?

A Relational People

It's all about relationships.

Call it what you will—a religion, a civilization, a way of life—Judaism is built on relationships. Born of a relationship between God and Abraham and Sarah, a pact literally marked in the flesh of males and symbolically celebrated in the hearts of females on the eighth day of life in a ceremony called *brit*, "covenant," we Jews are a relational people.

Rabbi Richard Address has developed what he calls a "theology of relationships" based on the Hebrew word *tzelem*, "image." By deconstructing the three-letter root of this word, Rabbi Address teaches that the *tzadi* stands for *tzelem*—God created human beings in God's "image"; every human being has the capacity to be like God, to enter into a sacred relationship with God as God's partner on earth. The *lamed* stands for *lev*, "heart." At the heart of relationships is love—love of oneself, love of others, love of community. The *mem* stands for *mitzvot*, the actions that one does in order to build relationships with others, including God. Uniqueness, love, and deed form the three-pronged chord of a theology of relationships.

The dialogical construct of relationships requires a rejection of aloneness in favor of response to the Other. "Response" is the root of "responsibility." Relationships, serious relationships, always come with responsibilities, demands, obligations, commitments.

In Jewish tradition, there are many commandments. There are the Top Ten … and 613 others that are pretty famous. These *mitzvot* are designed to shape our lives—to give meaning and purpose, belonging and blessing to what we do.

Yet, one of the imperatives in Judaism is the most unexpected, the most engaging, at least to me: we are commanded to love.

Consider these two well-known biblical imperatives:

> *V'ahavta et Adonai Elohecha …*
> You shall love Adonai your God
>
> *B'khol l'vav'kha …*
> With all your heart
>
> *Uv'khol nafsh'kha …*
> And with all your soul
>
> *Uv'khol m'odekha …*
> And with all your powers.
> DEUTERONOMY 6:5

> *V'ahvata l'rei'akha kamokha*
> You shall love your neighbor as yourself.
> LEVITICUS 19:18

This is striking. We are commanded to love God and to love our neighbor. How can one be *commanded* to love?

Why this imperative to "love"? Because love is at the heart of relationship.

To love an Other, you must love your Self.

To love an Other, you must put yourself in the Other's shoes. You must see the world through her or his eyes.

Even to love *The* Other—God—you must see yourself as God sees you.

That is the meaning of "walking with God." Rabbi Harold Schulweis teaches that instead of surrendering to a power beyond ourselves, we are to be in relationship with God. As much as we are looking for God, God is looking for us. As Abraham Joshua Heschel taught, God is in search of "man." In Judaism, what we want from God, God wants from us. It's a mirror—reflected right back at us. This is the meaning of being created in the image of God; we are a reflection of the Divine.

To see ourselves in God's shoes is to be like God. How? The key teaching is in the Talmud (*Sotah* 14a):

> Just as God clothed the naked (Adam and Eve), you clothe the naked. Just as God comforted the sick (Abraham after his self-circumcision at the age of ninety-nine), you comfort the sick. Just as God buried the dead (Moses), you bury the dead.

Be God's eyes and ears, hands and feet, heart and soul.

Wrestle with God all you want; don't worry—God can take it. It's in our DNA, it's in our very name—*b'nei Yisra-El*, the descendants of the one (Jacob) who wrestled with God.

In the end, the purpose of Judaism—the purpose of relationships—is to love the other and the Other, the thou and the Thou. When you do, you find *meaning*—an understanding of the significance of life; you find *purpose*—an imperative to do what you are put on earth to do during your life; you find *belonging*—a community of people who will be there for you and with you; and you find *blessing*—a feeling of deep satisfaction and gratitude, a calendar and life cycle of opportunities to celebrate the gifts of life. It *is* all about relationships … and creating and deepening them is the challenge to our Jewish communal institutions. It is time to set about the task. This is the moment to broaden our vision to embrace a Relational Judaism for the twenty-first century.

An Invitation to Action

To join with others in sharing best practices, principles, strategies, and conversation about Relational Judaism, I invite you to visit http:// myrelationaljudaism.org and/or my Facebook page and/or follow me on Twitter "@RonWolfson" and/or contact me at rwolfson@ajula.edu. I look forward to meeting you!

In Gratitude

I am extraordinarily blessed to be in relationship with a who's who of remarkable leaders of the Jewish people. When I set about my research for Relational Judaism, my guiding principle was the same as the Rabbis of the Talmud: *Puk hazei mai amma davar*, "Go out and see what the people are doing" (*Berakhot* 45a, *Eruvin* 14b). The many site visits, chats over coffee or frozen yogurt, phone and Skype conversations, and opportunities to share ideas and experiences with these friends form the foundation of this vision. My thanks to you all, each one of you a passionate advocate for shifting the Jewish communal paradigm from programmatic to relational.

To rabbis: Harold Schulweis, Noah Farkas, Ed Feinstein, Sharon Brous, Greg Litcofsky, Joshua Hoffman, Dara Frimmer, Joel Nickerson, Stephanie Kolin, David Wolpe, Gordon Freeman, Charles Simon, Richard Address, Will Berkovitz, Dovid Eliezrie, Moshe Bryski, Peter Berg, Rachael Bregman, Esther Lederman, Jay Kornsgold, Julie Schoenfeld, Jan Kaufman, David Ellenson, Robert Wexler, Elliot Dorff, Bradley Shavit Artson, Ryan Bauer, Carla Fenves, Alan Silverstein, Danny Zemel, Karyn Kedar, Joseph Telushkin, Peter Rubinstein, Danny Freelander, Elyse Frishman, Michael Holzman, David Stern, Jonah Pesner, Rick Jacobs, Steve Wernick, Noa Kushner, Rachel Nussbaum, Lizzi Heydemann, Gayle Pomerantz, Jonathan Blake, Alyson Solomon, Dan Smokler, Wes Gardenswartz, Daniel Brenner, David Levy, David Paskin, Kerry Olitzky, Angela Buchdahl, Hershey Novack, Ron Stern, Eli Herscher, Ken Chasen, Phil Warmflash, Aryeh Azriel, Aaron Spiegel, David Booth, Dan Judson, Janet Marder, Lydia Medwin, Laura Baum, Elie Kaunfer, David Komerofsky, Zoë Klein, Rachel Steiner, David-Seth Kirshner, Stuart Kelman, Baruch HaLevi, Philip Ohriner, Steven Carr

Reuben, Elie Spitz, Ami Hersh, Dan Moskovitz, Joy Levitt, Jill Jacobs, and Ari Moffic.

To colleagues: Bernie Marcus, Jay Kaiman, Arnie Eisen, Abe Foxman, Allan Finkelstein, Jerry Silverman, John Ruskay, Graham Hoffman, Margo Sack, Esther Netter, Amy Klein, Mike Benjamin, Lisa Colton, David Cygielman, Rachael Himovitz, Daniel Horwitz, Jonathan Jacoby, Beryl Geber, Mike Benjamin, Sacha Litman, Daniel Chiat, Gabby Kozak, Melissa Balaban, Michael Brooks, Chip Edelsberg, Josh Miller, Josh Fiegelson, Lisa Farber Miller, Jon Woocher, Jeannie Appleman, Harlene Appelman, Cyd Weissman, Abby Pitkowsky, Rachel Gildiner, Brad Sugar, Rachel Kaplan, Debra Markovic, Rhoda Weisman, Rachel Brodie, Steven M. Cohen, Janice Kamenir-Reznik, David Chrzan, Anne Krumm, Rick Warren, Doug Pagitt, Josh Furman, Shawn Landres, Steve Windmueller, Isa Aron, Wayne Firestone, Marie Koley, Robyn Faintich, Vicky Kelman, Joan Wolchansky, Pam Edelman, Linda Zimmerman, Joel Lurie Grishaver, Jo Kay, Shellie Dickstein, Sharie Calderone, Nancy Parkes, Rachel Stern, Rick Recht, Craig Taubman, Debi Mishael, Lisa Soble Siegmann, Laura Hyman, Randy Green, Ed Sachs, Richard Siegel, Daniel Inlender, Simon Greer, Josh Mason-Barkin, Yoni Sarason, Daniel Libenson, Susannah Sagan, Arlene Miller, Yechiel Hoffman, Michael Ungar, Charles Lowenhaupt, Larry Moses, Bruce Powell, Tzivia Getzug Schwartz, Beryl Weiner, Meir Lakein, Heather Wolfson, Macy B. Hart, Jay Sanderson, Lila Foldes, Sue Fishkoff, Lori Yadin, Lee Meyerhoff Hendler, Amy Dorsch, Rachel Levin, Andrew Kessler, David Elcott, Stuart Himmelfarb, Terry Rosenberg, Bill and Sandy Goodglick, Ellen Frankel, Sandy Rechtschaffen, Cindy Chazan, Gary Wexler, Andy Paller, Jill Seigerman, Morlie Levin, Joel Frankel, Caren Seligman, Howard Stahl, David Suissa, and Annie and Ian Graham.

To my students in the Ziegler School of Rabbinic Studies at the American Jewish University who have afforded me a wonderful opportunity to explore these ideas with a group of bright future rabbis of America. In the spring of 2012, they included Sara Metz, Joshua Corber, Elan Babchuck, and Daniel Kaiman.

To my colleagues at the American Jewish University—Dr. Robert Wexler, Dr. Stuart Sigman, and Dr. Miriam Heller Stern—who graciously accepted my proposal for sabbatical to enable this work. *Todah rabbah.*

For nearly twenty years, Larry Hoffman has been my partner in shaping the work of Synagogue 2000 and Synagogue 3000. Our conversations overflow with stimulating intellectual ideas and passionate prognostications of communal trends, challenges, and opportunities. We have gathered around us a terrific team: Jodi Berman Kustanovich, Rabbi Jessica Zimmerman, Aaron Spiegel, Steven M. Cohen, and a dedicated board of directors led by Larry Smith. Synagogue 3000/Next *Dor* continues its work due to the support of the Marcus Foundation, led by the visionary philanthropist Bernie Marcus and its remarkable executive director, Jay Kaiman. My thanks to all who make this sacred work possible.

Rabbi Myer S. Kripke is ninety-nine years young as of this writing. Each week, the editor of the *Jewish Press* in Omaha places the name of that week's Torah portion next to his oversized rocker in his apartment at the Rose Blumkin Jewish Home. On Tuesdays, Rabbi Kripke dictates his weekly *d'var Torah* by heart. It is the most eagerly read column in the paper. His philanthropy may have made him famous, but it is his passion for teaching that is the true hallmark of his rabbinate. Thank you, my dear rabbi, for generously supporting this research and writing.

The folks at Jewish Lights Publishing are everything an author desires: encouraging, supportive, flexible, and supremely professional. Stuart M. Matlins is not simply a publisher of books; he has become one of the most important Jewish educators of our time. His capable staff—Emily Wichland, Barbara Heise, Heather Pelham, Tim Holtz, and Kelly O'Neill—are the best.

I turned to the incomparable book editor Ilana Kurshan, who responded to my "pleas" and my "please" to focus her keen eye on this manuscript. Her deep understanding of Jewish communal life and her excellent literary skills have improved the work immeasurably. Thank you, Ilana.

My most important relationships are, of course, with those in my loving and supportive family. Bob and Sibby Wolfson, Doug and Sara Wolfson, Michael Wolfson, Havi Wolfson Hall, David Hall, Ellie

Brooklyn Hall, and Gabriel Elijah Hall always offer an encouraging word. My parents, Alan and Bernice, may they rest in peace, first modeled for me how to engage others and treat every human being as a *b'tzelem Elohim*, a reflection of the Divine—how lucky I have been to have had these remarkable people in my life. Finally, I am blessed to live my life in relationship with the sweetest person I know, Susie Wolfson, the best wife in the United States of America … and the world! I love you!

Finally, to my readers, may you be granted the power to transform the shape of Judaism, inspired by the stories you hear, the relationships you create, and the communities you build. God bless you!

Notes

Introduction

1. Ron Wolfson, *The Spirituality of Welcoming: How to Transform Your Synagogue into a Sacred Community* (Woodstock, VT: Jewish Lights Publishing, 2006), 9–10.

2. Mordecai Kaplan, *Judaism as a Civilization: Toward a Reconstruction of American-Jewish Life*, reprint ed. (Philadelphia: Jewish Publication Society, 2010), 3–4.

3. Ibid., 178.

4. *National Jewish Population Survey 2000–01: Strength, Challenge and Diversity in the American Jewish Population* (New York: United Jewish Communities, 2003), www.jewishfederations.org/page.aspx?id=33650.

Chapter 1: Shifting the Shape of Jewish Engagement

1. Steven M. Cohen, Jacob B. Ukeles, and Ron Miller, *Jewish Community Study of New York: 2011* (New York: UJA-Federation of New York, 2012), www.ujafedny.org/jewish-community-study-of-new-york-2011.

2. Jacob B. Ukeles and Ron Miller, *Jewish Community Study of New York: 2002* (New York: UJA-Federation of New York, 2004), www.ujafedny.org/jewish-community-study-2002.

3. David Hartman, "Rabbi David Hartman Talks about Mordecai Kaplan," Winter 2009 Pomrenze Lecture Series, Shalom Hartman Institute, Jerusalem, Israel, www.youtube.com/watch?v=WTDkeABMZag.

4. Walter Isaacson, *Steve Jobs* (New York: Simon and Schuster, 2011), 567.

Chapter 2: Toward a Relational Judaism

1. Barack Obama, *The Audacity of Hope* (New York: Crown, 2006), 85–86.

2. Emmanuel Levinas, *Totality and Infinity: An Essay on Exteriority* (Pittsburgh: Duquesne University Press, 1969).

3. Martin Buber, *I and Thou* (New York: Touchstone, 1971).

4. David Wolpe, "A Manifesto for the Jewish Future," *Jewish Journal*, December 1, 2005, www.jewishjournal.com/articles/item/a_manifesto_for_the_future_20051202.

5. Joseph B. Soloveitchik, *The Lonely Man of Faith* (Jerusalem: Maggid, 2011).

6. Arnold M. Eisen, *Taking Hold of Torah: Jewish Commitment and Community in America* (Bloomington, IN: Indiana University Press, 1997), 95.

7. Ibid., 97.

8. Ibid., 98.

9. Ibid., 100.

10. Ibid.

11. Gordon M. Freeman, *Trusting* (unpublished manuscript).

Chapter 3: The Nine Levels of Relationship

1. Ed Feinstein, Yom Kippur Sermon, 2005; www.vbs.org/page.cfm?p=836&newsid=128.

2. Kenneth J. Gergen, *Relational Being* (New York: Oxford University Press, 2009), xv.

3. Martin Buber, *Tales of the Hasidim*, vol. 1, *The Early Masters* (New York: Schocken Books, 1947), 251.

4. Robert D. Putnam and David E. Campbell, *American Grace: How Religion Divides and Unites Us* (New York: Simon and Schuster, 2010).

5. Rick Warren, *The Purpose-Driven Life: What on Earth Am I Here For?* (Grand Rapids, MI: Zondervan, 1995).

6. David Brooks, *The Social Animal: The Hidden Sources of Love, Character, and Achievement* (New York: Random House, 2012), ix.

7. Synagogue 3000 Synagogue Studies Institute, FACT survey; http://synagogue3000.org/reform-and-conservative-congregations-different-strengths-different-challenges.

8. George Herbert Mead, *Mind, Self and Society* (Chicago: University of Chicago Press, 1967).

9. Herbert Blumer, *Symbolic Interactionism: Perspective and Method* (Berkeley: University of California Press, 1986).

10. Martin Buber, *I and Thou* (New York: Touchstone, 1971).

11. Tony Bayfield, "Forty Years On: New Vision, New Agenda: Judaism as Relational Religion" (lecture, Bromley Reform Synagogue, Bromley, UK, November 14, 2004), http://news.reformjudaism.org.uk/assembly-of-rabbis/forty-years-on-new-vision-new-agenda-judaism-as-relational-religion.html.

12. Arnold M. Eisen and Steven M. Cohen, *The Jew Within: Self, Family, and Community in America* (Bloomington, IN: Indiana University Press, 2000), 185.

13. Karen L. Fingerman and Frank F. Furstenberg, "You Can Go Home Again," *New York Times*, May 31, 2012, www.nytimes.com/2012/05/31/opinion/the-parent-trap.html?_r=1.

14. Putnam and Campbell, *American Grace*, 174.

15. Steven M. Cohen, Jacob B. Ukeles, and Ron Miller, *Jewish Community Study of New York: 2011* (New York: UJA-Federation of New York, 2012), www.ujafedny.org/jewish-community-study-of-new-york-2011.

16. Jack Wertheimer, "Whatever Happened to the Jewish People?" *Commentary*, June 2006.

17. Ibid.

18. Eugene B. Borowitz, quoted in ibid.

19 Ronald G. Wolfson, "A Description and Analysis of an Innovative Living Experience in Israel: The Dream and the Reality." PhD diss., Washington University, St. Louis, Missouri, 1974.

20. American Jewish Committee Survey of American Jewish Opinion, March 14–27, 2012; www.ajc.org/surveys.

21. Ibid.

22. Dennis Overbye, "Physicists Find Elusive Particle Seen as Key to Universe," *New York Times*, July 4, 2012.

23. Dorothy K. Kripke and Christine Tripp, *Let's Talk about God* (Los Angeles: Torah Aura Productions, 2003), 12–13, 31.

24. Richard Rubenstein, *After Auschwitz: Radical Theology and Contemporary Judaism* (Indianapolis: Bobbs-Merrill, 1966).

25. Harold S. Kushner, *When Bad Things Happen to Good People* (New York: Schocken Books, 1981).

26. Bradley Shavit Artson, "On the Way: A Presentation of Process Theology," *Conservative Judaism* (Fall–Winter 2010–11).

27. David Wolpe, "Musings," *Jewish Week*, April 20, 2012.

Chapter 4: Transforming Programmatic Institutions into Relational Communities: Six Case Studies

1. Steven F. Windmueller, "Jewishness in the World: A Chabad Definition," *Menorah Review*, no. 77 (Summer/Fall 2012).

2. Joseph Telushkin, "What the Rebbe Taught," *Jewish Week*, June 12, 2012.

3. Jonathan Sacks, Address to Chabad *Shluchim Kinus*, November 2011, www.chabad.org/multimedia/media_cdo/aid/1690783/jewish/A-Story-in-Three-Acts.htm.

4. Steven M. Cohen, Ezra Kopelowitz, Jack Ukeles, and Minna Wolf, *Assessing the Impact of Senior Jewish Educators and Campus Entrepreneurs Initiative Interns on the Jewish Engagement of College Students—Two Year Summary: 2008–2010* (Research Success Technologies, Ukeles Associates, November 2, 2010).

5. "Relationship-Based Engagement and Growth," *Student Guide, Hillel: The Foundation for Jewish Campus Life* (unpublished).

6. Jonah Pesner, "Calling Jewish Activists: Synagogues Need You and You Need Them," *Zeek: A Jewish Journal of Thought and Culture*, December 20, 2011.

7. Jill Jacobs, *Where Justice Dwells: A Hands-On Guide to Doing Social Justice in Your Community* (Woodstock, VT: Jewish Lights Publishing, 2011), 5–6.

8. Steven M. Cohen and Lawrence A. Hoffman, "Different Growth for Different Folks: The ND Pilot Sites in Action," *S3K Report*, no. 10 (April 2011), http://synagogue3000.org/ different-growth-different-folks-nd-pilot-sites-action.

9. Ibid., 6.

10. Kenneth J. Gergen, *Relational Being* (New York: Oxford University Press, 2009), 400.

Chapter 5: The Twelve Principles of Relational Engagement

1. Richard Address, *Seekers of Meaning: Baby Boomers, Judaism, and the Pursuit of Healthy Aging* (New York: URJ Press, 2012), 25.

2. Martin Buber, *I and Thou* (New York: Touchstone, 1971), 26.

3. Ibid., 67.

4. Dennis S. Ross, *God in Our Relationships: Spirituality between People from the Teachings of Martin Buber* (Woodstock, VT: Jewish Lights Publishing, 2003), xv.

5. Kenneth J. Gergen, *Realities and Relationships: Soundings in Social Construction* (Cambridge, MA: Harvard University Press, 1997), 186.

6. Sherry Turkle, "The Flight from Conversation," *New York Times*, April 22, 2012, www.nytimes.com/2012/04/22/opinion/sunday/the-flight-from-conversation.html?_r=1&pagewanted=all.

7. Lizette Alvarez, "For Young Jews, a Service Says, 'Please Do Text,'" *New York Times*, September 17, 2012, www.nytimes.com/2012/09/18/us/ for-young-jews-a-service-says-please-do-text.html?_r=0).

8. "The Mitzvah Initiative," The Jewish Theological Seminary, www.jtsa.edu/ Conservative_Judaism/Mitzvah_Initiative.xml.

9. Nicolas Bourriaud, *Relational Aesthetics* (Dijon, France: Les Presse Du Reel, 1998), 14.

10. Barry Chazan, "The Philosophy of Informal Jewish Education," *Encyclopedia of Informal Education*, 2003. www.infed.org/informaleducation/informal_ jewish_education.htm.

11. Joseph Reimer, "A Response to Barry Chazan: The Philosophy of Informal Jewish Education," *Encyclopedia of Informal Education*, 2003. www.infed. org/informaljewisheducation/informal_jewish_education_reply.htm.

12. Daniel J. Libenson, "Jewish Education for a Time of Wandering," *Zeek*, January 10, 2012, http://zeek.forward.com/articles/117450.

13. David Brooks, "The Relationship School," *New York Times*, March 22, 2012, www.nytimes.com/2012/03/23/opinion/brooks-the-relationship-school. html.

14. Carmine Gallo, *The Apple Experience: Secrets to Building Insanely Great Customer Loyalty* (New York: McGraw-Hill, 2012), 91.

15. Charles Simon, *Building a Successful Volunteer Culture: Finding Meaning in Service in the Jewish Community* (Woodstock, VT: Jewish Lights Publishing, 2009), 41.

16. David M. Elcott, *Baby Boomers, Public Service, and Minority Communities: A Case Study of the Jewish Community in the United States* (New York: Berman Jewish Policy Archive, Research Center for Leadership in Action, NYU Wagner, Spring 2010), http://bjpa.org/Publications/details. cfm?PublicationID=5154.

17. Ibid., 20.

18. Ibid., 35.

19. "Passport to Liberal Judaism," Liberal Judaism, www.liberaljudaism.org/ youngadults/passport-to-liberal-judaism.html.

20. Dan Judson, "Scrapping Synagogue Dues: A Case Study of One Synagogue That Radically Altered Their Dues System and Found More Money, More Members and More Harmony," *eJewish Philanthropy*, http:// ejewishphilanthropy.com/scrapping-synagogue-dues-a-case-study.

21. Baruch HaLevi and Ellen Frankel, *Revolution of Jewish Spirit: How to Revive Ruakh in Your Spiritual Life, Transform Your Synagogue & Inspire Your Jewish Community* (Woodstock, VT: Jewish Lights Publishing, 2012), 157–58.

22. Josh Nathan-Kazis, "Synagogue Dues Don't Raise More Money Than Church Gifts," *Forward*, September 7, 2010, www.forward.com/ articles/131095/#.

23. R. I. M. Dunbar, "Neocortex Size as a Constraint on Group Size in Primates," *Journal of Human Evolution* 22, no. 6 (June 1992): 469–93.

24. *Northern New Jersey Jewish News*, October 22, 2009.

Chapter 6 The Challenges Ahead

1. Aaron Bisno. "It's Time for a Courageous Conversation," *eJewish Philanthropy*, May 8, 2011.

2. Steven Windmueller, "A Game Plan for Renewal: The Demise of National Movements and Their Rebirth," *eJewish Philanthropy*, July 25, 2012, http:// ejewishphilanthropy.com/a-game-plan-for-renewal-the-demise-of-national- movements-and-their-rebirth.

3. Robert D. Putnam and David E. Campbell, *American Grace: How Religion Divides and Unites Us* (New York: Simon and Schuster, 2010), 148.

4. Kerry Olitzky, "Community Struggling to Meet the Needs of Jewish Identity Survey's 'Others,'" *Jewish Telegraphic Agency*, June 28, 2012.

Selected Bibliography

Address, Richard. *Seekers of Meaning: Baby Boomers, Judaism and the Pursuit of Healthy Aging*. New York: URJ Press, 2012.

Aron, Isa, Steven M. Cohen, Lawrence A. Hoffman, and Ari Y. Kelman. *Sacred Strategies: Transforming Synagogues from Functional to Visionary*. Herndon, VA: Alban Institute, 2010.

Artson, Bradley Shavit. "On the Way: A Presentation of Process Theology." *Conservative Judaism*, Fall–Winter 2010–11.

Bayfield, Tony. "Forty Years On: New Vision, New Agenda: Judaism as Relational Religion." Lecture, Bromley Reform Synagogue, Bromley, UK, November 14, 2004. http://news.reformjudaism.org.uk/assembly-of-rabbis/forty-years-on-new-vision-new-agenda-judaism-as-relational-religion.html.

Behar, Howard. *It's Not about the Coffee: Leadership Principles from a Life at Starbucks*. New York: Penguin, 2007.

Bisno, Aaron. "It's Time for a Courageous Conversation." *eJewish Philanthropy*, May 8, 2011.

Blumer, Herbert. *Symbolic Interactionism: Perspective and Method*. Berkeley: University of California Press, 1986.

Bourriaud, Nicolas. *Relational Aesthetics*. Dijon, France: Les Presse Du Reel, 1998.

Brooks, David. "The Relationship School." *New York Times*, March 22, 2012. www.nytimes.com/2012/03/23/opinion/brooks-the-relationship-school.html.

———. *The Social Animal: The Hidden Sources of Love, Character and Achievement*. New York: Random House, 2011.

Buber, Martin. *I and Thou*. New York: Touchstone, 1971.

———. *Tales of the Hasidim*. New York: Schocken Books, 1947.

Callahan, Raymond E. *Education and the Cult of Efficiency*. Chicago: University of Chicago Press, 1964.

Chazan, Barry. "The Philosophy of Informal Jewish Education." *Encyclopedia of Informal Education*, 2003. www.infed.org/informaljewisheducation/informal_jewish_education.htm.

Christensen, Clayton M. *The Innovator's Dilemma*. Reprint ed. New York: HarperBusiness, 2011.

Cohen, Steven M., and Arnold M. Eisen. *The Jew Within: Self, Family and Community in America*. Bloomington: Indiana University Press, 2000.

Cohen, Steven M., and Lawrence A. Hoffman. "Different Growth for Different Folks: The ND Pilot Sites in Action." *S3K Report*, no. 10 (April 2011). http://synagogue3000.org/different-growth-different-folks-nd-pilot-sites-action.

Cohen, Steven M., and Lawrence A. Hoffman. "Reform and Conservative Congregations: Different Strengths, Different Challenges." *S3K Report*, no. 11 (March 2012). http://synagogue3000.org/reform-and-conservative-congregations-different-strengths-different-challenges.

Cohen, Steven M., Ezra Kopelowitz, Jack Ukeles, and Minna Wolf. *Assessing the Impact of Senior Jewish Educators and Campus Entrepreneurs Initiative Interns on the Jewish Engagement of College Students—Two Year Summary: 2008–2010.* Research Success Technologies, Ukeles Associates, November 2, 2010.

Cohen, Steven M., Jacob B. Ukeles, and Ron Miller. *Jewish Community Study of New York: 2011.* New York: UJA-Federation of New York, 2012. www.ujafedny.org.jewish-community-study-of-new-york-2011.

Dorff, Elliot N. *The Unfolding Tradition: Jewish Law After Sinai*. New York: Aviv Press, 2005.

Drath, Wilfred. *The Deep Blue Sea: Rethinking the Source of Leadership*. San Francisco: Jossey-Bass, 2001.

Dunbar, R. I. M. "Neocortex Size as a Constraint on Group Size in Primates." *Journal of Human Evolution* 22, no. 6 (June 1992): 469–93.

Eisen, Arnold M. *Taking Hold of Torah: Jewish Commitment and Community in America*. Bloomington: Indiana University Press, 1997.

Elcott, David. *Baby Boomers, Public Service, and Minority Communities: A Case Study of the Jewish Community in the United States*. New York: Berman Jewish Policy Archive, Research Center for Leadership in Action, NYU Wagner, Spring 2010. http://bjpa.org/Publications/details.cfm?PublicationID=5154.

Fingerman, Karen L., and Frank F. Furstenberg. "You Can Go Home Again." *New York Times*, May 31, 2012. www.nytimes.com/2012/05/31/opinion/the-parent-trap.html?_r=1.

Fishkoff, Sue. *The Rebbe's Army*. New York: Schocken Books, 2003.

Freeman, Gordon. *Trusting*. In press.

Frei, Francis, and Anne Morriss. *Uncommon Service: How to Win by Putting Customers at the Core of Your Business*. Boston: Harvard Business Review Press, 2012.

Friedman, Thomas L. "Help Wanted." *New York Times*, December 17, 2011.

Gallo, Carmine. *The Apple Experience: Secrets to Building Insanely Great Customer Loyalty*. New York: McGraw-Hill, 2012.

Gergen, Kenneth J. *Realities and Relationships: Soundings in Social Construction*. Cambridge, MA: Harvard University Press, 1997.

————. *Relational Being.* New York: Oxford University Press, 2009.

————. *The Saturated Self: Dilemmas of Identity in Contemporary Life.* New York: Basic Books, 1992.

Gladwell, Malcolm. *The Tipping Point: How Little Things Make a Big Difference.* New York: Little, Brown, 2000.

HaLevi, Baruch, and Ellen Frankel. *Revolution of Jewish Spirit: How to Revive Ruakh in Your Spiritual Life, Transform Your Synagogue & Inspire Your Jewish Community.* Woodstock, VT: Jewish Lights Publishing, 2012.

Hartman, David. "Rabbi David Hartman Talks about Mordecai Kaplan." Winter 2009 Pomrenze lecture Series, Shalom Hartman Institute, Jerusalem, Israel. www.youtube.com/watch?v=WTDkeABMZag.

Heilman, Samuel, and Menachem Friedman. *The Rebbe: The Life and Afterlife of Menachem Mendel Schneerson.* Princeton, NJ: Princeton University Press, 2010.

Hemmert, Fabian. *The Shape-Shifting Future of the Mobile Phone.* February 2010. www.ted.com/talks/fabian_hemmert_the_shape_shifting_future_of_the_mobile_phone.html.

Herring, Hayim. *Tomorrow's Synagogue Today: Creating Vibrant Centers of Jewish Life.* Herndon, VA: Alban Institute, 2012.

Heschel, Abraham Joshua. *God in Search of Man: A Philosophy of Judaism.* New York: Farrar, Straus and Cudahy, 1955.

Hoffman, Lawrence A. *Rethinking Synagogues: A New Vocabulary for Congregational Life.* Woodstock, VT: Jewish Lights Publishing, 2006.

Holman, Peggy. *Engaging Emergence: Turning Upheaval into Opportunity.* San Francisco: Barrett-Koehler Publishers, 2010.

Holman, Peggy, Tom Devane, and Steven Cady. *The Change Handbook.* San Francisco: Barrett-Koehler Publishers, 2007.

Isaacson, Walter. *Steve Jobs.* New York: Simon and Schuster, 2011.

Jacobs, Jill. *Where Justice Dwells: A Hands-On Guide to Doing Social Justice in Your Community.* Woodstock, VT: Jewish Lights Publishing, 2011.

Judson, Dan. "Scrapping Synagogue Dues: A Case Study of One Synagogue That Radically Altered Their Dues System and Found More Money, More Members and More Harmony." *eJewish Philanthropy.* http://ejewishphilanthropy.com/scrapping-synagogue-dues-a-case-study.

Kaleem, Jaweed. "Southern Jewish Communities Recruit Newcomers, Offer Incentives as Populations Dwindle." *Huffington Post,* June 15, 2012. www.huffingtonpost.com/2012/06/15/southern-jewish-recruit-population_n_1578825.html.

Kaplan, Mordecai. *Judaism as a Civilization: Toward a Reconstruction of American-Jewish Life.* Reprint ed. Philadelphia: Jewish Publication Society, 2010.

Katz, Maya Balakirsky. *The Visual World of Chabad*. Cambridge: Cambridge University Press, 2010.

Kaunfer, Elie. *Empowered Judaism: What Independent Minyanim Can Teach Us about Building Vibrant Jewish Communities*. Woodstock, VT: Jewish Lights Publishing, 2010.

Kegan, Robert. *The Evolving Self*. Cambridge, MA: Harvard University Press, 1982.

Kripke, Dorothy K., and Christine Tripp. *Let's Talk About God*. Los Angeles: Torah Aura Productions, 2003.

Kuhn, Thomas S. *The Structure of Scientific Revolutions*. 4th ed. Chicago: University of Chicago Press, 2012.

Lencioni, Patrick. *Five Temptations of a CEO: A Leadership Fable*. San Francisco: Jossey-Bass, 2008.

Levin, Morlie. "They're Shown It But Can They Own It? Peoplehood in the 21st Century." *Nurturing Jewish Peoplehood in the 21st Century: What Should We Do Differently?* Peoplehood Papers, vol. 8. Center for Jewish Peoplehood Education, June 2012.

Levinas, Emmanuel. *Totality and Infinity: An Essay on Exteriority*. Pittsburgh, PA: Duquesne University Press, 1969.

Libenson, Daniel J. "Jewish Education for a Time of Wandering." *Zeek: A Jewish Journal of Thought and Culture*, January 10, 2012, http://zeek.forward.com/articles/117450.

McLaren, Brian. *Finding Our Way Again*. Nashville: Thomas Nelson, 2008.

Mead, George Herbert. *Mind, Self and Society*. Chicago: University of Chicago Press, 1967.

Miller, Jon D. "Active, Balanced and Happy: These Young Americans Are Not Bowling Alone." *Generation X Report* 1, no. 1 (Fall 2011).

Nathan-Kazis, Josh. "Synagogue Dues Don't Raise More Money Than Church Gifts." *Forward*, September 7, 2010. www.forward.com/articles/131095/#.

National Jewish Population Survey 2000–01: Strength, Challenge and Diversity in the American Jewish Population. New York: United Jewish Communities, 2003. www.jewishfederations.org/page.aspx?id=33650.

Obama, Barack. *The Audacity of Hope*. New York: Crown, 2006.

Olitzky, Kerry. "Community Struggling to Meet the Needs of Jewish Identity Surveys 'Others.'" *Jewish Telegraphic Agency*, June 28, 2012.

Pesner, Jonah. "Calling Jewish Activists: Synagogues Need You and You Need Them." *Zeek: A Jewish Journal of Thought and Culture*, December 20, 2011.

Peterson, Christopher. *A Life Worth Living*. University of Michigan video. http://michigantoday.umich.edu/story.php?id=7853.

Putnam, Robert D., and David E. Campbell. *American Grace: How Religion Divides and Unites Us*. New York: Simon and Schuster, 2010.

Reimer, Joseph. "A Response to Barry Chazan: The Philosophy of Informal Jewish Education." *Encyclopedia of Informal Education*, 2003. www.infed.org/informaljewisheducation/informal_jewish_education_reply.htm.

Ross, Dennis S. *God in Our Relationships: Spirituality between People from the Teachings of Martin Buber.* Woodstock, VT: Jewish Lights Publishing, 2003.

Rubenstein, Richard. *After Auschwitz: Radical Theology and Contemporary Judaism.* Indianapolis: Bobbs-Merrill, 1966.

Sacks, Jonathan. Address to Chabad *Shluchim Kinus.* November 2011. www.chabad.org/multimedia/media_cdo/aid/1690783/jewish/A-Story-in-Three-Acts.htm.

Sarna, Nahum. *Genesis.* JPS Torah Commentary. Philadelphia: Jewish Publication Society, 1989.

Schulweis, Harold M. "Globalism and Judaism." Sermon, Rosh Hashanah, 2004. www.jewishworldwatch.org/aboutjww/sermon.html.

———. "Restructuring the Synagogue: The Creation of Havurot in the Synagogue." www.vbs.org/cf_news/view.cfm?newsid=192.

Schwarz, Sidney. *Jewish Megatrends: Charting the Course of the American Jewish Future.* Woodstock, VT: Jewish Lights Publishing, 2013.

Seidman, Dov. *How: Why How We Do Anything Means Everything.* Hoboken, NJ: Wiley, 2007.

Sheskin, Ira M. *Comparisons of Jewish Communities: A Compendium of Tables and Bar Charts.* Berman Institute–North American Jewish Data Bank, University of Connecticut, no. 5, May 2012. www.jewishdatabank.org/Archive/Comparisons_of_Jewish_Communities_Section_36_Summary_Measures.pdf.

Simon, Charles. *Building a Successful Volunteer Culture: Finding Meaning in Service in the Jewish Community.* Woodstock, VT: Jewish Lights Publishing, 2009.

Soloveitchik, Joseph B. *The Lonely Man of Faith.* Jerusalem: Maggid, 2011.

Spitz, Elie Kaplan. *Does the Soul Survive?: A Jewish Journey to Belief in Afterlife, Past Lives & Living with Purpose.* Woodstock, VT: Jewish Lights Publishing, 2002.

Turkle, Sherry. *Alone Together: Why We Expect More from Technology and Less from Each Other.* New York: Basic Books, 2006.

———. "The Flight from Conversation." *New York Times*, April 22, 2012. www.nytimes.com/2012/04/22/opinion/sunday/the-flight-from-conversation.html?_r=1&pagewanted=all).

Warren, Rick. *The Purpose Driven Church.* Grand Rapids, MI: Zondervan, 2002.

———. *The Purpose Driven Life: What on Earth Am I Here For?* Grand Rapids, MI: Zondervan, 1995.

Wertheimer, Jack. "Whatever Happened to the Jewish People?" *Commentary*, June 2006.

Windmueller, Steven. "A Game Plan for Renewal: The Demise of National Movements and Their Rebirth." *eJewish Philanthropy*, July 25, 2012. http://

ejewishphilanthropy.com/a-game-plan-for-renewal-the-demise-of-national-movements-and-their-rebirth.

———. "Jewishness in the World; A Chabad Definition." *Menorah Review*, no. 77. Summer/Fall 2012.

———. "New Economic Challenges, New Opportunities: The Unfolding of the Third American Jewish Revolution." *eJewish Philanthropy*, May 30, 2012. http://ejewishphilanthropy.com/the-unfolding-of-the-third-american-jewish-revolution.

———. "Unpacking Chabad: Their Ten Core Elements of Success." *eJewish Philanthropy*, August 2, 2012. http://ejewishphilanthropy.com/unpacking-chabad-their-ten-core-elements-for-success.

Wolfson, Ronald G. "A Description and Analysis of an Innovative Living Experience in Israel: The Dream and the Reality." PhD diss., Washington University, St. Louis, Missouri, 1974.

———. *Be Like God: God's To-Do List for Kids*. Woodstock, VT: Jewish Lights Publishing, 2012.

———. *God's To-Do List: 103 Ways to Be an Angel and Do God's Work on Earth*. Woodstock, VT: Jewish Lights Publishing, 2006.

———. *The Spirituality of Welcoming: How to Transform Your Synagogue into a Sacred Community*. Woodstock, VT: Jewish Lights Publishing, 2006.

Wolpe, David. "A Manifesto for the Future." *Jewish Journal*, December 1, 2005. www.jewishjournal.com/articles/item/a_manifesto_for_the_future_20051202.

Index

Bible Study / Midrash

The Book of Job: Annotated & Explained
Translation and Annotation by Donald Kraus; Foreword by Dr. Marc Brettler
Clarifies for today's readers what Job is, how to overcome difficulties in the text, and what it may mean for us. Features fresh translation and probing commentary.
5½ x 8½, 256 pp, Quality PB, 978-1-59473-389-5 **$16.99**

Masking and Unmasking Ourselves: Interpreting Biblical Texts on Clothing & Identity *By Dr. Norman J. Cohen*
Presents ten Bible stories that involve clothing in an essential way, as a means of learning about the text, its characters and their interactions.
6 x 9, 240 pp, HC, 978-1-58023-461-0 **$24.99**

The Other Talmud—*The Yerushalmi:* Unlocking the Secrets of The Talmud of Israel for Judaism Today *By Rabbi Judith Z. Abrams, PhD*
A fascinating—and stimulating—look at "the other Talmud" and the possibilities for Jewish life reflected there. 6 x 9, 256 pp, HC, 978-1-58023-463-4 **$24.99**

The Torah Revolution: Fourteen Truths That Changed the World
By Rabbi Reuven Hammer, PhD A unique look at the Torah and the revolutionary teachings of Moses embedded within it that gave birth to Judaism and influenced the world. 6 x 9, 240 pp, HC, 978-1-58023-457-3 **$24.99**

Ecclesiastes: Annotated & Explained
Translation and Annotation by Rabbi Rami Shapiro; Foreword by Rev. Barbara Cawthorne Crafton
5½ x 8½, 160 pp, Quality PB, 978-1-59473-287-4 **$16.99**

Ethics of the Sages: Pirke Avot—Annotated & Explained *Translation and Annotation by Rabbi Rami Shapiro* 5½ x 8½, 192 pp, Quality PB, 978-1-59473-207-2 **$16.99**

The Genesis of Leadership: What the Bible Teaches Us about Vision, Values and Leading Change *By Rabbi Nathan Laufer; Foreword by Senator Joseph I. Lieberman*
6 x 9, 288 pp, Quality PB, 978-1-58023-352-1 **$18.99**

Hineini in Our Lives: Learning How to Respond to Others through 14 Biblical Texts and Personal Stories *By Rabbi Norman J. Cohen, PhD* 6 x 9, 240 pp, Quality PB, 978-1-58023-274-6 **$16.99**

A Man's Responsibility: A Jewish Guide to Being a Son, a Partner in Marriage, a Father and a Community Leader *By Rabbi Joseph B. Meszler* 6 x 9, 192 pp, Quality PB, 978-1-58023-435-1 **$16.99**

The Modern Men's Torah Commentary: New Insights from Jewish Men on the 54 Weekly Torah Portions *Edited by Rabbi Jeffrey K. Salkin*
6 x 9, 368 pp, HC, 978-1-58023-395-8 **$24.99**

Moses and the Journey to Leadership: Timeless Lessons of Effective Management from the Bible and Today's Leaders *By Rabbi Norman J. Cohen, PhD*
6 x 9, 240 pp, Quality PB, 978-1-58023-351-4 **$18.99**; HC, 978-1-58023-227-2 **$21.99**

Proverbs: Annotated & Explained
Translation and Annotation by Rabbi Rami Shapiro
5½ x 8½, 288 pp, Quality PB, 978-1-59473-310-9 **$16.99**

Righteous Gentiles in the Hebrew Bible: Ancient Role Models for Sacred Relationships
By Rabbi Jeffrey K. Salkin; Foreword by Rabbi Harold M. Schulweis;
Preface by Phyllis Tickle 6 x 9, 192 pp, Quality PB, 978-1-58023-364-4 **$18.99**

Sage Tales: Wisdom and Wonder from the Rabbis of the Talmud
By Rabbi Burton L. Visotzky 6 x 9, 256 pp, HC, 978-1-58023-456-6 **$24.99**

The Wisdom of Judaism: An Introduction to the Values of the Talmud
By Rabbi Dov Peretz Elkins 6 x 9, 192 pp, Quality PB, 978-1-58023-327-9 **$16.99**

Or phone, fax, mail or e-mail to: **JEWISH LIGHTS Publishing**
Sunset Farm Offices, Route 4 • P.O. Box 237 • Woodstock, Vermont 05091
Tel: (802) 457-4000 • Fax: (802) 457-4004 • www.jewishlights.com
Credit card orders: (800) 962-4544 (8:30AM–5:30PM EST Monday–Friday)
Generous discounts on quantity orders. SATISFACTION GUARANTEED. Prices subject to change.

Bar / Bat Mitzvah

The Mitzvah Project Book
Making Mitzvah Part of Your Bar/Bat Mitzvah ... and Your Life
By Liz Suneby and Diane Heiman; Foreword by Rabbi Jeffrey K. Salkin; Preface by Rabbi Sharon Brous
The go-to source for Jewish young adults and their families looking to make the world a better place through good deeds—big or small.
6 x 9, 224 pp, Quality PB Original, 978-1-58023-458-0 **$16.99** For ages 11–13

The Bar/Bat Mitzvah Memory Book, 2nd Edition: An Album for Treasuring the Spiritual Celebration
By Rabbi Jeffrey K. Salkin and Nina Salkin
8 x 10, 48 pp, 2-color text, Deluxe HC, ribbon marker, 978-1-58023-263-0 **$19.99**

For Kids—Putting God on Your Guest List, 2nd Edition: How to Claim the Spiritual Meaning of Your Bar or Bat Mitzvah *By Rabbi Jeffrey K. Salkin*
6 x 9, 144 pp, Quality PB, 978-1-58023-308-8 **$15.99** For ages 11–13

The Jewish Prophet: Visionary Words from Moses and Miriam to Henrietta Szold and A. J. Heschel *By Rabbi Dr. Michael J. Shire*
6½ x 8½, 128 pp, 123 full-color illus., HC, 978-1-58023-168-8 **$14.95**

Putting God on the Guest List, 3rd Edition: How to Reclaim the Spiritual Meaning of Your Child's Bar or Bat Mitzvah *By Rabbi Jeffrey K. Salkin*
6 x 9, 224 pp, Quality PB, 978-1-58023-222-7 **$16.99**; HC, 978-1-58023-260-9 **$24.99**

Putting God on the Guest List Teacher's Guide
8½ x 11, 48 pp, PB, 978-1-58023-226-5 **$8.99**

Teens / Young Adults

Text Messages: A Torah Commentary for Teens
Edited by Rabbi Jeffrey K. Salkin
Shows today's teens how each Torah portion contains worlds of meaning for them, for what they are going through in their lives, and how they can shape their Jewish identity as they enter adulthood.
6 x 9, 304 pp (est), HC, 978-1-58023-507-5 **$24.99**

Hannah Senesh: Her Life and Diary, the First Complete Edition
By Hannah Senesh; Foreword by Marge Piercy; Preface by Eitan Senesh; Afterword by Roberta Grossman
6 x 9, 368 pp, b/w photos, Quality PB, 978-1-58023-342-2 **$19.99**

I Am Jewish: Personal Reflections Inspired by the Last Words of Daniel Pearl
Edited by Judea and Ruth Pearl 6 x 9, 304 pp, Deluxe PB w/ flaps, 978-1-58023-259-3 $18.99
Download a free copy of the *I Am Jewish Teacher's Guide* at www.jewishlights.com.

The JGirl's Guide: The Young Jewish Woman's Handbook for Coming of Age
By Penina Adelman, Ali Feldman and Shulamit Reinharz
6 x 9, 240 pp, Quality PB, 978-1-58023-215-9 **$14.99** For ages 11 & up

The JGirl's Teacher's and Parent's Guide
8½ x 11, 56 pp, PB, 978-1-58023-225-8 **$8.99**

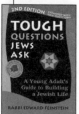

Tough Questions Jews Ask, 2nd Edition: A Young Adult's Guide to Building a Jewish Life *By Rabbi Edward Feinstein*
6 x 9, 160 pp, Quality PB, 978-1-58023-454-2 **$16.99** For ages 11 & up

Tough Questions Jews Ask Teacher's Guide
8½ x 11, 72 pp, PB, 978-1-58023-187-9 **$8.95**

Pre-Teens

Be Like God: God's To-Do List for Kids
By Dr. Ron Wolfson
Encourages kids ages eight through twelve to use their God-given superpowers to find the many ways they can make a difference in the lives of others and find meaning and purpose for their own.
7 x 9, 144 pp, Quality PB, 978-1-58023-510-5 **$15.99** For ages 8–12

The Book of Miracles: A Young Person's Guide to Jewish Spiritual Awareness
By Lawrence Kushner, with all-new illustrations by the author.
6 x 9, 96 pp, 2-color illus., HC, 978-1-879045-78-1 **$16.95** For ages 9–13

Congregation Resources

A Practical Guide to Rabbinic Counseling
Edited by Rabbi Yisrael N. Levitz, PhD, and Rabbi Abraham J. Twerski, MD
Provides rabbis with the requisite knowledge and practical guidelines for some of the most common counseling situations.
6 x 9, 432 pp, HC, 978-1-58023-562-4 **$40.00**

Professional Spiritual & Pastoral Care: A Practical Clergy and Chaplain's Handbook
Edited by Rabbi Stephen B. Roberts, MBA, MHL, BCJC
An essential resource integrating the classic foundations of pastoral care with the latest approaches to spiritual care, specifically intended for professionals who work or spend time with congregants in acute care hospitals, behavioral health facilities, rehabilitation centers and long-term care facilities.
6 x 9, 480 pp, HC, 978-1-59473-312-3 **$50.00**

Reimagining Leadership in Jewish Organizations: Ten Practical Lessons to Help You Implement Change and Achieve Your Goals
By Dr. Misha Galperin
Serves as a practical guidepost for lay and professional leaders to evaluate the current paradigm with insights from the world of business, psychology and research in Jewish demographics and sociology. Supported by vignettes from the field that illustrate the successes of the lessons as well as the consequences of not implementing them.
6 x 9, 192 pp, Quality PB, 978-1-58023-492-4 **$16.99**

Empowered Judaism: What Independent Minyanim Can Teach Us about Building Vibrant Jewish Communities
By Rabbi Elie Kaunfer; Foreword by Prof. Jonathan D. Sarna
6 x 9, 224 pp, Quality PB, 978-1-58023-412-2 **$18.99**

Building a Successful Volunteer Culture: Finding Meaning in Service in the Jewish Community *By Rabbi Charles Simon; Foreword by Shelley Lindauer; Preface by Dr. Ron Wolfson*
6 x 9, 192 pp, Quality PB, 978-1-58023-408-5 **$16.99**

The Case for Jewish Peoplehood: Can We Be One?
By Dr. Erica Brown and Dr. Misha Galperin; Foreword by Rabbi Joseph Telushkin
6 x 9, 224 pp, HC, 978-1-58023-401-6 **$21.99**

Finding a Spiritual Home: How a New Generation of Jews Can Transform the American Synagogue *By Rabbi Sidney Schwarz*
6 x 9, 352 pp, Quality PB, 978-1-58023-185-5 **$19.95**

Inspired Jewish Leadership: Practical Approaches to Building Strong Communities
By Dr. Erica Brown 6 x 9, 256 pp, HC, 978-1-58023-361-3 **$27.99**

Jewish Pastoral Care, 2nd Edition: A Practical Handbook from Traditional & Contemporary Sources *Edited by Rabbi Dayle A. Friedman, MSW, MAJCS, BCC*
6 x 9, 528 pp, Quality PB, 978-1-58023-427-6 **$35.00**

Jewish Spiritual Direction: An Innovative Guide from Traditional and Contemporary Sources
Edited by Rabbi Howard A. Addison, PhD, and Barbara Eve Breitman, MSW
6 x 9, 368 pp, HC, 978-1-58023-230-2 **$30.00**

Rethinking Synagogues: A New Vocabulary for Congregational Life
By Rabbi Lawrence A. Hoffman, PhD 6 x 9, 240 pp, Quality PB, 978-1-58023-248-7 **$19.99**

Spiritual Community: The Power to Restore Hope, Commitment and Joy
By Rabbi David A. Teutsch, PhD
5½ x 8½, 144 pp, HC, 978-1-58023-270-8 **$19.99**

Spiritual Boredom: Rediscovering the Wonder of Judaism *By Dr. Erica Brown*
6 x 9, 208 pp, HC, 978-1-58023-405-4 **$21.99**

The Spirituality of Welcoming: How to Transform Your Congregation into a Sacred Community *By Dr. Ron Wolfson* 6 x 9, 224 pp, Quality PB, 978-1-58023-244-9 **$19.99**

Children's Books

Around the World in One Shabbat
Jewish People Celebrate the Sabbath Together
By Durga Yael Bernhard
Takes your child on a colorful adventure to share the many ways Jewish people celebrate Shabbat around the world.
11 x 8½, 32 pp, Full-color illus., HC, 978-1-58023-433-7 **$18.99** *For ages 3–6*

It's a ... It's a ... It's a Mitzvah
By Liz Suneby and Diane Heiman; Full-color Illus. by Laurel Molk
Join Mitzvah Meerkat and friends as they introduce children to the everyday kindnesses that mark the beginning of a Jewish journey and a lifetime commitment to *tikkun olam* (repairing the world). 9 x 12, 32 pp, Full-color illus., HC, 978-1-58023-509-9 **$18.99** *For ages 3–6*

What You Will See Inside a Synagogue
By Rabbi Lawrence A. Hoffman, PhD, and Dr. Ron Wolfson; Full-color photos by Bill Aron
A colorful, fun-to-read introduction that explains the ways and whys of Jewish worship and religious life. 8½ x 10½, 32 pp, Full-color photos, Quality PB, 978-1-59473-256-0 **$8.99** *For ages 6 & up*
(A book from SkyLight Paths, Jewish Lights' sister imprint)

Because Nothing Looks Like God
By Lawrence Kushner and Karen Kushner
Real-life examples of happiness and sadness—from goodnight stories, to the hope and fear felt the first time at bat, to the closing moments of someone's life—invite parents and children to explore, together, the questions we all have about God, no matter what our age. 11 x 8½, 32 pp, Full-color illus., HC, 978-1-58023-092-6 **$18.99** *For ages 4 & up*

The Book of Miracles: A Young Person's Guide to Jewish Spiritual Awareness
Written and illus. by Lawrence Kushner
Easy-to-read, imaginatively illustrated book encourages kids' awareness of their own spirituality. Revealing the essence of Judaism in a language they can understand and enjoy. 6 x 9, 96 pp, 2-color illus., HC, 978-1-879045-78-1 **$16.95** *For ages 9–13*

In God's Hands   *By Lawrence Kushner and Gary Schmidt*
Brings new life to a traditional Jewish folktale, reminding parents and kids of all faiths and all backgrounds that each of us has the power to make the world a better place—working ordinary miracles with our everyday deeds.
9 x 12, 32 pp, Full-color illus., HC, 978-1-58023-224-1 **$16.99** For ages 5 & up

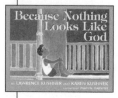

In Our Image: God's First Creatures
By Nancy Sohn Swartz
A playful new twist to the Genesis story, God asks all of nature to offer gifts to humankind—with a promise that the humans would care for creation in return. 9 x 12, 32 pp, Full-color illus., HC, 978-1-879045-99-6 **$16.95** *For ages 4 & up*

The Jewish Family Fun Book, 2nd Ed.
Holiday Projects, Everyday Activities, and Travel Ideas with Jewish Themes
By Danielle Dardashti and Roni Sarig
The complete sourcebook for families wanting to put a new spin on activities for Jewish holidays, holy days and the everyday. It offers dozens of easy-to-do activities that bring Jewish tradition to life for kids of all ages.
6 x 9, 304 pp, w/ 70+ b/w illus., Quality PB, 978-1-58023-333-0 **$18.99**

The Kids' Fun Book of Jewish Time   *By Emily Sper*
A unique way to introduce children to the Jewish calendar—night and day, the seven-day week, Shabbat, the Hebrew months, seasons and dates.
9 x 7½, 24 pp, Full-color illus., HC, 978-1-58023-311-8 **$16.99** *For ages 3–6*

What Makes Someone a Jew?   *By Lauren Seidman*
Reflects the changing face of American Judaism. Helps preschoolers and young readers (ages 3–6) understand that you don't have to look a certain way to be Jewish. 10 x 8½, 32 pp, Full-color photos, Quality PB, 978-1-58023-321-7 **$8.99** *For ages 3–6*

When a Grandparent Dies: A Kid's Own Remembering Workbook for
Dealing with Shiva and the Year Beyond   *By Nechama Liss-Levinson*
8 x 10, 48 pp, 2-color text, HC, 978-1-879045-44-6 **$15.95** *For ages 7–13*

Life Cycle
Marriage / Parenting / Family / Aging

The New Jewish Baby Album: Creating and Celebrating the Beginning of a Spiritual Life—A Jewish Lights Companion
By the Editors at Jewish Lights; Foreword by Anita Diamant; Preface by Rabbi Sandy Eisenberg Sasso
A spiritual keepsake that will be treasured for generations. More than just a memory book, *shows you how—and why it's important*—to create a Jewish home and a Jewish life. 8 x 10, 64 pp, Deluxe Padded HC, Full-color illus., 978-1-58023-138-1 **$19.95**

The Jewish Pregnancy Book: A Resource for the Soul, Body & Mind during Pregnancy, Birth & the First Three Months *By Sandy Falk, MD, and Rabbi Daniel Judson, with Steven A. Rapp* Medical information, prayers and rituals for each stage of pregnancy. 7 x 10, 208 pp, b/w photos, Quality PB, 978-1-58023-178-7 **$16.95**

Celebrating Your New Jewish Daughter: Creating Jewish Ways to Welcome Baby Girls into the Covenant—New and Traditional Ceremonies *By Debra Nussbaum Cohen; Foreword by Rabbi Sandy Eisenberg Sasso* 6 x 9, 272 pp, Quality PB, 978-1-58023-090-2 **$18.95**

The New Jewish Baby Book, 2nd Edition: Names, Ceremonies & Customs—A Guide for Today's Families *By Anita Diamant* 6 x 9, 320 pp, Quality PB, 978-1-58023-251-7 **$19.99**

Parenting as a Spiritual Journey: Deepening Ordinary and Extraordinary Events into Sacred Occasions *By Rabbi Nancy Fuchs-Kreimer, PhD*
6 x 9, 224 pp, Quality PB, 978-1-58023-016-2 **$17.99**

Parenting Jewish Teens: A Guide for the Perplexed
By Joanne Doades Explores the questions and issues that shape the world in which today's Jewish teenagers live and offers constructive advice to parents.
6 x 9, 176 pp, Quality PB, 978-1-58023-305-7 **$16.99**

Judaism for Two: A Spiritual Guide for Strengthening and Celebrating Your Loving Relationship *By Rabbi Nancy Fuchs-Kreimer, PhD, and Rabbi Nancy H. Wiener, DMin; Foreword by Rabbi Elliot N. Dorff, PhD*
Addresses the ways Jewish teachings can enhance and strengthen committed relationships. 6 x 9, 224 pp, Quality PB, 978-1-58023-254-8 **$16.99**

The Creative Jewish Wedding Book, 2nd Edition: A Hands-On Guide to New & Old Traditions, Ceremonies & Celebrations *By Gabrielle Kaplan-Mayer*
9 x 9, 288 pp, b/w photos, Quality PB, 978-1-58023-398-9 **$19.99**

Divorce Is a Mitzvah: A Practical Guide to Finding Wholeness and Holiness When Your Marriage Dies *By Rabbi Perry Netter; Afterword by Rabbi Laura Geller*
6 x 9, 224 pp, Quality PB, 978-1-58023-172-5 **$16.95**

Embracing the Covenant: Converts to Judaism Talk About Why & How
By Rabbi Allan Berkowitz and Patti Moskovitz 6 x 9, 192 pp, Quality PB, 978-1-879045-50-7 **$16.95**

The Guide to Jewish Interfaith Family Life: An InterfaithFamily.com Handbook
Edited by Ronnie Friedland and Edmund Case
6 x 9, 384 pp, Quality PB, 978-1-58023-153-4 **$18.95**

A Heart of Wisdom: Making the Jewish Journey from Midlife through the Elder Years
Edited by Susan Berrin; Foreword by Rabbi Harold Kushner
6 x 9, 384 pp, Quality PB, 978-1-58023-051-3 **$18.95**

Introducing My Faith and My Community: The Jewish Outreach Institute Guide for the Christian in a Jewish Interfaith Relationship
By Rabbi Kerry M. Olitzky 6 x 9, 176 pp, Quality PB, 978-1-58023-192-3 **$16.99**

Making a Successful Jewish Interfaith Marriage: The Jewish Outreach Institute Guide to Opportunities, Challenges and Resources *By Rabbi Kerry M. Olitzky with Joan Peterson Littman*
6 x 9, 176 pp, Quality PB, 978-1-58023-170-1 **$16.95**

A Man's Responsibility: A Jewish Guide to Being a Son, a Partner in Marriage, a Father and a Community Leader *By Rabbi Joseph B. Meszler*
6 x 9, 192 pp, Quality PB, 978-1-58023-435-1 **$16.99**; HC, 978-1-58023-362-0 **$21.99**

So That Your Values Live On: Ethical Wills and How to Prepare Them
Edited by Rabbi Jack Riemer and Rabbi Nathaniel Stampfer
6 x 9, 272 pp, Quality PB, 978-1-879045-34-7 **$18.99**

Social Justice

Where Justice Dwells
A Hands-On Guide to Doing Social Justice in Your Jewish Community
By Rabbi Jill Jacobs; Foreword by Rabbi David Saperstein
Provides ways to envision and act on your own ideals of social justice.
7 x 9, 288 pp, Quality PB Original, 978-1-58023-453-5 **$24.99**

There Shall Be No Needy
Pursuing Social Justice through Jewish Law and Tradition
By Rabbi Jill Jacobs; Foreword by Rabbi Elliot N. Dorff, PhD; Preface by Simon Greer
Confronts the most pressing issues of twenty-first-century America from a deeply
Jewish perspective. 6 x 9, 288 pp, Quality PB, 978-1-58023-425-2 **$16.99**
There Shall Be No Needy Teacher's Guide 8½ x 11, 56 pp, PB, 978-1-58023-429-0 **$8.99**

Conscience
The Duty to Obey and the Duty to Disobey
By Rabbi Harold M. Schulweis
Examines the idea of conscience and the role conscience plays in our relationships
to government, law, ethics, religion, human nature, God—and to each other.
6 x 9, 160 pp, Quality PB, 978-1-58023-419-1 **$16.99**; HC, 978-1-58023-375-0 **$19.99**

Judaism and Justice
The Jewish Passion to Repair the World
By Rabbi Sidney Schwarz; Foreword by Ruth Messinger
Explores the relationship between Judaism, social justice and the Jewish identity
of American Jews. 6 x 9, 352 pp, Quality PB, 978-1-58023-353-8 **$19.99**

Spirituality / Women's Interest

New Jewish Feminism
Probing the Past, Forging the Future
Edited by Rabbi Elyse Goldstein; Foreword by Anita Diamant
Looks at the growth and accomplishments of Jewish feminism and what they
mean for Jewish women today and tomorrow.
6 x 9, 480 pp, HC, 978-1-58023-359-0 **$24.99**

The Divine Feminine in Biblical Wisdom Literature
Selections Annotated & Explained
Translation & Annotation by Rabbi Rami Shapiro
5½ x 8½, 240 pp, Quality PB, 978-1-59473-109-9 **$16.99**
(A book from SkyLight Paths, Jewish Lights' sister imprint)

The Quotable Jewish Woman
Wisdom, Inspiration & Humor from the Mind & Heart
Edited by Elaine Bernstein Partnow
6 x 9, 496 pp, Quality PB, 978-1-58023-236-4 **$19.99**

The Women's Haftarah Commentary
New Insights from Women Rabbis on the 54 Weekly Haftarah Portions,
the 5 Megillot & Special Shabbatot
Edited by Rabbi Elyse Goldstein
Illuminates the historical significance of female portrayals in the Haftarah and the
Five Megillot. 6 x 9, 560 pp, Quality PB, 978-1-58023-371-2 **$19.99**

The Women's Torah Commentary
New Insights from Women Rabbis on the 54 Weekly Torah Portions
Edited by Rabbi Elyse Goldstein
Over fifty women rabbis offer inspiring insights on the Torah, in a week-by-week format.
6 x 9, 496 pp, Quality PB, 978-1-58023-370-5 **$19.99**; HC, 978-1-58023-076-6 **$34.95**

> See Passover for *The Women's Passover Companion: Women's Reflections on
> the Festival of Freedom* and *The Women's Seder Sourcebook: Rituals &
> Readings for Use at the Passover Seder.*

Theology / Philosophy / The Way Into... Series

The Way Into... series offers an accessible and highly usable "guided tour" of the Jewish faith, people, history and beliefs—in total, an introduction to Judaism that will enable you to understand and interact with the sacred texts of the Jewish tradition. Each volume is written by a leading contemporary scholar and teacher, and explores one key aspect of Judaism. The Way Into... series enables all readers to achieve a real sense of Jewish cultural literacy through guided study.

The Way Into Encountering God in Judaism
By Rabbi Neil Gillman, PhD
For everyone who wants to understand how Jews have encountered God throughout history and today.
6 x 9, 240 pp, Quality PB, 978-1-58023-199-2 **$18.99**; HC, 978-1-58023-025-4 **$21.95**
Also Available: **The Jewish Approach to God:** A Brief Introduction for Christians
  By Rabbi Neil Gillman, PhD
  5½ x 8½, 192 pp, Quality PB, 978-1-58023-190-9 **$16.95**

The Way Into Jewish Mystical Tradition
By Rabbi Lawrence Kushner
Allows readers to interact directly with the sacred mystical texts of the Jewish tradition. An accessible introduction to the concepts of Jewish mysticism, their religious and spiritual significance, and how they relate to life today.
6 x 9, 224 pp, Quality PB, 978-1-58023-200-5 **$18.99**; HC, 978-1-58023-029-2 **$21.95**

The Way Into Jewish Prayer
By Rabbi Lawrence A. Hoffman, PhD
Opens the door to 3,000 years of Jewish prayer, making anyone feel at home in the Jewish way of communicating with God.
6 x 9, 208 pp, Quality PB, 978-1-58023-201-2 **$18.99**

The Way Into Jewish Prayer Teacher's Guide
By Rabbi Jennifer Ossakow Goldsmith
8½ x 11, 42 pp, PB, 978-1-58023-345-3 **$8.99**
Download a free copy at www.jewishlights.com.

The Way Into Judaism and the Environment
By Jeremy Benstein, PhD
Explores the ways in which Judaism contributes to contemporary social-environmental issues, the extent to which Judaism is part of the problem and how it can be part of the solution.
6 x 9, 288 pp, Quality PB, 978-1-58023-368-2 **$18.99**; HC, 978-1-58023-268-5 **$24.99**

The Way Into Tikkun Olam (Repairing the World)
By Rabbi Elliot N. Dorff, PhD
An accessible introduction to the Jewish concept of the individual's responsibility to care for others and repair the world.
6 x 9, 304 pp, Quality PB, 978-1-58023-328-6 **$18.99**

The Way Into Torah
By Rabbi Norman J. Cohen, PhD
Helps guide you in the exploration of the origins and development of Torah, explains why it should be studied and how to do it.
6 x 9, 176 pp, Quality PB, 978-1-58023-198-5 **$16.99**

The Way Into the Varieties of Jewishness
By Sylvia Barack Fishman, PhD
Explores the religious and historical understanding of what it has meant to be Jewish from ancient times to the present controversy over "Who is a Jew?"
6 x 9, 288 pp, Quality PB, 978-1-58023-367-5 **$18.99**; HC, 978-1-58023-030-8 **$24.99**

Theology / Philosophy

From Defender to Critic: The Search for a New Jewish Self
By Dr. David Hartman
A daring self-examination of Hartman's goals, which were not to strip halakha of its authority but to create a space for questioning and critique that allows for the traditionally religious Jew to act out a moral life in tune with modern experience. 6 x 9, 336 pp, HC, 978-1-58023-515-0 **$35.00**

Our Religious Brains: What Cognitive Science Reveals about Belief, Morality, Community and Our Relationship with God
By Rabbi Ralph D. Mecklenburger; Foreword by Dr. Howard Kelfer; Preface by Dr. Neil Gillman
This is a groundbreaking, accessible look at the implications of cognitive science for religion and theology, intended for laypeople. 6 x 9, 224 pp, HC, 978-1-58023-508-2 **$24.99**

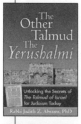

The Other Talmud—*The Yerushalmi*: Unlocking the Secrets of The Talmud of Israel for Judaism Today By *Rabbi Judith Z. Abrams, PhD*
A fascinating—and stimulating—look at "the other Talmud" and the possibilities for Jewish life reflected there. 6 x 9, 256 pp, HC, 978-1-58023-463-4 **$24.99**

The Way of Man: According to Hasidic Teaching
By Martin Buber; New Translation and Introduction by Rabbi Bernard H. Mehlman and Dr. Gabriel E. Padawer; Foreword by Paul Mendes-Flohr
An accessible and engaging new translation of Buber's classic work—available as an e-book only. E-book, 978-1-58023-601-0 Digital List Price **$14.99**

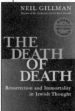

The Death of Death: Resurrection and Immortality in Jewish Thought
By Rabbi Neil Gillman, PhD 6 x 9, 336 pp, Quality PB, 978-1-58023-081-0 **$18.95**

Doing Jewish Theology: God, Torah & Israel in Modern Judaism *By Rabbi Neil Gillman, PhD*
6 x 9, 304 pp, Quality PB, 978-1-58023-439-9 **$18.99**; HC, 978-1-58023-322-4 **$24.99**

A Heart of Many Rooms: Celebrating the Many Voices within Judaism
By Dr. David Hartman 6 x 9, 352 pp, Quality PB, 978-1-58023-156-5 **$19.95**

The God Who Hates Lies: Confronting & Rethinking Jewish Tradition
By Dr. David Hartman with Charlie Buckholtz 6 x 9, 208 pp, HC, 978-1-58023-455-9 **$24.99**

Jewish Theology in Our Time: A New Generation Explores the Foundations and Future of Jewish Belief *Edited by Rabbi Elliot J. Cosgrove, PhD; Foreword by Rabbi David J. Wolpe; Preface by Rabbi Carole B. Balin, PhD* 6 x 9, 240 pp, HC, 978-1-58023-413-9 **$24.99**

Maimonides—Essential Teachings on Jewish Faith & Ethics: The Book of Knowledge & the Thirteen Principles of Faith—Annotated & Explained
Translation and Annotation by Rabbi Marc D. Angel, PhD
5½ x 8½, 224 pp, Quality PB Original, 978-1-59473-311-6 **$18.99***

Maimonides, Spinoza and Us: Toward an Intellectually Vibrant Judaism
By Rabbi Marc D. Angel, PhD 6 x 9, 224 pp, HC, 978-1-58023-411-5 **$24.99**

A Touch of the Sacred: A Theologian's Informal Guide to Jewish Belief
By Dr. Eugene B. Borowitz and Frances W. Schwartz
6 x 9, 256 pp, Quality PB, 978-1-58023-416-0 **$16.99**; HC, 978-1-58023-337-8 **$21.99**

Traces of God: Seeing God in Torah, History and Everyday Life *By Rabbi Neil Gillman, PhD*
6 x 9, 240 pp, Quality PB, 978-1-58023-369-9 **$16.99**

Your Word Is Fire: The Hasidic Masters on Contemplative Prayer
Edited and translated by Rabbi Arthur Green, PhD, and Barry W. Holtz
6 x 9, 160 pp, Quality PB, 978-1-879045-25-5 **$16.99**

I Am Jewish
Personal Reflections Inspired by the Last Words of Daniel Pearl

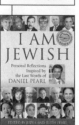

Almost 150 Jews—both famous and not—from all walks of life, from all around the world, write about many aspects of their Judaism.
Edited by Judea and Ruth Pearl 6 x 9, 304 pp, Deluxe PB w/ flaps, 978-1-58023-259-3 **$18.99**
Download a free copy of the *I Am Jewish* Teacher's Guide at www.jewishlights.com.

Hannah Senesh: Her Life and Diary, The First Complete Edition
By Hannah Senesh; Foreword by Marge Piercy; Preface by Eitan Senesh; Afterword by Roberta Grossman
6 x 9, 368 pp, b/w photos, Quality PB, 978-1-58023-342-2 **$19.99**

*****A book from SkyLight Paths, Jewish Lights' sister imprint*

Inspiration

God of Me: Imagining God throughout Your Lifetime
By Rabbi David Lyon Helps you cut through preconceived ideas of God and dogmas
that stifle your creativity when thinking about your personal relationship with
God. 6 x 9, 176 pp, Quality PB, 978-1-58023-452-8 **$16.99**

The God Upgrade: Finding Your 21st-Century Spirituality in Judaism's
5,000-Year-Old Tradition *By Rabbi Jamie Korngold; Foreword by Rabbi Harold M. Schulweis*
A provocative look at how our changing God concepts have shaped every aspect
of Judaism. 6 x 9, 176 pp, Quality PB, 978-1-58023-443-6 **$15.99**

The Seven Questions You're Asked in Heaven: Reviewing and
Renewing Your Life on Earth *By Dr. Ron Wolfson* An intriguing and entertaining
resource for living a life that matters. 6 x 9, 176 pp, Quality PB, 978-1-58023-407-8 **$16.99**

Happiness and the Human Spirit: The Spirituality of Becoming the
Best You Can Be *By Rabbi Abraham J. Twerski, MD*
Shows you that true happiness is attainable once you stop looking outside yourself for
the source. 6 x 9, 176 pp, Quality PB, 978-1-58023-404-7 **$16.99**; HC, 978-1-58023-343-9 **$19.99**

A Formula for Proper Living: Practical Lessons from Life and Torah
By Rabbi Abraham J. Twerski, MD 6 x 9, 144 pp, HC, 978-1-58023-402-3 **$19.99**

The Bridge to Forgiveness: Stories and Prayers for Finding God and Restoring
Wholeness *By Rabbi Karyn D. Kedar* 6 x 9, 176 pp, Quality PB, 978-1-58023-451-1 **$16.99**

The Empty Chair: Finding Hope and Joy—Timeless Wisdom from a Hasidic Master,
Rebbe Nachman of Breslov *Adapted by Moshe Mykoff and the Breslov Research Institute*
4 x 6, 128 pp, Deluxe PB w/ flaps, 978-1-879045-67-5 **$9.99**

The Gentle Weapon: Prayers for Everyday and Not-So-Everyday Moments—
Timeless Wisdom from the Teachings of the Hasidic Master, Rebbe Nachman of Breslov
Adapted by Moshe Mykoff and S. C. Mizrahi, together with the Breslov Research Institute
4 x 6, 144 pp, Deluxe PB w/ flaps, 978-1-58023-022-3 **$9.99**

God Whispers: Stories of the Soul, Lessons of the Heart *By Rabbi Karyn D. Kedar*
6 x 9, 176 pp, Quality PB, 978-1-58023-088-9 **$15.95**

God's To-Do List: 103 Ways to Be an Angel and Do God's Work on Earth
By Dr. Ron Wolfson 6 x 9, 144 pp, Quality PB, 978-1-58023-301-9 **$16.99**

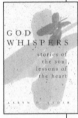

Jewish Stories from Heaven and Earth: Inspiring Tales to Nourish the Heart and
Soul *Edited by Rabbi Dov Peretz Elkins* 6 x 9, 304 pp, Quality PB, 978-1-58023-363-7 **$16.99**

Life's Daily Blessings: Inspiring Reflections on Gratitude and Joy for Every Day, Based
on Jewish Wisdom *By Rabbi Kerry M. Olitzky* 4½ x 6½, 368 pp, Quality PB, 978-1-58023-396-5 **$16.99**

Restful Reflections: Nighttime Inspiration to Calm the Soul, Based on Jewish Wisdom
By Rabbi Kerry M. Olitzky and Rabbi Lori Forman-Jacobi 5 x 8, 352 pp, Quality PB, 978-1-58023-091-9 **$16.99**

Sacred Intentions: Morning Inspiration to Strengthen the Spirit, Based on Jewish Wisdom
By Rabbi Kerry M. Olitzky and Rabbi Lori Forman-Jacobi 4½ x 6½, 448 pp, Quality PB, 978-1-58023-061-2 **$16.99**

Kabbalah / Mysticism

Jewish Mysticism and the Spiritual Life: Classical Texts,
Contemporary Reflections *Edited by Dr. Lawrence Fine, Dr. Eitan Fishbane and Rabbi Or N. Rose*
Inspirational and thought-provoking materials for contemplation, discussion and
action. 6 x 9, 256 pp, HC, 978-1-58023-434-4 **$24.99**

Ehyeh: A Kabbalah for Tomorrow
By Rabbi Arthur Green, PhD 6 x 9, 224 pp, Quality PB, 978-1-58023-213-5 **$18.99**

The Gift of Kabbalah: Discovering the Secrets of Heaven, Renewing Your Life on Earth
By Tamar Frankiel, PhD 6 x 9, 256 pp, Quality PB, 978-1-58023-141-1 **$16.95**

Seek My Face: A Jewish Mystical Theology *By Rabbi Arthur Green, PhD*
6 x 9, 304 pp, Quality PB, 978-1-58023-130-5 **$19.95**

Zohar: Annotated & Explained *Translation & Annotation by Dr. Daniel C. Matt; Foreword by
Andrew Harvey* 5½ x 8½, 176 pp, Quality PB, 978-1-893361-51-5 **$16.99**
(A book from SkyLight Paths, Jewish Lights' sister imprint)

See also *The Way Into Jewish Mystical Tradition* in The Way Into... Series.

Spirituality / Prayer

Making Prayer Real: Leading Jewish Spiritual Voices on Why Prayer Is Difficult and What to Do about It *By Rabbi Mike Comins*
A new and different response to the challenges of Jewish prayer, with "best prayer practices" from Jewish spiritual leaders of all denominations.
6 x 9, 320 pp, Quality PB, 978-1-58023-417-7 **$18.99**

Witnesses to the One: The Spiritual History of the *Sh'ma*
By Rabbi Joseph B. Meszler; Foreword by Rabbi Elyse Goldstein
6 x 9, 176 pp, Quality PB, 978-1-58023-400-9 **$16.99**; HC, 978-1-58023-309-5 **$19.99**

My People's Prayer Book Series: Traditional Prayers, Modern Commentaries *Edited by Rabbi Lawrence A. Hoffman, PhD*
Provides diverse and exciting commentary to the traditional liturgy. Will help you find new wisdom in Jewish prayer, and bring liturgy into your life. Each book includes Hebrew text, modern translations and commentaries from all perspectives of the Jewish world.

Vol. 1—The *Sh'ma* and Its Blessings
7 x 10, 168 pp, HC, 978-1-879045-79-8 **$29.99**
Vol. 2—The *Amidah* 7 x 10, 240 pp, HC, 978-1-879045-80-4 **$24.95**
Vol. 3—*P'sukei D'zimrah* (Morning Psalms)
7 x 10, 240 pp, HC, 978-1-879045-81-1 **$29.99**
Vol. 4—*Seder K'riat Hatorah* (The Torah Service)
7 x 10, 264 pp, HC, 978-1-879045-82-8 **$29.99**
Vol. 5—*Birkhot Hashachar* (Morning Blessings)
7 x 10, 240 pp, HC, 978-1-879045-83-5 **$24.95**
Vol. 6—*Tachanun* and Concluding Prayers
7 x 10, 240 pp, HC, 978-1-879045-84-2 **$24.95**
Vol. 7—Shabbat at Home 7 x 10, 240 pp, HC, 978-1-879045-85-9 **$24.95**
Vol. 8—*Kabbalat Shabbat* (Welcoming Shabbat in the Synagogue)
7 x 10, 240 pp, HC, 978-1-58023-121-3 **$24.99**
Vol. 9—Welcoming the Night: *Minchah* and *Ma'ariv* (Afternoon and Evening Prayer) 7 x 10, 272 pp, HC, 978-1-58023-262-3 **$24.99**
Vol. 10—Shabbat Morning: *Shacharit* and *Musaf* (Morning and Additional Services) 7 x 10, 240 pp, HC, 978-1-58023-240-1 **$29.99**

Spirituality / Lawrence Kushner

I'm God; You're Not: Observations on Organized Religion & Other Disguises of the Ego
6 x 9, 256 pp, Quality PB, 978-1-58023-513-6 **$18.99**; HC, 978-1-58023-441-2 **$21.99**

The Book of Letters: A Mystical Hebrew Alphabet
Popular HC Edition, 6 x 9, 80 pp, 2-color text, 978-1-879045-00-2 **$24.95**
Collector's Limited Edition, 9 x 12, 80 pp, gold-foil-embossed pages, w/ limited-edition silkscreened print, 978-1-879045-04-0 **$349.00**

The Book of Miracles: A Young Person's Guide to Jewish Spiritual Awareness
6 x 9, 96 pp, 2-color illus., HC, 978-1-879045-78-1 **$16.95** *For ages 9–13*

The Book of Words: Talking Spiritual Life, Living Spiritual Talk
6 x 9, 160 pp, Quality PB, 978-1-58023-020-9 **$18.99**

Eyes Remade for Wonder: A Lawrence Kushner Reader *Introduction by Thomas Moore*
6 x 9, 240 pp, Quality PB, 978-1-58023-042-1 **$18.95**

God Was in This Place & I, i Did Not Know: Finding Self, Spirituality and Ultimate Meaning 6 x 9, 192 pp, Quality PB, 978-1-879045-33-0 **$16.95**

Honey from the Rock: An Introduction to Jewish Mysticism
6 x 9, 176 pp, Quality PB, 978-1-58023-073-5 **$16.95**

Invisible Lines of Connection: Sacred Stories of the Ordinary
5½ x 8½, 160 pp, Quality PB, 978-1-879045-98-9 **$16.99**

Jewish Spirituality: A Brief Introduction for Christians
5½ x 8½, 112 pp, Quality PB, 978-1-58023-150-3 **$12.95**

The River of Light: Jewish Mystical Awareness
6 x 9, 192 pp, Quality PB, 978-1-58023-096-4 **$18.99**

The Way Into Jewish Mystical Tradition
6 x 9, 224 pp, Quality PB, 978-1-58023-200-5 **$18.99**; HC, 978-1-58023-029-2 **$21.95**

Spirituality

The Jewish Lights Spirituality Handbook: A Guide to Understanding, Exploring & Living a Spiritual Life *Edited by Stuart M. Matlins*
What exactly is "Jewish" about spirituality? How do I make it a part of my life? Fifty of today's foremost spiritual leaders share their ideas and experience with us.
6 x 9, 456 pp, Quality PB, 978-1-58023-093-3 **$19.99**

The Sabbath Soul: Mystical Reflections on the Transformative Power of Holy Time *Selection, Translation and Commentary by Eitan Fishbane, PhD*
Explores the writings of mystical masters of Hasidism. Provides translations and interpretations of a wide range of Hasidic sources previously unavailable in English that reflect the spiritual transformation that takes place on the seventh day.
6 x 9, 208 pp, Quality PB, 978-1-58023-459-7 **$18.99**

Repentance: The Meaning and Practice of *Teshuvah*
By Dr. Louis E. Newman; Foreword by Rabbi Harold M. Schulweis; Preface by Rabbi Karyn D. Kedar
Examines both the practical and philosophical dimensions of *teshuvah*, Judaism's core religious-moral teaching on repentance, and its value for us—Jews and non-Jews alike—today. 6 x 9, 256 pp, HC, 978-1-58023-426-9 **$24.99**

Aleph-Bet Yoga: Embodying the Hebrew Letters for Physical and Spiritual Well-Being
By Steven A. Rapp; Foreword by Tamar Frankiel, PhD, and Judy Greenfeld; Preface by Hart Lazer
7 x 10, 128 pp, b/w photos, Quality PB, Lay-flat binding, 978-1-58023-162-6 **$16.95**

A Book of Life: Embracing Judaism as a Spiritual Practice
By Rabbi Michael Strassfeld 6 x 9, 544 pp, Quality PB, 978-1-58023-247-0 **$19.99**

Bringing the Psalms to Life: How to Understand and Use the Book of Psalms
By Rabbi Daniel F. Polish, PhD 6 x 9, 208 pp, Quality PB, 978-1-58023-157-2 **$16.95**

Does the Soul Survive? A Jewish Journey to Belief in Afterlife, Past Lives & Living with Purpose *By Rabbi Elie Kaplan Spitz; Foreword by Brian L. Weiss, MD*
6 x 9, 288 pp, Quality PB, 978-1-58023-165-7 **$18.99**

Entering the Temple of Dreams: Jewish Prayers, Movements and Meditations for the End of the Day *By Tamar Frankiel, PhD, and Judy Greenfeld*
7 x 10, 192 pp, illus., Quality PB, 978-1-58023-079-7 **$16.95**

First Steps to a New Jewish Spirit: Reb Zalman's Guide to Recapturing the Intimacy & Ecstasy in Your Relationship with God *By Rabbi Zalman M. Schachter-Shalomi with Donald Gropman* 6 x 9, 144 pp, Quality PB, 978-1-58023-182-4 **$16.95**

Foundations of Sephardic Spirituality: The Inner Life of Jews of the Ottoman Empire
By Rabbi Marc D. Angel, PhD 6 x 9, 224 pp, Quality PB, 978-1-58023-341-5 **$18.99**

God & the Big Bang: Discovering Harmony between Science & Spirituality
By Dr. Daniel C. Matt 6 x 9, 216 pp, Quality PB, 978-1-879045-89-7 **$18.99**

God in Our Relationships: Spirituality between People from the Teachings of Martin Buber *By Rabbi Dennis S. Ross* 5½ x 8½, 160 pp, Quality PB, 978-1-58023-147-3 **$16.95**

Judaism, Physics and God: Searching for Sacred Metaphors in a Post-Einstein World
By Rabbi David W. Nelson 6 x 9, 352 pp, Quality PB, inc. reader's discussion guide,
978-1-58023-306-4 **$18.99**; HC, 352 pp, 978-1-58023-252-4 **$24.99**

Meaning & Mitzvah: Daily Practices for Reclaiming Judaism through Prayer, God, Torah, Hebrew, Mitzvot and Peoplehood *By Rabbi Goldie Milgram*
7 x 9, 336 pp, Quality PB, 978-1-58023-256-2 **$19.99**

Minding the Temple of the Soul: Balancing Body, Mind, and Spirit through Traditional Jewish Prayer, Movement, and Meditation *By Tamar Frankiel, PhD, and Judy Greenfeld*
7 x 10, 184 pp, Illus., Quality PB, 978-1-879045-64-4 **$18.99**

One God Clapping: The Spiritual Path of a Zen Rabbi *By Rabbi Alan Lew with Sherril Jaffe*
5½ x 8½, 336 pp, Quality PB, 978-1-58023-115-2 **$16.95**

The Soul of the Story: Meetings with Remarkable People
By Rabbi David Zeller 6 x 9, 288 pp, HC, 978-1-58023-272-2 **$21.99**

***Tanya,* the Masterpiece of Hasidic Wisdom:** Selections Annotated & Explained
Translation & Annotation by Rabbi Rami Shapiro; Foreword by Rabbi Zalman M. Schachter-Shalomi
5½ x 8½, 240 pp, Quality PB, 978-1-59473-275-1 **$16.95**

These Are the Words, 2nd Edition: A Vocabulary of Jewish Spiritual Life
By Rabbi Arthur Green, PhD 6 x 9, 320 pp, Quality PB, 978-1-58023-494-8 **$19.99**

About Jewish Lights

People of all faiths and backgrounds yearn for books that attract, engage, educate, and spiritually inspire.

Our principal goal is to stimulate thought and help all people learn about who the Jewish People are, where they come from, and what the future can be made to hold. While people of our diverse Jewish heritage are the primary audience, our books speak to people in the Christian world as well and will broaden their understanding of Judaism and the roots of their own faith.

We bring to you authors who are at the forefront of spiritual thought and experience. While each has something different to say, they all say it in a voice that you can hear.

Our books are designed to welcome you and then to engage, stimulate, and inspire. We judge our success not only by whether or not our books are beautiful and commercially successful, but by whether or not they make a difference in your life.

For your information and convenience, at the back of this book we have provided a list of other Jewish Lights books you might find interesting and useful. They cover all the categories of your life:

Bar/Bat Mitzvah	Life Cycle
Bible Study / Midrash	Meditation
Children's Books	Men's Interest
Congregation Resources	Parenting
Current Events / History	Prayer / Ritual / Sacred Practice
Ecology / Environment	Social Justice
Fiction: Mystery, Science Fiction	Spirituality
Grief / Healing	Theology / Philosophy
Holidays / Holy Days	Travel
Inspiration	Twelve Steps
Kabbalah / Mysticism / Enneagram	Women's Interest

Stuart M. Matlins, Publisher

Or phone, fax, mail or e-mail to: **JEWISH LIGHTS Publishing**
Sunset Farm Offices, Route 4 • P.O. Box 237 • Woodstock, Vermont 05091
Tel: (802) 457-4000 • Fax: (802) 457-4004 • www.jewishlights.com
Credit card orders: (800) 962-4544 (8:30AM–5:30PM EST Monday–Friday)
Generous discounts on quantity orders. SATISFACTION GUARANTEED. Prices subject to change.

For more information about each book, visit our website at www.jewishlights.com